In the hallway, the assistant fire chiefs grew uncomfortable. Something was not right. Joe Rod and Jim Lawrence had been in tight situations before, and this one had begun to prickle the hair on their necks. The fire on the girl's bed had been extinguished some time ago, and no hot spots or residual burning had been found in her room.

So where the devil was all this smoke coming from? They turned to the end of the hall, where a final door stood. There had been no evidence of anything wrong there.

But the fire serpent that had been slumbering in that back room while firefighters were looking elsewhere was about to burst forth with a vengeance. As Rod and Lawrence watched in dread, smoke seeped out above the door and hovered in a thickening bank on the ceiling of the hallway.

Then, in an instant, the door turned black and all hell broke loose. . . .

St. Martin's Paperbacks Titles
by Don Davis

THE MILWAUKEE MURDERS
THE NANNY MURDER TRIAL

THE NANNY MURDER TRIAL

Don Davis

ST. MARTIN'S PAPERBACKS

THE NANNY MURDER TRIAL

Copyright © 1993 by Don Davis.

Front cover photo credits: top photo by Richard Harbus/Associated Press; bottom by Laura Seitz/Gannett Suburban Newspapers.

ISBN: 0–312–95085–3

Printed in the United States of America

St. Martin's Paperbacks edition/April 1993

10 9 8 7 6 5 4 3 2 1

For Robin

Acknowledgments

A NUMBER OF PEOPLE WERE KIND ENOUGH TO LEND ME THEIR time and expertise in writing this book. Without them, these pages never would have come together.

Joyce Eggington, my rival, became a mentor. Henry Alter provided unexpected assistance and friendship. Special thanks go to the guys from Switzerland who helped me interpret events—Rico Carisch, Stefan Ragaz, Sacha Wigdorovits, George Simor, and, in Wettingen, Daniel Benz.

Laura Brevetti went the extra step to provide guidance, as did Chris Rush. If anyone needs a top investigator, call Rush at (212) 951-0735. Interpreter Maya Hess was amazing, and Carmine Surace was a pal. Bruce Johnson and Marie Solimando at the Mount Pleasant Police Department were courteous and helpful, even when they did not have to be. Numerous people in White Plains and Mount Pleasant helped on an anonymous basis, and I value their comments. Judge Donald Silverman squeezed time out of a busy schedule for an important talk.

Patrice K. Johnson of the Gannett Suburban Newspapers displayed extraordinary kindness in sharing her information, as did Marlene Aig of the Associated Press, freelancer Mary Meenan, and Bryna Taubman, a nifty writer. Thanks also to Fiona, Kari, and Lisbet at the Sheraton in Nanuet.

My editor, Charlie Spicer, gave freely of his time and encouragement. My agent, Mark Joly, kept the tigers at bay so I could write. Ken Englade fixed my computer on deadline at the expense of his golf game.

My wife Robin was the most important person in the whole process, and but for her understanding and help, I would be lost. Russ and Randy gave pep talks when I needed them. In the background, always, is the support from the people in Savannah, Irma and Eric Johnson and their clan, Maureen and Robert Alonso and theirs. I owe you all a Low Country Boil dinner at Thunderbolt.

Blitz, R.I.P.

PREFACE

SCOTT CARPENTER CAREFULLY NOSED HIS BLUE AND WHITE PA-
trol car through the gathering wet December dusk. It was
the worst time of day for drivers, that evil little zone that
isn't quite daylight and not yet dark, and most of the people behind steering wheels were only now deciding to
turn on their headlights. At five P.M. the presence of his
police cruiser on the roads helped jog the memories of
motorists hurrying home from work.

He shifted his weight as he drove, adjusting his black
leather jacket while his eyes roamed the winter gloom
gathering beyond his windshield. He had checked in for
his night shift at the Mount Pleasant police station, on the
bottom floor of Town Hall Plaza, was briefed and then
headed out to patrol Post Five, three square miles where
the hamlets of Valhalla and Thornwood bump together.

He anticipated that the biggest problem on that Monday evening would be traffic. Rivers of automobiles
flowed north out of New York City, and the commuter
railway stations would soon set free hundreds of more
automobiles. The usual tributary of cars would branch
into his area. Tired people, frustrated after a day of work,
would be doubly frustrated at the near gridlock that
could bloom along the road network that linked New
York to Westchester County. They all wanted to get
home, to get some suburban peace and quiet.

1

While darkness might herald the start of another night of bright lights or criminal activity down in the Big Apple, depending on one's economic status, such was not the case in Westchester. This wasn't The City. It was genteel neighborhoods, old families, big lawns, and small-town life carefully hidden only a few dozen miles north of the garishness of Times Square. It was a haven for those souls lucky enough to taste New York in the daytime and escape it by nightfall.

Officer Scott Carpenter had only been on the police force for two years and a few months, but he was comfortable as a cop. He readily looked the part, spreading a solid 195 pounds over a five feet, ten inch body, a physique that gave him a football player's squareness. Everything about him seemed trim and shipshape, from the flat brush cut of his dark brown hair, worn almost in Marine Corps whitewall style, so severe that he had no sideburns, to his muscular legs. Even the small mustache was trimmed short and ruler even. When young officer Carpenter appeared, the big pistol with the rubber hand grip bouncing at his waist, just behind the metal handcuffs, his presence left no doubt. This was a cop.

Appearances are not everything. Carpenter seemed an idealized version of a young police officer, but like every cop who had ever pinned on a badge, he had lessons yet to learn. He was about to learn a big one about tragedy and chaos. For while he may have thought that Monday, December 2, 1991, was going to be another quiet evening, he was wrong.

When the radio crackled, it was loud in the closed confines of the automobile, because the windows were up to shield against the new winter's cold. The disembodied, businesslike voice of Sergeant Robert Gardner, running the communications console for the shift, came into the patrol car over a square speaker. "Respond to Five West Lake Drive. Ten-five," was the terse order. Ten-five. Police radio code for a fire.

Carpenter acknowledged the message, then stomped the accelerator, even as he flipped on the flashing lights atop his cruiser and punched the siren to shrieking. He was about a mile and a half from 5 West Lake, and began a speeding weave through the homeward-bound traffic.

He shut down the lights and the wailer as he pulled up at the curb on the corner of West Lake and Nanny Hagen Road, where a house at the end of a broad, deep lawn seemed caught in a pancake of curling smoke.

As Carpenter jumped from his car, he saw that he was not the first badge there. The white Chevrolet Blazer truck of the Thornwood fire chief Greg Wind was already in the driveway, and Wind was on the front lawn, watching the billowing masses of smoke and looking sad beyond belief. In a soft voice, the fire chief told the policeman there was a dead baby in the ground-floor nursery.

Carpenter spun away and took off at a run, hurtling flat out into the burning structure, hoping his speed could carry him to the trapped infant. The front door was funneling out a cloud of choking smoke, and the policeman held his breath as he dashed through. But only a few steps later he had to stop. His watering eyes felt scalded. When he had to take a breath, his lungs filled with smoke, robbing him of oxygen. Heat smashed against his exposed flesh. He was wearing only his uniform, not the flame-proof gear of a firefighter. He had no breathing apparatus, no shield for his face. Only a dozen feet into the house, the dirty river of smoke had become an impenetrable wall. If he stayed longer, he risked becoming a victim himself.

Carpenter staggered back toward safety, his shoulders brushing the walls of the narrow hallway, then he found the open front door and was out in the cold night air. He could breathe. He was racked by coughs, but he was alive.

The policeman snatched the portable radio from his belt to call for reinforcements, but the walkie-talkie, which he had checked before leaving the station, emitted only growls and squeaks. Disgusted, he put it away. A neighbor offered a car telephone, and Carpenter dialed Gardner at the station, telling the sergeant that there was a "DOA" —a dead on arrival—at the fire scene. Detectives and medical examiners were needed as soon as possible.

He became aware of other people. A young woman standing in the driveway was crying, babbling hysterically in a strange language. The only thing he could understand was "cats," a word she kept repeating over and over. The chief was still there. John Gallagher, a friend of Carpenter's brother, rushed up and began yelling something. And beyond him, some help had arrived in the form of firefighters and officer Bobby Miliambro.

The smoke, blowing away to the right as it was caught on the wind, had abated during the four minutes since Carpenter had been thrown back. He and Miliambro grabbed their flashlights and went inside the house to find that baby.

Miliambro led the way, and Carpenter followed as chaos rose behind them. They checked different areas of the large family room at the front of the house, then moved to the third door on the left in the hall, their flashlights cutting cones of brightness through curling fingers of smoke.

Although they could breathe, the two young officers remembered their training. Smoke rises. Things would be better near the floor. They dropped to their hands and knees to reach fresher air and crawled into the baby's nursery. A dim light shone above the fog of moving smoke, giving the scene a surrealistic feeling.

On the rug, Carpenter noticed a large, heat-warped plastic bottle, the sort that is used to hold soft drinks. A partially burned box of stick matches lay nearby.

The flashlight beams swept across something in the far left corner of the room, and Carpenter, the youngest officer on the Mount Pleasant Police Department, stared in

4

shock. He crawled closer, wanting to disbelieve his eyes. Months later his voice would still drop to a whisper when he recalled that awful moment.

"I saw a really charred, smoldering doll in the corner of the bedroom," he said. Edging nearer, he realized the burned thing in a car carrier melted flat by the intense heat was not a doll at all.

"It was a baby," he said. "A human baby."

PART ONE

Fire

Chapter One

DECEMBER 2, 1991

ON WHAT WOULD BE THE WORST DAY OF HIS LIFE, THE ALARM shook Bill Fischer awake at five A.M. He lay still, shrouded in darkness, while he got his bearings. Waking up was not a problem, for he was a morning person, but getting out of bed, knowing that winter was waiting just outside, was a chore for anyone. The hardest thing about staying in good physical condition at the age of forty-eight was getting out of a warm bed on a cold morning to go exercise.

It was Monday. His wife Denise was still asleep next to him, and the house at 5 West Lake Drive was quiet as his feet hit the carpet of the master bedroom. Downstairs, their baby daughter, Kristie, only three months old, was having baby dreams in her nursery. He automatically cocked an ear to the monitor on his bedroom wall. The device was linked to an audio transmitter in the baby's room, allowing the parents to hear even a whimper, any sign of distress. It remained quiet this morning.

A similar monitor was in the bedroom of the Swiss nanny, Olivia Riner, who had come to America specifically to care for Kristie. Her room was directly across the narrow hallway from the baby. Olivia, too, would be asleep at such an early hour. Denise had gone to extraordinary lengths to hire the quiet au pair, and the choice seemed to have paid off, for Olivia had almost become a

9

member of the family in the short month that she had lived with them. Bill and Denise felt comfortable leaving the baby in her care.

It did not take Bill long to dress that morning, for it was just casual stuff, since he was headed to the YMCA for his thrice-weekly workout. He left the bedroom and moved through the dark house with ease, as if every light were burning brightly. Fischer had lived in his two-story home for twenty-two years, did most of the work, including the recent remodeling, by himself, and knew every screw and nail by its first name.

Passing the kitchen, he moved through the large upstairs living room, with the big fireplace and cabinet against the wall. Then he veered right and descended the twenty steps to the lower floor, where the only bathroom in the house was located. His motion brought a mild bit of attention from the family's four cats, but no more than that. They stirred, ears pricked at the sudden movement, but soon went back to sleep, preferring to leave any early affection involving Bill to Snuffy, the big black dog with whom they shared the house. Snuffy would go to work with Bill, leaving the house to the cats during the day, an arrangement precisely to the liking of the quartet of felines that bore the names Oliver, O.J., Fleetwood, and Kabuki.

By the calendar, winter was officially still twenty days away. But along the Hudson River Valley a deep chill had already begun to seep down from Canada. The nights were cold, below freezing, and snow flurries were displacing the needles of icy rain that had soaked Westchester County with monotonous regularity. As Fischer stepped outside, his breath ballooned before him on the frosty morning and a crescent moon rose in the east.

He walked to the long macadam driveway, where three vehicles were parked, drops of water beading on their hoods and streaking the windows. Denise's little 1986 Honda Civic was beneath the open carport beside the house. Midway up the drive, half on and half off the blacktop, sat the big Ford pickup truck that belonged to John Gallagher, the longtime boyfriend of twenty-two-year-old Leah Fischer, Bill's daughter by an earlier marriage. The two kids had spent the night at John's house.

Fischer opened the door of his 1980 Chevy Blazer, and Snuffy, his red collar a lone stripe of brightness against the morning dark, jumped in. Bill slid behind the wheel and gunned the big engine to life. With his mechanic's ear, he listened to how the Blazer was running, almost able to see in his mind's eye the gasoline flowing into the fuel pump, the spark plugs firing, the camshaft spinning. Bill Fischer and his brother Bob had inherited the repair garage that had been in his family for three generations. He knew how motor vehicles worked. The Blazer hummed perfectly. Fischer switched on the heater, put on the lights, released the brakes, and headed for the Y.

If all went well, he and Snuffy would be at work by 7:30 A.M., ready for another day in the trenches of the automobile repair business.

About seven A.M., a 1989 Toyota Corolla pulled into the driveway, stopping close behind the pickup truck. John Gallagher, a tall, red-haired young man, got out of the driver's side, and Leah Fischer stepped from the passenger seat. He was twenty-six years of age and had known Leah since a mutual friend introduced them in 1987. Except for a seven-month stretch of silence following an argument in 1988, the two had dated steadily ever since and were almost inseparable. Their families had long ago grown accustomed to the fact that John and Leah were much more than friends, and that, as healthy young adults, they frequently spent the night together.

Yesterday, the Sunday that followed the Thanksgiving holiday, John had picked Leah up at her house, but was so late that a plan for an early brunch had changed into a late three o'clock meal at a nearby motor inn. They left his pickup in the driveway, and with John at the wheel, took the Toyota. After the meal, they made the thirty-minute drive to his house in nearby Mahopac, only twenty-four miles away, where they spent the night in the Gallagher family home.

Arriving back in Thornwood on Monday morning, they saw the Blazer was gone, meaning Bill was off for his workout. Denise would still be asleep, as would the baby and the nanny, so Leah and John were quiet as they went through the unlocked front door. Only a swish of cornstalks hanging on the door as a symbol of the holiday announced their arrival. They walked down the hall to the last door on the right, opened it and stepped into Leah's bedroom, where clothes and other items were strewn over the full-sized platform bed against the wall. Leah had exchanged strong words about the condition of her bedroom with her stepmother, and, as a compromise, it was decided Leah would keep the door closed. Privacy ensured tranquility. Two feet above the bed was a narrow window, which she kept locked and covered by metal blinds.

Leah set about getting ready for the day. While John had several changes of clothing and work boots in the deep closet of her bedroom, Leah did not keep clothes at his house and had to return home each morning to dress. A receptionist and secretary, she had to be at work by 8:30 A.M.

John, a mechanic at White Plains Jaguar, had to punch in thirty minutes earlier. He kissed her good-bye, left the house, and climbed into the Ford truck. It was a beautifully maintained vehicle, with light green trim over a cream body, which he had purchased, used, the previous year. He would stop by the deli on the way in and grab a cup of coffee, driving his U.S.-built Ford to his job at the exclusive foreign car repair shop.

An hour later, as the sun was trying to brighten the drab morning, Leah joined the throngs of people heading to work. She drove the Japanese-made Toyota to her job at a White Plains dealership selling American Fords.

* * *

The cats and the girls—Denise, baby Kristie, and Olivia, the nanny—were getting up and about. Denise would be the next to leave.

An attractive and slim woman with honey-blond hair cut above the collar and swept back on the sides, she was slightly taller than Bill, her husband of only five months. They had met when she took her car into Fischer's Garage for some work in the spring of 1988, when both were recovering from first marriages that had not worked.

Bill's divorce became final the next year, and in the summer of 1990 Denise had moved into the marvelous old house with the cathedral ceilings and spacious lawn, as her new husband set about remodeling to suit their needs. A new master bedroom suite was added upstairs, and the downstairs reconfigured to make room for some changes in the family. Bill's son Troy had moved out and settled in Manhattan, leaving one of the three downstairs bedrooms vacant.

When Denise became pregnant, things really began to change. She had strong ideas of how her new family should be, ideas that harkened to an older day in some ways, but were very modern in others. For instance, she decreed that John Gallagher could no longer sleep over at the Fischer home, even if he was confined to a family room couch. But at the same time, she planned to resume her career as a certified public accountant after the baby was born. Like many accountants, she wore glasses to ease the strain on eyes that scanned numbers all day, round lenses with dark brown shell frames.

Something novel happened in this middle-class Westchester County neighborhood. Denise Fischer had brought in a trained person whose sole job was to take care of the baby.

She had worked hard to get just the right person. While doing her homework, Denise learned that an estimated 8.5 million children under the age of thirteen are left each day in the care of nonfamily members, and the chance of something terrible happening was not insignificant. People, it seemed, put more effort into choosing a new car or television set than in picking just the right person to care for their children, so she took every precaution to find someone special, someone with love in their heart for children, someone who would not be looking at the baby as a paycheck.

Denise wanted someone mature and experienced, preferably a European with a knowledge of English, someone who had been to the United States. She discovered the E.F. Foundation, a giant Swedish nonprofit agency that is a leader in the peculiar industry of finding positions for European au pair girls, who exchange their work at low salaries for a chance to live in a foreign country. The Fischers were put in touch with one particular girl from Switzerland with outstanding credentials, who could communicate in English and had actually worked as a medical assistant for a pediatrician. There were a few telephone interviews, and shortly after Kristie was born on September 11 in the White Plains Hospital, the decision was made to hire Olivia Riner, a nineteen-year-old girl whose last name was pronounced as Reener. Into the little hamlet of Thornwood, New York, came a rare sight: a Swiss nanny.

When Olivia stepped off the plane after her long sojourn across the Atlantic Ocean on November 1, Denise, who spoke a little German, and Bill Fischer were there to meet her. The house was ready. Bill and Denise had moved into the upstairs bedroom; Leah took over their old corner bedroom, the largest of those downstairs; the room where Troy had lived had been converted into a nursery, and Leah's old bedroom had been prepared as the quarters for the au pair.

Denise was quite taken with Olivia, but left nothing to chance. The girl turned twenty on November 5 and seemed well up to the task of caring for Kristie. But being so far away from Switzerland had made her homesick, and Denise wanted to be absolutely sure Olivia was completely ready before going back to work herself.

Throughout November, Denise Fischer stayed home, helping the shy and quiet Olivia learn the ropes of being in America. Emphasis was placed on how she should react in case of an emergency, particularly a fire. She was shown where the fire extinguishers were kept. Bill even activated the smoke detectors so Olivia would know that shrieking alarm sound. She was given written instructions on whom to call. Denise told her the main rule was that in case of fire, Olivia was to get the baby out of the house.

Finally, at the end of November, Denise felt comfortable enough to return to her job. She and Bill had watched closely as the au pair warmed to the baby, to the animals in the house, and to the Fischers themselves. The girl had been hired through a leading agency, she had been through the homesickness phase, Denise had coached her side by side with little Kristie throughout the month. It was time to get on with life.

Denise went back to work as a CPA with a firm in Stamford, Connecticut, and on Monday, December 2, she was in a hurry to get to the office. The end of the year can be almost as busy for an accountant as the mid-April income-tax filing deadline nightmare. As she drove away from home, she relaxed in the knowledge that the baby was being taken care of by a pretty, white, Swiss girl with a shy smile and a gentle touch.

Olivia had been screened by the au pair agency and had passed Denise's careful overview once she was at the Fischer household. The girl genuinely cared for the baby.

The house at 5 West Lake Drive in Thornwood was very far from the third-floor apartment in Wettingen, Switzerland, where Olivia had grown up. At times Olivia Riner felt the distance was as far as the earth to the moon. When she had registered with her community police on November 1, to tell them she was moving to America to be an au pair, the decision had seemed well thought out. She had been to the United States twice before, and had even visited Disney World. It is not unusual for a young Swiss person to travel during their postschooling years, to take a look at the world before settling down in picturesque, isolated Switzerland.

When she arrived in New York, despite the welcome from Denise and Bill, despite the warmth of the child who would be in her charge, and the four cats and one dog that she instantly loved, an overwhelming sense of loneliness wrapped around her like a dank, heavy coat. The changes to her personal life were immense, and in her bedroom at night she confided her private thoughts to her diary. She longed for her home in the Aargau and the view of the Jura mountains. Instead, she was in a place she did not know, and only a handful of people even knew her name. As she turned twenty years of age, Olivia was burdened by loneliness.

Time, however, changes one's outlook, and Olivia was no exception. By the start of her second month on the job, for which she was paid one hundred American dollars a week and given free room and board, she was able to tell her diary that she was satisfied. Life had settled into a rhythm, she was adjusting to the freewheeling style of American life—as contrasted to the more controlled actions of the Swiss—and she had begun to enjoy herself. Best of all, she wrote, was little Kristie, who was not an anchor around her neck, but more like a little sister, or perhaps even her own baby.

In talking with other au pairs, she discovered her job seemed excellent by comparison. Some girls found upon arrival that they had many children to care for, had to do maid's work, and that family tensions could become overwhelming. It was not unusual for a European au pair to take one good look at things in a household, pack her bag and leave as soon as possible. Olivia couldn't imagine that happening here. She had been accepted into the family, had even been encouraged to bring another German-speaking au pair to share a happy American holiday called Thanksgiving, and was required only to care for the baby between the hours of nine A.M. and five P.M., five days a week. That was all. It was a dream job, working just the way the au pair situation was supposed to work. Before she knew it, a month flew past in her one-year agreement with the Fischers. She took care of the baby with ease, because Kristie had such a sweet disposition. Olivia had graduated from Juventus, a vocational school in Zurich, trained as a physician's assistant. In Switzerland she had worked for a pediatrician and later with a primary care provider, before signing up with the E.F. Foundation to experience the American lifestyle.

This Monday morning was little different than the others on West Lake Drive, except that Denise had finally gone back to work, and Olivia and Kristie were alone with the cats. She gave the baby a morning bottle and straightened both of their rooms, which faced each other directly across the hall. Olivia could lie in her bed and see Kristie either in the crib or the car seat on the floor. The baby did not like to take her daytime naps flat in the crib, but rather preferred to lean up in the cushioned car seat.

One true thing about babies anywhere, Switzerland or New York, is they will make a mess now and then. The ecology-conscious Fischers allowed plastic disposable diapers to be used on Kristie when they went out, but at home, cloth diapers were the rule. That meant that the washing machine in the laundry room was kept busy, with Olivia doing a load of baby clothes almost every day.

That did not bother her. It was expected. She knew how to take care of babies, so life was, overall, pleasant.

Fischer's Garage, at 873 North Broadway in North White Plains, has the look of an old fire station, with a big roll-up door that yawns directly onto the busy four-lane street. The red-brick front is old and dark, and looks like the false sets seen in old Western movies. The roof is hidden from view, as the brickwork takes on a stair-step effect. The car bay is on the left, the office on the right.

But the front is deceiving, for the building is constructed into a steep hillside and drops down another full floor. The garage, in the family for three generations, is owned by the Fischer brothers, who took over when their father decided to retire and go fishing every day possible.

It was extraordinarily convenient to Bill's home. All he had to do was drive the short distance up North Broadway to connect either with Columbus Avenue, which sweeps into Thornwood, or go a bit farther north to where West Lake Drive begins on the edge of Mount Pleasant, and turn left across the long Kensico Reservoir dam. Columbus was quicker, with a higher speed limit. Ten minutes maximum on most days.

Because of the proximity, Fischer occasionally would spend his lunch hour at home instead of around the shop, and on this particular Monday he had a double reason for doing so. Not only would he be able to enjoy the midday break in a setting more tranquil than the garage, but he would be able to check on how Kristie and Olivia were getting along.

Leaving Snuffy at the shop, he drove home about 1:30 P.M., intentionally not telephoning ahead to alert Olivia that he was on the way. An unexpected visit would be best, just like the snap inspections he had endured during his Navy days. He drove his Blazer all the way up the macadam drive and parked beneath the carport, got out and walked around to the front door, which they kept unlocked for ease of entrance. The corn decoration whisked against the wood as he opened the front door.

Nobody was in the family room, so he walked down the narrow hallway, past the empty laundry room and bathroom on the left, and stuck his head into the nursery. Olivia was seated on the floor, her back to him, folding clothes. Beside her, Kristie lay on a blanket, her little hand dancing around the rings of a colorful jungle gym. "Hi," Bill said quietly. When he spoke, Olivia turned around, and the baby, recognizing Daddy's voice, beamed him a bright smile.

He went back toward the front of the house and up the stairs to the kitchen, made lunch and sat down to read the newspaper. South Africa's Nelson Mandela was in New York, and the juicy testimony was beginning in the Palm Beach trial of William Kennedy Smith, who was accused of raping a woman he had met at a bar. The abrasive John Sununu was preparing to resign as White House chief of staff. On the sports page, baseball slugger Bobby Bonilla was now the richest player in the game, with a new contract that would pay him $5.8 million every year.

Downstairs, Kristie had become restless, first wanting to play with the little mobile and then not wanting it. She would stay on her stomach, then want to be on her back. At the table in the dining area, Bill heard the baby fuss.

To quiet Kristie, Olivia picked her up. Baby fingers found a baby mouth, and Kristie stopped making noise in order to munch on them contentedly. Olivia wiped away some drool as she held the infant close. She reached for an eight-ounce bottle of formula and soon Kristie, well fed, began to nod off. Olivia put a pacifier in the baby's mouth and laid her in the gray car seat for a nap.

After forty-five minutes Bill finished both his meal and paper and walked back downstairs. Kristie was asleep in the car seat, her head leaning against a soft cloth diaper that Olivia had rolled up to use as a pillow. He gazed at his daughter with unabashed love. The sleeping baby, dressed in a long-sleeve, lime-green coverall with white stripes on the wrist, was a gift to a man of his age. When she would be sixteen, in the year 2008, Bill would be sixty-four years old and a year from retirement. She probably would drive him crazy with loud music and strange clothes and boyfriends. But he didn't care. His new daughter was something special.

He turned and saw Olivia across the hall in her room, lost in another of the books she always seemed to be reading. Her back was toward him, and he cleared his throat and said aloud that he was leaving. "See you later," Fischer said. Olivia smiled over her shoulder.

In ten minutes he was back at the red-brick garage. Olivia resumed her book and minding the baby.

Only four hours later, the world at 5 West Lake Drive would explode.

Chapter Two

NIGHTFALL

FOR OLIVIA RINER, THE AFTERNOON HOURS SPED PAST IN AN environment and routine that had become familiar. One good thing about working with Kristie was she did not have to dress up. Instead she was comfortable on this crisp winter evening in black slacks and a purple sweatshirt that she wore over a white camisole. Purple sneakers with playful white designs around the soles were on her feet. By four P.M. Olivia was resting in the big lounge chair in the downstairs family room, feeding a four-ounce bottle of formula to the baby in her arms. The television set was on because Kristie seemed to enjoy the flashing colors. Olivia's workday would be over in an hour, when the Fischers arrived home, and she wanted to have Kristie clean, rested, and ready to see them.

Through the three tall windows along the front of the house, she saw the propane gas delivery man pass by to fill the tanks. She had not heard his big truck arrive, but that was not unusual, with the television set playing background noise. The Swiss nanny continued to rock the baby, soothing it with her soft, accented voice, speaking in both English and her Swiss-German. The propane man, his job finished, passed by again, heading back to the truck. Olivia had not budged from the chair, sitting in a wedge of light from the lamp overhead.

Kristie was almost asleep, eyes closed and her head lolling to one side. Olivia rose and carried the baby to the nursery. There, she changed the wet diaper, snapped up the short-sleeve little T-shirt and the coveralls, then put her into the plastic car carrier for a nap. She rolled a diaper and put it beside the baby's head. The car carrier sat in the far left corner of the nursery, directly in line with the closed window covered by curtains tied back at the middle. To the side was a long, white dresser, over which a small lamp cast a dim light. By the time Olivia moved away, going to the laundry to do another wash, Kristie was off in baby dreamland.

When she exited into the hallway, the four cats began telling her it was time for their evening meal, rubbing against her ankles and making impatient noises. She loved animals and spent a minute playing with them before going over to the storage closet beside the front door where their food was kept, along with myriad other items, from fishing poles to some of the solvents Bill had used in remodeling the house. She opened a can of tuna and placed it on the floor.

She rolled O.J. onto his back and ran a hand through the soft hair on the orange cat's stomach. Fleetwood and Kabuki, gray-striped tabbies, meandered about, licking their paws. Oliver, ever the loner, stalked away, heading for Olivia's bedroom and a quick nap.

Suddenly, the cats in the family room started behaving strangely, moving toward the front door and mewling, as if they wanted to go outside, then prowling stiffly about when Olivia went to open it. With a loud yowl Oliver came bounding out of the bedroom, running as if being chased by an angry dog. It was not the stop-and-go run of a playful cat, but a dash propelled by sheer terror.

Olivia walked the short distance to her room and her blue eyes flew open in astonished fear. Her bed was on fire!

Snapping flames leapt from a circle in the middle of her blanket, and the smoke leaned toward the window on the far wall. It was December and the weather outside was cold. The window had been closed, and now it was open, the pane pushed to the side about ten inches. She flipped the light switch. Nothing happened. The room remained dark, except for the fierce yellow-orange glow of the flames.

A million thoughts crowded through her mind as the fire began to burn brighter, mocking her stillness. Bill and Denise had showed her a fire extinguisher. Where was it? There were a couple of them. Where? The flames, catching hold, dug into the spread and the smoke turned dark. The kitchen! There was a fire extinguisher upstairs!

The nanny twisted away and ran through the family room, pounding up the angled stairway. She grabbed the bright red canister and rushed back down, turning the corner into the hallway at a run, her eyes locked on the smoky interior of her room.

Olivia hooked a finger through a ring that would activate the fire extinguisher, pointed the nozzle toward the circle of fire and pressed the trigger. Just as with the light switch, nothing happened. The fire danced merrily on.

She made a little noise of fear in her throat and jiggled the canister, pulling the trigger again. This time it worked, releasing the inert nitrogen gas that combined with three pounds of dry ammonium phosphate powder and blew out in a white cloud at 195 pounds per square inch of pressure. Olivia moved toward the flames as the extinguisher roared like a passing train. The fire was smothered, leaving a scorched circle about a foot in diameter in the middle of her bed.

Olivia stepped back into her doorway, the heavy extinguisher dangling from her hand. She was exhausted, as if she had carried a great weight, but the crisis was over. She could not have been more wrong.

When she turned around, she saw the unbelievable had happened. The door to the baby's room was closed and smoke was curling beneath it. She tried the knob and it was locked.

KRISTIE!

She tried again, shaking the knob, which was hot in her hand. Smoke gathered at her feet, wrapping her in its gray haze. She was descending into an uncontrolled hell, sinking, helpless and scared. For behind the locked portal, in there with the merciless fire goblin, was Kristie Fischer, and the baby was in mortal danger.

Olivia shook herself under control. The telephone! The emergency numbers were on her desk. The light in her room still would not work. She charged into the darkness, the smoldering smell from her bed haunting her panicked movements as her blind fingers sought to find the slip of paper Denise had carefully printed.

The hamlet of Thornwood is officially part of the town of Mount Pleasant, a place where some miracles of modern technology have not yet arrived. The records at the Mount Pleasant Police Department are not computerized and there is no direct dial 911 emergency code by which a person can summon help. Although Denise Fischer had jotted down the telephone numbers of the police and fire departments, the primary number at the top of the paper instructed Olivia to dial O. An operator would answer and help.

She could not use the telephone on her desk. She could not even see it, much less dial. The nanny hurried to the family room, grabbed a receiver and dialed zero, as instructed.

It was 5:10 P.M. When the deep-voiced operator answered, Olivia told him there was a fire. As the smoke alarms screeched, the operator told her to hold on, then immediately connected her with the wrong police department. Instead of going into the Mount Pleasant police station only a few miles away, the frantic girl's call was transferred to the police department in Pleasantville, a neighboring community.

PLEASANTVILLE OFFICER: Police department.
RINER: Hi. Fire.
OFFICER: Where is this, ma'am?
RINER: Five West Lake Drive.

OFFICER: Where?

RINER: In Thornwood.

OFFICER: What's the address?

RINER: West Lake Drive.

OFFICER: What number on West Lake Drive?

RINER: Five.

OFFICER: Five West Lake Drive, you have a fire?

RINER: Yes.

OFFICER: Okay. I'll get 'em out. I'll send the fire department. What's your name, ma'am?

RINER: Riner.

OFFICER: Leland?

RINER: Riner.

As the emergency telephone call concluded, the operator came back on the line and asked Olivia if she wanted to call anyone else. Smoke was gathering behind her as she gave the operator the number for Fischer's Garage five miles away, in North White Plains. A man answered and fetched Bill.

She was frantic when he came on the line, crying, "Fire. Fire." Bill asked if she had called the fire department, and the operator's voice broke into the conversation to tell him that, yes, the authorities had been notified. Bill Fischer told Olivia that he was on the way.

Then the nightmare deepened. As she hung up the receiver, thinking that help, possibly rescue, was on the way, the telephone rang beneath her fingertips. With precious seconds ticking away, the emergency call had been turned over by Pleasantville to the Mount Pleasant police, where the desk sergeant had leafed through a worn set of Rolodex cards that listed the addresses for every street in town. He found a problem.

Olivia grabbed the ringing phone as her eyes began to burn from the smoke.

RINER: Yes.

MT. PLEASANT OFFICER: All right. What's your address?

RINER: Five West Lake Drive.
OFFICER: There is no Five West Lake Drive.

Her heart fell in disbelief. She was talking to a policeman only a few miles away and was being told that she was not where she was! The number tacked on the side of the house at the top of the outside stairs was a 5. She received mail at 5 West Lake Drive. Bill and Denise had told her this was 5 West Lake Drive, but now the policeman, at this worst of times, was telling her there was no such place! Near the duty sergeant's desk at the police station, a large Dictaphone 5500 reel-to-reel tape recorder slowly turned, recording the conversation.

RINER: No? Yes. In Thornwood.
OFFICER: What is your address, please?
RINER: Five West Lake Drive.
OFFICER: Five West Lake Drive? What street are you near?
RINER: Nanny Hagen Road.
OFFICER: You're near Nanny Hagen?
RINER: Nanny Hagen. Yes.
OFFICER: How far off Nanny Hagen?
RINER: What?
OFFICER: How far are you off from Nanny Hagen?
RINER: It's the next street, and then you come *(inaudible)* Nanny Hagen and then West Lake Drive is the right, right.
OFFICER: Yeah. How far in on West Lake?
RINER: The first, the corner, and then the second.
OFFICER: Is it right near Nanny Hagen?
RINER: Yes *(inaudible)* Nanny Hagen.
OFFICER: Ah boy. Do you have any smoke in the house?

This was finally too much for Olivia. She had just put out a fire on her bed, Kristie was locked in a burning room and she needed help, but all she was getting were questions and more questions. The overwhelmed nanny began to tremble and weep, and had to fight to make her voice heard.

RINER: Yes!
OFFICER: Okay.
RINER: Good.

At last, she felt. The message had gotten through. The firefighters would come now. She was wrong. The policeman spoke again.

OFFICER: Ha ... Ma'am, I don't have a Five West Lake Drive. Can you tell me exactly where the house is?

She could no longer fight the panic and fear. In a broken voice, Olivia, her determination wilting in the face of bureaucracy, choked out in a tight voice, "The baby's in the room!"

OFFICER: All right.

With that inconclusive comment, the policeman hung up the telephone, never saying help was on the way. Olivia ran back upstairs to turn on all the lights to act as a beacon that could guide the fire trucks to the place the policeman said was not there.

John Gallagher had cleaned his tools after a day of working on foreign automobiles at Big Dee Auto Sales—White Plains Jaguar at 499 Old Tarrytown Road. He was looking forward to meeting Leah Fischer within half an hour. She would get off work about the same time, but it would take her longer to get home. They would meet at her house. He punched out at twenty minutes before five o'clock, and with time to spare, talked with a couple of fellow mechanics before heading out.

He knew the back route to 5 West Lake Drive by heart,

having figured out the path of least resistance between where he worked and where his girlfriend lived.

The building where he worked was another of those built around the contours of Westchester County's rolling hills. A road led from behind the building, beside a tall fence that separated it from the telephone company offices next door, and Gallagher gunned his truck up the incline to Old Tarrytown Road and hung a right to the stop sign, where he turned left onto Hillside. Crossing the bridge to where Hillside came to a dead end at the Valhalla Fire Department, he swung onto Legion Drive, then caught Columbus all the way through Valhalla to Nanny Hagen in Thornwood. A right turn up Nanny Hagen and in seconds he would be at West Lake Drive. He arrived at the first driveway on the left at 5:15 P.M.

A bag of automobile parts on the seat beside him toppled over as he turned into the drive. Pieces of metal clattered onto the floor. As Gallagher leaned over to catch them, he saw a glimmer of bright light flickering on the left side of the house. He pulled to a halt in his usual spot, halfway up the drive and with the right wheels on the grass, shut down his engine and turned off the headlights. Smoke alarms were screaming. He leapt from the truck and covered the thirty feet to the front door at a run. The motion light detected his presence and flashed on above him, bathing the stone patio in brightness.

Inside he saw Olivia Riner standing between the family room and the hallway, moving as if she were confused.

Olivia turned toward the sudden light and saw Gallagher coming up. She threw open the front door and cried, "Fire. Fire."

"Where's Kristie?"

"In the room! In the room."

Gallagher grabbed the fire extinguisher from Olivia's hands and dashed down the hall. He twisted the knob to the nursery but the door would not budge. He braced his back and with his right foot kicked open a portal to a scene of horror. Before him, on the floor, the baby was on fire. Flames were actually coming from the child, climbing the curtains and spreading to the wall.

Gallagher pointed the fire extinguisher and pulled the trigger. The device had only ten seconds of power, and Olivia had used some of it to suppress the fire in her room, but Gallagher did not know that. Holding the door open with his left foot, he used short bursts of the extinguisher while he yelled to ask Olivia why she had locked the door. He could not hear her reply over the noise of the fire and the whooshing extinguisher, which he waved toward the flames he saw on the baby, on the curtains, on the wall, and behind the door. By the time the extinguisher sputtered to empty, the fire was out.

Gallagher, still carrying the empty red canister, left. There was nothing else he could do. He went outside to the front patio, where Olivia stood alone.

Chapter Three

ANSWERING THE CALL

THE FIRE CALL WENT OUT AT 5:18 P.M. AND SET THE SIREN hooting at the Westchester County Fire Services training center. Normally, Henry Flavin would have ignored it. A volunteer with the Valhalla Fire Department for a dozen years, his job now was not so much to pump water, but to teach fire suppression techniques to new volunteers throughout the county. The siren continued to wail and wail, finally catching his attention, and he decided to go to the scene. Instead of grabbing a hard hat or a hose, Flavin picked up a video camera and set out for 5 West Lake Drive in Thornwood, hoping to shoot some footage that could be used in a training film. That decision, six months later, would have an unexpectedly important impact on the drama beginning to unfold.

Off-duty Mount Pleasant police sergeant Brian Dwyer was alerted by a radio page and immediately shifted into his alternate persona of volunteer firefighter. The nononsense Dwyer, a cop for twenty-three years and a firefighter for twenty-six, took off for the Thornwood Fire Department at 770 Congress Street. There he struggled into his heavy, fireproof turnout gear—the cumbersome coat, visored helmet, and rubber boots—as other volunteers began to assemble. He climbed into the front seat of the yellow-green fire truck, beside the driver, and three firefighters jumped aboard as it roared out for the one and one-half mile dash uphill to the burning house. As a former plainclothes detective who also had served as chief of the volunteer fire department, Dwyer brought special skills and experience to the scene. He went about the business of firefighting with the eyes of a cop.

Another former Thornwood fire chief heard the call over a radio scanner. Although retired from that strenuous profession, George Fries still maintained an active interest in what was happening in his hometown. He worked as superintendent of the Mount Pleasant Water Department, and his wife Kathryn had just been reelected to a new term as Mount Pleasant's town clerk, a job she had held for ten years. On Monday night he was at home, ready to settle down for the evening, when the alarm growled over the scanner. It took a few moments for the information to soak in. Fries could not believe the address that was being broadcast. 5 West Lake Drive was the Fischer home— right next door! Not waiting to throw a jacket over his red flannel shirt, he grabbed a big flashlight and headed out the door and then to the right, toward the line of trees and heavy shrubs that separated the two properties.

Fries broke through the thick foliage barrier as John Gallagher was leaving the house, trailing a plume of smoke. Looking across the dark lawn, he saw a Chevrolet Blazer charging up the drive with lights flashing on its roof. Fire Chief Greg Wind, in a yellow jacket, jumped out. Olivia Riner and John Gallagher were standing outside the door, and after talking with them, Wind and Fries went in together. Moments later they came back out, their faces grim.

Less than a minute later officer Scott Carpenter pulled up in his marked patrol car. The fires were out, but when the policeman was told there was a baby, probably dead, still inside the house, Carpenter made his futile attempt to gain entry, only to be forced back by heavy smoke.

* * *

The big flat nose of the Thornwood Volunteer Fire Department truck hove into view. Trained firefighters were finally on the scene, and an engine from the neighboring Hawthorne volunteer unit was on its way. Putting on portable oxygen packs and pulling the visors down on their helmets, a team headed into the tunnel of smoke venting from the front door and laid a length of hose down the straight, tiled hallway. A charge of eighty pounds per square inch of water pressure rushed through and inflated the hose, bulging it rigid. Since the fires appeared to be out, the big nozzle was kept closed.

Dwyer, pulling on his thick gloves, walked over to Chief Wind, who told him about the dead infant inside. With Wind leading the way, the two men entered the smoky house and turned into the nursery. Dwyer saw the charred spot around the burned carrier and the little corpse lying in the middle of the fire pattern. The baby was dead. As he stepped back, he did not like the way things seemed in this house. His cop's antennae started to vibrate with the possibility that a crime had been committed. As they left, Dwyer told Wind that the area must be secured for a police investigation.

The scene was becoming chaotic as Mount Pleasant patrolman Robert Miliambro, another young officer, drove up in his police car, parked on Nanny Hagen Road, and hurried over. People were milling about the driveway. The Pleasantville Ambulance Corps medics were giving oxygen to an hysterical young woman he did not know, and firefighters were hustling around the house, laying hose. Miliambro noticed that the unmarked car of his boss, Lieutenant Lewis Alagno, who lived only two houses away, was already there.

Knowing little about what had happened, he found Scott Carpenter on the lawn, and the two officers headed into the smoke, which instead of clearing out after the fires, seemed constant, even growing in volume. Stepping over the hose in the hallway, they went through the open door of the nursery, dropped to their hands and knees and made their way across the floor to the carrier seat and baby.

When he backed out of the room, Miliambro, just as Dwyer had done before him, told Chief Wind that the room was to be off limits until an investigation could be conducted. Then he pulled the door to the baby's bedroom closed, and the lock that had been dislodged by Gallagher's kick again snapped into place.

From his telephone at the police station, Sergeant Gardner placed another call. With a dead body at the scene, he had to get a detective over there.

Although there were three detectives in the department, a scheduling quirk had left Bruce Johnson working alone that Monday. He had checked out at the end of his eight A.M. to four P.M. tour, but he was tagged to catch any evening call. Johnson worked in plainclothes, but on that afternoon, with temperatures dropping over the area, he had already swapped his dress slacks, shirt, and shoes for a more comfortable and warmer flannel shirt, jeans, and sneakers. The 5:25 P.M. telephone call placed him back on duty. Without knowing it, Johnson was answering a summons that would change his life.

In his twenty-one years on the Mount Pleasant police force, investigating cases that could be mean and cruel, or bizarre enough to be laughable, Johnson had handled many cases and had seen many unpleasant things. Standing six feet, two inches tall and weighing 225 pounds, he had muscles if they were needed, but like many big men confident of their strength, he preferred to use his brain. A detective for the past six years, his job was to investigate, gather evidence and question suspects, not to wrestle somebody to the ground. Thornwood averaged about one murder a year, and Bruce Johnson had his share. He was a veteran cop who could keep his emotions in tight rein while conducting an investigation. As he tucked his 9mm Smith & Wesson pistol beneath his shirt and into the holster on his right hip, pulled on a jacket and headed for headquarters to round up the needed equipment, Johnson thought this Monday night episode would be just another routine piece of work. Instead, he was walking into a mystery to rival anything a screenwriter could dream up for a television police drama.

While Johnson went to Town Hall Plaza to pick up a video camera, a 35mm still camera, a Polaroid instant camera, and four shiny metal cans that would be used to hold evidence, the investigation was already under way back at 5 West Lake Drive.

Patrolman Scott Carpenter, a little spiral notebook in hand, walked over to the girl being helped by the paramedics. He recognized some of the people in the driveway—Fries, Wind, and Gallagher—but did not know Olivia Riner, who was crying her eyes out. Cats, she was saying, over and over. It was all that he could make out from her gibberish. Some foreign language, it sounded like. Something about cats.

An anguished Bill Fischer saw the signs of catastrophe even before he arrived at his house about 5:30 P.M. Vehicles were everywhere, emergency lights rotating on their roofs, painting the trees red and blue. A crowd of people milled about in the darkness, flashes of light reflecting bright and silver from the broad luminescent strips on the coats of the firefighters. His house, his home of twenty-two years, the place that he had just painstakingly remodeled for his new wife and baby, was surrounded in a haze of twirling smoke that hung overhead like something evil. Fear gnawed at his guts. He nosed his Blazer around the parked fire engine and noticed that John Gallagher's pickup was parked in its usual place.

As Fischer shut off his truck, Gallagher, breathless and excited, came running up. "You'd better get up there," he said.

Fischer started across the lawn toward the open door,

but an alert firefighter moved forward to block his path. "No," the man told Bill Fischer, with a sad look. "You'd better not go inside."

At that moment, on the cold and wet evening of December 2, Bill Fischer's heart broke. His shoulders sagged as he turned to the knot of people on the driveway and saw the weeping au pair.

"Olivia, what happened?" he asked, quietly.

Olivia began to speak in English. She had known John Gallagher vaguely, as Leah's boyfriend, but the arrival of Bill put her in touch with the first person she actually knew and trusted in the surging crowd of men and women appearing at the fire scene. She picked her way through the English language and told him that she had been feeding the cats and had closed Kristie's door and went to her room and saw fire on her bed and had called the police and . . .

What was said beyond that was lost in the emotion overwhelming the two of them, as Bill Fischer reached out to comfort Olivia, who at once was reduced to incoherence and began to cry. Those would be the last words Bill Fischer and Olivia Riner would ever say to each other.

When he turned, Fischer saw his daughter Leah had arrived, and he reached for her, telling her that her baby half sister had died in the fire. Around them the soft mist creating glittering halos of moisture around the bright lights gave way to rain.

Brian Dwyer needed to confirm his personal observations in the nursery. From what he had seen, Dwyer was already convinced that the fires had not been accidental. If they had been set intentionally, the crime would be arson. And if the arson caused the death of the baby, it would be murder. He wanted to verify his suspicions with another policeman.

Carpenter was standing over by the Fischers. Dwyer,

still wearing his firefighter gear but doing a necessary police chore, told Miliambro to follow him inside.

It was getting crowded in there. Assistant Thornwood fire chiefs Joe Rod and Jim Lawrence were checking the interior, as some of their men opened windows on the ground floor and others worked outside. No more flames had been found, but the inspection was incomplete.

The door to the baby's room was locked, but Miliambro disassembled his ballpoint pen and used its narrow brass ink cartridge to pick the lock. Inside the room, Dwyer pointed out the condition of the baby, the melted carrier seat, the burn pattern, and the heat-warped plastic beverage container that had melted into the carpet. Miliambro nodded in agreement. This fire had been deliberately set.

Outside, the weather worsened. Lieutenant Alagno, the senior police officer at the scene, moved over to where Carpenter stood with Olivia, the medical personnel, Bill and Leah Fischer, and John Gallagher. George and Katie Fries had volunteered their house as a command post, and Alagno accepted the offer. He suggested that Carpenter take everyone next door and get them out of the rain.

Bill Fischer shook off the idea. He, Leah, and John would await the arrival of Denise, who was hurrying home from Connecticut. He neither knew nor cared that it was raining.

Carpenter, accompanied by the ambulance corps personnel toting an oxygen tank, took Olivia to the Fries residence, where she sat down at the dining room table. The officer took out his spiral notebook again and began to question the girl, the sole witness to the tragedy.

"What happened over there? " Carpenter asked. Once again the dark-haired girl tried to compose herself while sobbing into a twisted white tissue, and murmured something about cats.

Bruce Johnson piloted his big unmarked Ford to a stop about 5:40 P.M., having listened to the chatter on the high-band frequency of his two-way radio. He had no flashing lights or siren going, and parked in an out-of-the-way area so as not to add to the confusion. The wet, cold air slapped his face as he got out and looked over the busy scene before him. The house was rectangular, with the narrow end facing the street, and set back about seventy-five yards from West Lake Drive. Big trees were on all sides, illuminated by the big lights that had been hooked to grumbling emergency generators.

The house had two stories, with a wooden outside stairway on the left that reached up from a macadam driveway to a patio that stretched around much of the second floor. Thick evergreens, trimmed back to be low, fat bushes, hugged the sides. There was plenty of glass in front, three long panes flanking the front door, and big windows and sliding doors upstairs. The sharply pitched roof slanted off to both sides of the sand-colored house with dark brown trim. A row of thick bushes bordered the front stone patio.

It was not the first time he had seen the house. Bruce Johnson had passed it hundreds of times because he had grown up in the neighborhood, prior to going to college and becoming a cop for the Town of Mount Pleasant twenty-one years ago. The index card at the station might not have shown the location of 5 West Lake Drive, but Johnson could have driven there with his eyes closed.

He saw plenty of familiar faces, and the activity, to him, did not seem unusual. He had been a volunteer fireman with the Thornwood department until 1984, hanging up his rubber boots after fifteen years on that job. There was nothing untoward happening here, in the judgment of an experienced officer.

Sergeant Dwyer and Lieutenant Alagno closed on him, along with patrolman Miliambro. When Johnson wanted to know who had been watching the baby, Miliambro replied, "The au pair." Now that was something different.

As the designated investigator, Johnson needed to see

what had happened, but with the firefighters still working inside, Dwyer guided the little group of policemen around to the left side of the house, to a low window behind a large bush. A ragged hole about a foot in diameter had somehow been torn in the glass.

Cautiously, Johnson bent over. The house was built into a slanted hill, and while the front was level with the lawn, the slope continued to incline toward the back of the house, and the windows on the lower floor were close to the dirt. The detective noticed the rectangular windows were an older style, broad wooden frames fitted into metal tracks. The two panes could slide sideways, to open in fair weather. This was definitely not fair weather. Johnson checked, and the side edges where the panes met in the middle were flush, secured by a lock.

He looked carefully at the hole in the glass, then stuck his head through it. He could see the baby in what looked like a car seat that had been burned so badly it lay flat in the midst of a burned circle. He saw a changing table against the far wall, a crib, a white dresser beside the carrier, and, on the far left, an open closet. It was enough. Johnson had seen worse in his career, but not by much.

In the hallway, the assistant fire chiefs grew uncomfortable. Something was not right. Joe Rod and Jim Lawrence had been in tight situations before, and this one had begun to prickle the hair on their necks. The little fire on the girl's bed had obviously been extinguished some time ago, and no hot spots or residual burning had been found in her room. The conflagration in the nursery, as horrible as it had been, also had been extinguished for some time.

So, then, just where the devil was all this smoke coming from? They turned to the end of the hall, where a final door stood. It was the bedroom of Leah Fischer. There had been no evidence of anything wrong there.

But the fire serpent that had been slumbering in that back room while firefighters were looking elsewhere was about to burst forth with a vengeance. As Rod and Lawrence watched in dread, smoke seeped out above the door and hovered in a thickening bank on the ceiling of the hallway.

Then, in an instant, the door turned black and all hell broke loose.

Chapter Four

DOUBTS

THE FIRE COOKED UNNOTICED IN LEAH'S ROOM, KEPT ALIVE
by the slightest hint of a draft, burning in a horseshoe
pattern around the sides and foot of her full-sized platform bed. It followed the path of least resistance, circulat-
ing to the ceiling and then banking down in a superheated
cloud of smoke and vapor.

It grew stronger in the enclosed room, with layers of
red-hot smoke transforming into a burnable gas. The
polyurethane mattress burned, dripping globs of plastic
onto the rug. A secretarial chair smoldered into a twist of
metal as the hungry fire ate the plastic stuffing in the seat
and backrest. Papers, pictures, loose articles, and everything in its path became fuel. The curious flames tasted a
small draft of air coming over the closed plywood door of
the closet and were drawn toward it. Fire soon ate
through the top of the door and devoured clothing on
hangers, dropping them into the smoldering heap of shoes
and other debris on the floor.

Slowly, the vapors built toward the necessary temperature, and ignited automatically as explosive gases rolled
down in a thick cloud.

The narrow closet, which stretched across the rear of
the bottom floor of the house, linked Leah's room with
the back of the nursery closet, and the fire followed that
path. Only a thin piece of drywall kept it from emerging

into the baby's room, where the earlier fire had already left its deadly mark.

Outside, a firefighter knelt down to look into Leah's window and felt heat wash over his face. He put a palm to the wall, felt the burning heat inside and yelled, "We've got a fire here!" Suddenly the lull was over. The firefighters surged to alertness again, and the yelling men, clattering equipment, and roar of the fire churned into a horrible noise.

Henry Flavin was about ten feet away, videotaping the operation as more firefighters rushed up, their axes and Halgan steel crowbars raised to attack the fire demon that was once again on the prowl.

Joe Rod and Jim Lawrence knew what was about to happen. The blackening door signaled a big fire was coming out of that back bedroom in a matter of seconds. They looked back down the hallway and saw a team of men grab the primary attack hose, ready to slam 125 gallons-per-minute of water at the brewing firestorm. The hoses running beside the flanks of the house outside were swiftly maneuvered into position.

Lawrence saw the determined look on Rod's face and put a hand on his arm. They checked their oxygen equipment and flipped down the clear plastic face shields on their helmets. Joe Rod kicked the smoldering bedroom door as hard as he could.

The room flashed with the sudden flood of air into the oxygen-starved fire and ignited a holocaust. A huge tongue of flame roared into the hallway, and the two assistant chiefs backed away, crowding into the baby's room as the hose team surged past them. Other firefighters smashed the panes in Leah's window from outside and opened a second hose.

Bruce Johnson had just pulled his head from the nursery window when the fire exploded through the rear of the closet in the baby's room and raced across the ceiling. Flames licked out through the broken window. Brian Dwyer picked up a small aluminum ladder and swung it like a club to demolish the remaining glass in that pane, giving the hose team more access and at the same time venting the heat, smoke, and flames that were suddenly threatening the house. Windows on the upper floor cracked. The sound of breaking glass echoed through the night.

For the next forty-five minutes the firefighters would tangle with a caldron of flame, the third fire of the evening to strike the house. Henry Flavin dashed from point to point, camera on his shoulder.

But Bruce Johnson was not there to put out a fire. His job lay elsewhere. He stepped back and examined the left side of the house while the firefighters went about their job. A broad wooden staircase at the front corner led up to a second-floor patio that ran along the front, side, and rear. An evergreen bush, fat and prickly, stood just outside the window to the baby's room. He went around to the rear and saw more patio area upstairs. A tin garden shed was set back from the house. It was dark back there because the emergency lights hooked to the fire department generators were focused on the front. Johnson could not complete his circle around the right side of the house because of the firefighters attacking the flames in Leah's room through that window. The detective found Miliambro and asked who had been watching the baby when the fire started. He was told it was the au pair, who was in the house next door. Johnson walked away from the burning structure, fire thrusting from the lower windows in billowing orange-red clouds, and headed across to the Fries house, a home he had visited before as a friend.

The detective found the nanny seated at an oval dining table, with Scott Carpenter standing near her, his notebook on the table as he asked questions. Guided by Mrs. Fries, they had arrived about the same time the fire erupted on the right side of the Fischer residence, accompanied by five ambulance medical personnel arrayed in a semicircle around Olivia.

Carpenter, using a soft voice, asked her again what had happened. "I don't smoke or have no fire," she replied. For three minutes they had discussed the situation in the most general terms, with Olivia describing feeding the cats and how one ran from her room. He asked if she had a hot plate in her room, or anything that might start a fire. "I don't smoke. I have no fire," she said again.

Carpenter looked up as Johnson came over. "Hello, Bruce. How you doin'?" Johnson acknowledged the patrolman, then introduced himself as a detective to the disheveled girl sitting at the table. Carpenter folded his notebook, where he had listed Olivia's occupation as "opar," and left, without sharing any of his notes with Johnson.

The detective took a good look at the nanny. She was a small girl, he guessed about five-foot-three and maybe 120 pounds. Long brown hair hung over her shoulders, and a mass of thick bangs fell to just above dark eyebrows that accented striking eyes of glacial blue. Although her face was a bit pudgy and she had a trace of a double chin, the high cheekbones, fair skin, and sharp nose gave her a delicate appearance. Her mouth, which pulled down at the corners, had a short upper lip. She was dressed casually, in dark jeans, a purple sweatshirt with a hood, and purple sneakers. He noticed that her clothing reeked of smoke, she was emotionally distraught but did not appear injured, and she spoke English haltingly, with a strange accent. Johnson withheld making any judgment. For him, at this moment, Olivia Riner was a tabula rasa, a clean blank slate on which they—the witness and the interrogator—would write together. She had been in charge of the baby that had burned to death in the fire next door. Something terrible had happened over there, and it was Johnson's job to determine just what that might have been, putting together the puzzle, piece by piece, until he had the answer.

Behind the nanny stood several members of the Ambulance Corps in their distinctive orange jackets, including

Gail Wind, the fire chief's wife and an old friend of the detective. Johnson nodded to her. A dim bulb overhead placed the table in a circle of light. He chose a chair between the wall and the table and put a yellow pad between them on which to write. It was just a little after six o'clock, and as he began to question her, they could hear the racket outside. Some forty firefighters battled the inferno next door.

First he needed background information, her name, where she was from, that sort of thing. Her voice was quiet, almost too soft to be heard, and Olivia hardly moved, except for twisting a sodden tissue. She was respectful and polite, answering every question that came her way. Her language was a problem, but not insurmountable if one listened to her closely.

Olivia Riner told her story, just as she had to the first policeman. She would be telling that same tale for the next nine hours, almost without pause.

She said she had been feeding the cats in the laundry room, playing with one on the floor while another walked away, heading for her bedroom. Johnson made a visual note: when she talked about the animals, her demeanor brightened.

"Was anyone else in the house with you?"

"Yes. The only other one was Kristie," she replied in her awkward English.

"Anyone else?"

"No. If anyone else was there, I would have seen them."

Johnson made a mental note. She is firm on this point, that she was alone in the house with the child. He had her pick up the account of the cats moving around.

Oliver, she said, ran out of the bedroom, appearing very angry, and when she went to see what was the matter, she discovered her bed on fire. A smoke alarm began to scream as she ran upstairs to get the fire extinguisher and returned, noticing when she did that the window of her bedroom was opened. "I didn't open window," she

44

said. The orange fire was doused by the extinguisher, and she turned to find Kristie's door closed and locked. "Door is never locked!" she said, with emphasis. Johnson wrote it down.

He dialed back in time: Had anyone else been at the house that evening? No, she said. The propane gas delivery man had come about four P.M., but no one else. At 4:30 she had given Kristie a bottle while sitting on the floor with the baby in her lap. Then she moved the napping infant into the nursery and went to feed the cats. After opening the can of tuna, she returned to the baby's room and checked on Kristie. The baby was still asleep in the car seat. Moments later she noticed the cats patrolling the closed front door. When she opened it, Fleetwood and Kabuki reluctantly went out into the dampness but O.J. stayed in. Olivia sat in a reclining chair in the front corner of the family room, playing with O.J., when Oliver dashed from the hallway.

They jumped ahead to when she went into her bedroom. The window was open, pushed aside about ten inches, "I don't know how." The light in her room would not go on. When she turned, she discovered that the door to the baby's room had been closed, and when she tried to open it, she found the brass knob was locked. She described calling the operator on the telephone, giving the address of the fire, calling Bill at the garage and the man calling back, the man to whom she explained exactly where the house was located.

Then she had gone upstairs to turn on the lights on the top floor, while smoke filled the downstairs area. When she opened the front door, O.J. the cat dashed out just as John Gallagher ran into the room and called out, "Where's Kristie? " He ran down the hall, then came back outside and asked if the baby was in the crib. Olivia told him Kristie was in the car seat, and John rushed back inside. Then the neighbor man went in and out of the house, and the man came wearing the yellow jacket.

Johnson asked: "The window in your room was open?"

"I don't open window." Her crying had finally stopped and her voice was gaining clarity.

"Did you hear, or see, anyone else in the house?"

"No."

They went through it for an hour, back and forth through the story as if walking a familiar trail, checking the details of the tragic evening repeatedly, the nanny never moving from her chair. He felt she was being extraordinarily calm for such a situation. Olivia, however, was reacting as she would in Switzerland, where people are respectful to a fault when government officials are involved.

That she actually had a choice of whether to talk to policemen never crossed her mind. That she had a right to have an attorney present during questioning also was unimaginable to her. And she did not know that, at any moment, she could have risen from her seat and walked away from the inquisitive detective without penalty. A stranger in a strange land, she was dealing with the nuances of a legal system about which she knew nothing. So she continued to sit there. And Bruce Johnson, questions forming in his mind, continued the interrogation.

As the detective was winding down his first hour with Olivia, someone important arrived at the fire scene next door. Joseph Butler, the legendary arson investigator for the Westchester County District Attorney's Office, braked his car to a halt about seven P.M., joining the throng of vehicles already dotting West Lake Drive and Nanny Hagen Road.

A small round man, Butler had been going to fires for almost fifty years and was considered one of the state's top experts on their causes and effects. If this fire had indeed been an arson, Joe Butler would determine it beyond a doubt.

He spoke briefly with a few officials at the scene and

went inside the structure, which stank of dampness and smoke. The family room carpet was spongy from water that had surged into the house from the three big hoses.

Butler wandered in and out of the various rooms in no particular order, his eyes recording the evidence and his brain cataloging what he saw, cross-matching with the evidence he had seen at thousands of other fire sites and coming up with conclusions. In the room of the au pair, he saw the remains of a very localized burn atop the bed, and rubbing his palm around the discolored spot on the lacy, transparent material that covered a tufted blanket, felt the gritty yellow residue that could only have come from a fire extinguisher.

In Leah's gutted room Butler determined the fire had been severe, starting around the big bed and transmitting toward the door of the closet. The contents of the closet were destroyed.

The baby's room showed evidence of two fires, one obviously an extension from the ferocious blaze that devoured Leah's back bedroom and burned through to the closet in the nursery, charring the ceiling. That fire could not have ignited the other burn pattern he saw in the room, in the far left-hand corner before the window.

His years of experience cried out to him that he had discovered evidence of three separate fires, intentionally set, and caused by the ignition of some flammable liquid. After his initial inspection, Butler was ready to give details to the investigating police.

Brian Dwyer was going through another metamorphosis. The fire was out, and with permission from Lieutenant Alagno to file overtime, Dwyer became a full-time policeman again. While other firefighters would do the cleanup work, Dwyer would play a major role in the investigation. He went to the Fries residence, tapped on the front door and signaled Bruce Johnson to come outside. The detective left Olivia at the table.

Dwyer and Johnson crossed the two lawns and went

into 5 West Lake Drive, hurrying to escape a sudden torrential downpour that had closed over the area. As rain pelted down in sheets, a conference was held between Johnson the detective, Dwyer the police sergeant, Butler the arson special investigator, and patrolman Miliambro. Butler told Johnson the fires were not of accidental origin, but had been intentionally set. The detective began his personal tour of the interior of the residence. With a video camera, he taped the rooms as he went along, noting that all windows had been smashed out by firefighters. Rain was blowing in.

There was the burn pattern in the center of Olivia's bed and the remaining frames of her window were slid open all the way to the right. Butler said the pattern resulted from flammable liquid being poured on the bed.

In little Kristie's room he took particular note of the burned portion of carpet around the baby, which was still in the destroyed carrier. A melted plastic soda bottle and a box of Diamond matches were within the three-foot-wide pattern of char. Butler said an intentional fire had been set at that point too. Johnson looked at the window, and the frames still met in the middle, with the thumb-locking mechanism in the secure position.

In the gutted room of Leah Fischer, there was a U-shaped pattern of deep burn scars around the bed and evidence of another pour upon the bed itself. Those were the points of origin for that destructive fire, said Butler. The window, with the blinds torn down, could be plainly seen, and Johnson observed that the middle edges of the two frames were flush, meaning the window was totally closed and the lock secured.

In the laundry room a can of cat food lay in the sink. A pile of laundry was next to a recycling container filled with plastic one-liter soda bottles with blue bottoms. An empty red fire extinguisher was on the floor near the living room door. For half an hour Johnson roamed the fire-ravaged residence, upstairs and downstairs, taking 35mm photographs and videotaping the scene. He determined that the house had a deceptive design. For although it appeared large from the outside, the rooms actually were quite small. He could understand why Olivia insisted that she would have known if anyone else had entered the premises while she was there.

Something nagged at him. If she were accurate in that statement, and all of the windows were locked, except in her room, and the three fires were all set intentionally, with the doors closed to Leah's bedroom and the baby's room, then how in the world did someone get in and do so much damage without her knowing about it? A mystery indeed.

At 7:30 P.M. Johnson told Lieutenant Alagno he had seen enough. He was returning next door to continue interviewing the au pair. As he resumed his interview, one-on-one with the Swiss girl, Johnson looked up to see Bill and a weeping Denise Fischer being escorted into the den of the Fries home. Not a word was exchanged between the Fischers and their nanny.

Johnson tried to get things back on track, learning for the first time that the girl had been hired by the E.F. Au Pair agency, which had set up the employment with the Fischers. They ran through the story again, quickly. The baby was asleep, she was feeding the cats in the living room, Oliver ran out, she found the bed on fire . . .

Bruce Johnson paused, tuning her out without turning her off. It wasn't much, but it was worth following. At first she had said she had fed the cats in the laundry room, and now the nanny was saying that she fed them in the living room. A discrepancy, duly noted.

He pressed on whether she was alone, and Olivia replied in the affirmative once again. If anyone had been there, "I would have either heard them or seen them."

It was becoming too confusing to continue working in the pandemonium of the Fries household. The Fischers were in the back, firefighters and ambulance personnel came and went, people were using the phone. Too much was going on.

Olivia had not moved from the chair, but her feelings were in turmoil. She sat alone, abandoned by the Fischers, the people with whom she lived. This wasn't good, Johnson felt. The detective decided to transfer the interview to the police station, to find someplace quiet to start to sort out this dilemma.

They stepped into the cold night air. Olivia pulled the gray jacket that Katie Fries had loaned her over her shoulders. The rain had stopped and they walked to the edge of the road, where officer Carpenter was talking with Lieutenant Alagno. Johnson had her remain with Carpenter while he rounded up the car keys, then he opened the back door to the vehicle and Olivia got in. There was no cage separating the back from the front seat, no painted markings on the gray Ford LTD, no roof rack of emergency lights. Riding to the station were two very big policemen in the front seat and a frightened and confused twenty-year-old Swiss girl in the rear.

It took only about two minutes for Johnson to drive the short distance to Town Hall Plaza, whisking down to the intersection and left on Columbus Avenue. They arrived at the long, low concrete building just before eight P.M. During the brief ride, not a word was spoken.

Chapter Five

ARREST

THAT THERE WAS NO DIALOGUE IN THE CAR BETWEEN CARPENTER and Johnson was, in retrospect, important, for they were the only two Mount Pleasant policemen who had interviewed the girl in the back seat. But it went deeper than that. While Johnson was making his tour of the burned house, Carpenter had been sitting in his squad car, taking an official statement from John Gallagher. He had known Gallagher's brother, and so was acquainted with John, and had taken the initiative in finding out what the young man was doing at the fire scene. Gallagher had given the policeman a cigarette as the rain pounded on the car roof and the officer took notes detailing what Gallagher did and observed that evening. Carpenter put his notes in his briefcase and reported it to his boss, Lieutenant Alagno, who also was familiar with the man whom Carpenter had interviewed.

Johnson was not informed of that interview before taking Olivia to the police station. Carpenter's notes would remain, unseen and useless, in his briefcase until he got off work at midnight.

This unintentional conspiracy of silence could be viewed, in retrospect, as the first light kiss of wind from a hurricane of official incompetency that was inexorably surrounding the house at 5 West Lake Drive.

For the layperson the presence of all the badges and

credentialed experts, and the men and women in uniform, would indicate everything was under control. Just the opposite was true. As Johnson drove away, things were already bad and heading toward worse.

Police sergeant Dwyer, wearing his cop hat again, began gathering evidence, assisted by officer Miliambro. They saw some things, such as flammable liquids in a storage closet, and did not see others, such as a bloodstain on a door frame. They filled four protective cans with evidence, then stopped, because they only had four cans. The fire extinguisher, last seen in the family room, was retrieved from the front lawn. After the body of the baby was removed, the fire-flattened infant car seat remained untagged as evidence.

Arson investigator Joe Butler, busy searching for causes, ordered an "overhaul." Firefighters tossed outside everything in the stricken rooms to search for possible hot spots. To do this, Butler had the bedroom window frames ripped out to eliminate those bothersome middle segments so the burned mattresses could be pushed through.

The trashing of the rooms undoubtedly destroyed evidence, a common result when arson is involved with another crime. Long after the flames were doused, firefighters stomped through the house, tracking their big muddy boots on the floors and looking around out of curiosity when they ran out of official chores. Even officer Carpenter would later say that he, too, had been curious and had gone on a look-see ramble through the residence without a specific legal mission. Authority at the scene was split between Fire Chief Wind, Police Lieutenant Alagno, Butler, and the heads of various other departments. That was even before a pair of Westchester County assistant district attorneys showed up to weigh possible criminal charges. It wasn't so much a case of conflicting instructions as a lack of leadership that was turning the situation on its head. A uniformed cop was positioned on the lawn, but the usual yellow tape barrier that keeps a crime scene pristine for the investigators was never erected.

The incident was being treated in an astonishingly cavalier manner by the senior officials involved. No experts were summoned to dust for fingerprints, no forensic scientists came to help determine what evidence might be useful, no county or state crime response teams were asked to assist the small-town police force. No roadblocks were set up to interview passersby. No house-to-house questioning was done. No one stopped to declare: "Hey! An arson and possibly the murder of a three-month-old baby has been committed here. This is a crime scene and must be protected!"

Under the rules of the game, Johnson, the investigating detective, was in charge. But to think that Bruce Johnson, who had spent most of his evening next door interviewing a single witness, was actually in control of this bewildering situation was preposterous. In reality, he was barely in the information loop on some critical points.

In fact, no one took control at the scene of this awful crime. But they all were the best of friends.

Johnson made a left turn at the intersection of Nanny Hagen Road and Columbus Avenue and sped down the broad drive, his tires whispering on the wet road, finally curling left into the Town Hall Plaza parking lot and driving down the ramp to the front entrance of the police department. Carpenter was dismissed as soon as they walked into the lobby, and Johnson asked Betsy Hoagland, a female civilian dispatcher behind the glass booth on the right-hand side, to join them. Sergeant Gardner, who had made the original calls, remained on desk duty. Johnson and Olivia went through a door beside the booth and down a narrow hallway, past the empty offices of the chief and lieutenants, past the records room where the lack of computerization left old arrests, warrants, and other such paperwork hidden in big file cabinets. The hallway reached a dead end at a barred yellow door, the entrance to the three-cell detention area. Continuing, they soon entered the long, narrow, and cluttered room used by the detectives. Clearly it was a male domain—the gun with its bent barrel leaning against a wall, the machete stuck into something by a window, chains and manacles hanging from pegs, bursting file cabinets, a one-way mirror with its shade drawn beside the door, a display of headlines of solved crimes from the past.

Johnson's desk, a jumbled affair of papers and souvenirs that seemed to grudgingly make room for a black telephone, was halfway down the right wall, facing an identical steel desk. A small intercom was on the wall beside it. He sat in a swivel chair and Olivia sat in a straight-backed chair to his left. Hoagland brought over a chair from another desk, and the three of them sat at the points of an invisible triangle. The office had bright fluorescent lighting, and as Johnson took his place, he noticed he could see Olivia's face much better. He looked hard at those blue eyes, for he thought something appeared different under the bright lights. In a moment it came to him. Her eyelashes were dirty and uneven—as if singed by a fire! The right eyelash was worse than the left. He said nothing, but made a mental note.

He glanced at a clock. It was 7:50 P.M., and he began to question the young foreign woman once more, walking over the same ground as before. But this time he was definitely looking for inconsistencies. When Bruce Johnson saw the damaged eyelashes, Olivia Riner was promoted in his mind from the status of witness to that of suspect.

His questions now had a sharper, different purpose, and Olivia detected the change. She would sob and look into her lap, her voice trailing away. She had already told the big detective everything and told him again, over and over, and he wanted to know more. Johnson reached over and gently lifted her chin, raising her face. He wanted her looking at him, not at her feet, when she answered the questions.

He pulled a sheet from a yellow legal pad and began to work with Olivia to sketch the layout of the ground floor of the Fischer residence in long pencil marks. The front door opened into the downstairs family room, with a storage closet just to the left of the door, and the entryway to the staircase just beyond that. The hallway sliced the downstairs in half. On the left, after the stairs, was a laundry room, the only bathroom in the house, and the baby's room. On the right side of the hall was the furnace room, Olivia's bedroom, and Leah's bedroom. Leah's closet extended across the back of the house, all the way behind the nursery.

Then, with pencil points, fingers, and words, they went through the story once again.

At eight P.M. things quieted around 5 West Lake Drive, and Sergeant Brian Dwyer was taking photographs and gathering evidence. A specialist from the office of the county medical examiner had arrived and was removing the body of the baby from the burned carrier seat, as Dwyer and Miliambro, who was helping him, stood in the destroyed nursery and watched. As the tiny corpse was picked up, the burned diaper around its bottom fell off, landing in the center of the burn pattern surrounding the carrier.

Dwyer bent down and picked up the diaper. It had a peculiar odor, and using his firefighter training again, he detected the strong, pungent smell of a flammable liquid, probably something like paint thinner, emanating from the charred cloth. He wanted to be sure and extended it toward Miliambro. "What does that smell like? "

The officer took a whiff. "Paint thinner."

Dwyer went to find a telephone, as the baby's remains were placed in a special case and taken away.

Bruce Johnson listened to the voice in the receiver without changing expression. Dwyer told him they had discovered the baby's diaper had been doused in paint thinner.

Slim, almost gossamer threads of evidence were beginning to tighten around the girl seated before him. The questioning continued, while back at the house Dwyer and Miliambro went through the contents on the shelves of the storage closet. Several cans of burnable fluids were there, and the policemen stuffed them into plastic bags as evidence.

Scott Carpenter returned to the scene by nine P.M. and was sitting in his marked patrol car. Lieutenant Alagno wanted him to get fresh clothes for the au pair.

Two civilians approached his car and began to quiz him about what had happened. Carpenter was a bit hesitant, because he normally would not discuss a case with a civilian. When they identified themselves, however, he quickly complied.

James McCarty and Maryellen Martirano were assistant district attorneys for Westchester County. Martirano specialized in domestic violence and child abuse and had been summoned because a child had been involved in the fire. McCarty, a homicide specialist, was a heavy hitter in the D.A.'s office and was one of the prosecutors currently handling the explosive *Fatal Attraction* trial of Carolyn Warmus, a woman charged with the shooting death of her lover's wife.

After chatting with them, Carpenter went back into the house and performed the uncomfortable task of picking out some suitable clothes for Olivia Riner. It was not a job that he, nor probably most young men, could have done well. He did not color-coordinate or guess how the outfit might look together. He grabbed the first things he saw, a pair of tattered jeans festooned with big patches over the knees, and a dark sweatshirt emblazoned with the peculiar design of a woman wearing a big hat. Then the big cop had to pick up feminine underwear.

* * *

At headquarters two hours had passed swiftly as Johnson led Olivia through her story a few more times, gaining some new details. She had been to the United States twice before coming to live with the Fischers. For the American holiday of Thanksgiving, a barbecue was held at the Fischer house and Olivia was allowed to drive Denise's car the short distance to Marymount College in Tarrytown and bring back another German-speaking au pair as a guest. Olivia said she felt lucky that she only had to look after Kristie when the other girl told her she had to care for three children.

As Johnson continued to question her, Olivia continued to sob and twist her tissue and would not look at him, instead letting her chin sink into her chest.

Johnson was on the edge of a decision. He asked Olivia, as he had several times, if she wanted anything to eat or drink, or if she needed to visit the bathroom. No. She stayed put. Outside the detectives' office he had a brief talk with Lieutenant Alagno while thumbing through a copy of the New York penal code. The detective told the lieutenant that, after five hours of questioning, most of his doubts had vanished. She had been alone in the house, three separate fires had been set, the house was small enough for her to detect any intruders, the windows were locked in two of the three bedrooms, and flammable liquid of the sort used to set the fire in the baby's room was available from the storage closet. Alagno did not disagree.

For motive, Johnson theorized that something had happened to the baby while it was in Olivia's care that afternoon. Perhaps she dropped it, or it had suffocated, or who knows what, and she panicked enough to set the fires in an attempt to cover up the death. It was his call.

He went back into his office. Hoagland and Olivia were still seated. A few more questions. He asked if she was jealous of Leah's boyfriend or of Bill Fischer. No. Was she sexually active with anyone? No. Did she have a boyfriend? No.

Bruce Johnson paused, then reached for a battered, yellowing card amid the jumble on his desk. It contained the text of the Miranda rights to which every defendant is entitled. Then he told the brown-haired young woman that she was under arrest for arson in the third degree.

Chapter Six

DAZED AND CONFUSED

BEFORE READING OLIVIA HER LEGAL RIGHTS, WHICH, UNDER the U.S. Constitution, were the same for a Swiss national as a native-born American, Detective Johnson picked up one of the two tape recorders in the office, a Japanese-made Aiwa, placed it on a ledge beside his desk and turned it on. His first words gave the date and the time, 10:20 P.M., and he noted that he and Betsy Hoagland were in the room for an interview with Olivia Riner. No interpreter was present, and the young nanny was about to be thrust into a world that she clearly did not understand. She had cooperated with the police, answering all of their questions, and now this big man had said she was under arrest for the crime of arson, whatever that might be. Her fright at the fire had turned into worry, then into apprehension, and now she was back to fear. As close as she could figure, she was being called a criminal.

A cultural habit, in which a Swiss person helps authority figures, had played against her, and the language differences, which might be minor in ordinary conversation, soon stretched into an unbridgeable gap, as Johnson tried to explain her rights.

He told her she had the right to remain silent and that anything she said could be used against her in a court of law. She had the right to talk to a lawyer and have the lawyer present beside her, while she was being questioned. If she could not afford a lawyer, one could be appointed before she was questioned. She could exercise those rights at any time and not answer any questions. "Do you understand each of these rights that I have explained to you?" Johnson asked.

"Some I don't," she replied. From there it went straight downhill.

For instance, she did not understand the word "remain". At that point Hoagland, a civilian with no official standing whatever, joined the conversation. Instead of an officer of the law explaining the rights, a radio dispatcher was helping to perform that vital function. Hoagland said the term "remain silent" meant Olivia could "just be quiet."

There were a few other things Olivia said she didn't understand in the basic warnings; such as *lawyer*, and *court of law*, and *to hire*, and *decide*. Johnson's explanations were hardly crystal clear to the girl, such as when he defined a "court of law" as the "American judicial system." Eventually, however, Olivia said she thought she understood the rights and agreed to continue.

Johnson said he would be asking the same questions.

She said she would be giving the same answers. "I can't say anything different."

And off they went, once again going over the afternoon's events detail by detail, from the time Bill Fischer came home for lunch until the fire broke out three hours later. The tape machine recording this conversation was on the far side of the desk, at the detective's back, so his deep voice came through loud and clear, but her soft, strained replies were at times inaudible. Some legal observers would later comment that if Johnson would have placed the tape recorder between them, in plain sight, Olivia might have become more cautious in her replies.

Her language had lapsed under the strain into broken English, with nouns and verbs and adjectives getting mixed up, Olivia floundering to find the right words. The results were sentences such as, "She had not the plastic—

but we don't use this only when we go out. When she's home we use the cloth diapers. They're little, thin and bigger. I use the most time the bigger. And I make this and then she's a little bit fussy. She don't want to play mobiler [sic]—take the mobiler away." Clear as mud.

And still no one stepped in to question whether this line of inquiry should continue, without providing the girl with the kind of help tacitly implied in the Miranda warning.

Olivia described how much milk she had fed the baby, what the condition of the diapers were, how Kristie enjoyed hearing the sound of the television set, and how, just before she put the baby in the carrier on the floor of the nursery for a nap, "she sleep in my arms." She detailed how she fed the four cats and washed out the food cans from the morning and threw them into the recycling bin, how she was playing with O.J. before the noisy television when "I see Oliver run out of my room and I see Oliver run out and I go to look why and I see fire in my bed."

Here they hit another snag when the detective wanted to know how big that fire was. "How tall was [sic] the flames? "

"What? "

"A foot? One foot? "

"What's a foot? "

"Twelve inches."

"What's an inch? "

Johnson reached into his desk drawer and pulled out a wooden ruler, standing it on end to show the markings and indicate the height of an inch and a foot. He did not use the reverse side of the ruler, which was marked in the metric system the European girl would have instantly recognized.

She repeated the nightmare of calling an unresponsive police department for help and how the man called back to say there was no 5 West Lake Drive. "Don't get it and I must tell him where the others is," she said.

Back and forth they went, Johnson trying to think of every bit of detail. The horror of finding the baby's room locked, what was stored around the house, the color of the smoke, how she was alone in the house—these and dozens of other points were examined.

"You don't know how the fire started in your room . . ."

"No."

"Or anywhere else? "

"I don't know."

"What did you think? "

"I don't know . . . I don't know how the fire start."

Johnson decided it was enough. They had gone on record for more than an hour. He noted aloud that the time was 11:37 P.M., then turned off the Aiwa.

There was a new face in the room. Betsy Hoagland was replaced by Marie Solimando, a motherly looking woman with big eyes. She had been asleep when the desk sergeant telephoned her at 10:30 P.M. and asked her to come in. Solimando was now caught in a vise of divided feelings. A little baby had been killed, probably intentionally, and this quiet young woman seated across from her was accused of setting the deadly fire. Sometimes she was baffled by her job.

After making the tape, Johnson picked up a Polaroid camera and snapped a few shots of Olivia's face to try and capture the peculiar look of her eyebrows. The picture shows her with her head down, in a look of total submission. Then he gave Solimando instructions to have Olivia change her clothes, and he left the room.

The ordeal was embarrassing for both women. To ensure privacy, Solimando checked the blinds on the one-way mirror and the door to the room. Then, in the harsh lights of the detective's office, she had Olivia strip.

Solimando tried to be discreet. Only half of the girl's body was nude at any one time. When she finished taking off all of her clothes on top, she put on the sweatshirt, then replaced the jeans and panties. Solimando neatly folded the clothing and put them into a brown paper bag for laboratory analysis.

That, however, was not the end for the night. The tape recorder was put away, but now the questions took on a bludgeoning effect, as Alagno, Dwyer, and even a white-haired, craggy-faced man who identified himself as Police Chief Paul Oliva, joined in. Voices were raised. Accusations were made. Was she covering up for someone? Was she trying to protect John Gallagher? No, she cried. No. The brutal session went on without letup. There was no need for politeness now.

Midnight passed. One A.M. on December 3, a new day, swept by unnoticed. Two A.M. came and went. Then three A.M.

The police had their suspect and they wanted a confession. "They just plain hammered her," said one person who knew about the early morning session. "They went at her without mercy."

But they didn't get a confession. In the end the quiet girl was stronger than all the men who were verbally beating on her. She did not change her story.

She was never given access to a telephone to call for help before or during the interview. Finally Olivia was escorted out of the detectives' office. Only a few steps away were the jail cells. This time she turned to the right, straight into the heart of the steel beast.

The outer door rumbled back, clanking against its barrier. A small walkway spread in front of three cells; the two on the far end were open and used for male prisoners. They were empty. Olivia stepped into the third, used to detain women. It had a metal screen, with some holes in it, to shield the area of the stainless steel toilet with no seat. Along the right-hand wall, hanging about two feet off the floor, stretched a long wooden bench that would be her bed that night.

Olivia went inside and the barred steel door smacked shut behind her, separating her from the outside world. She had never been so alone in her life. She was a prisoner in a foreign country! She looked up at the cream-colored wall and saw that earlier inmates had scratched graffiti into the paint. One called for PIGS TO DIE, another said uncomplimentary things about Sergeant Dwyer and a third expressed her own wash of emotions at the time. From an old rock song by Led Zeppelin were scrawled the words, DAZED AND CONFUSED.

Just beyond the outside door a worried Marie Solimando adjusted a chair and began her nightlong vigil.

In the cold cell, alone and as far from her home in Switzerland as she could be, Olivia lay down on her stomach and buried her face in her arms. She was without friends, without family, and even without someone with whom she could communicate in her own language.

Quietly she began to cry, her shoulders shaking and the unanswered tears soaking into the sleeves of her black sweatshirt.

Chapter Seven

HOLLYWOOD NIGHTMARE

THE ARREST OF OLIVIA RINER WAS A FLASH OF FARAWAY LIGHT-ning and a rasp of distant thunder. A storm was coming.

The role of a nanny in society had deep, almost mystical, roots. Actress Julie Andrews was the model for the dream nanny, as she cavorted and sang amid clouds and love to establish the Hollywood version of nannydom. A household might be in chaos, but when the energetic nanny came on the scene, someone was able to take charge and straighten out the lives of all involved. A dirty-faced, magical *Mary Poppins* floated about beneath her umbrella, and Maria von Trapp made the hills come alive with *The Sound of Music*. These motion pictures were based on the idea that only the wealthy could afford a European nanny.

Reality caught up with the movies. In the 1980s and into the 1990s, the two-income household in America had led to farming out children to day care centers, to neighbors, to babysitters, and, for those who could afford it, to importing live-in nannies from other countries. Dad had to go to work, Mom had to go to work, so the child became someone else's responsibility. It was not long before horror stories began to appear about atrocities some child keepers visited upon the kids in their care. Money for substitute parenting purchased only a limited amount of love, and with state governments unable to keep up with the need for appropriate day care, enforcement of rules and prosecution of violators fell behind.

About the time the news began to spread of the Swiss nanny jailed in Westchester County, Hollywood was ready with another movie about nannies.

The Hand That Rocks the Cradle became a surprise overnight box office hit in January 1992, and pulled in some $50 million in its first four weeks. The perky Julie Andrews image was shattered by the terrifying portrayal of actress Rebecca De Mornay as a seemingly wonderful nanny who was really a monster.

De Mornay simply scared the hell out of parents across the nation and changed, probably forever, the image of babysitters. Moms and Dads who had given more thought to where to have dinner than to who was watching over their children had a wake-up call. About 75,000 nannies and au pairs were employed in the United States, most distributed through approximately 800 unregulated agencies to America's modern, middle-class, two-income households. Suddenly the bond between babysitter and family was something to be carefully examined. Parents began to wonder if they *really* knew the background of the au pair, babysitter, or nanny caring for their child.

In an alarming number of cases, the worst things that could happen to a child did. In Palmdale, California, the parents of two-year-old Stevie Lewis suspected a problem and hid a video camera in their home. They later viewed the horrendous sight of their nineteen-year-old nanny knocking the child on the head with a spoon for not eating yogurt and, holding an arm to arrest the impact, flinging the tot to the floor. In Colorado, day care provider Heidi Jensen was trimming her poodle with an electric clipper when she allegedly became annoyed with the crying of ten-month-old Jacqueline Rosenfield. Police charged she grabbed the child and smashed her on the head repeatedly with the clippers, fracturing the baby's skull. Jensen was charged with felony child abuse and second-degree murder. The trial is pending.

THE NANNY MURDER TRIAL

WHO'S ROCKING THE CRADLE? A HIT MOVIE STRIKES A NERVE, roared a headline in *People* magazine. THE NANNY NIGHTMARE, chimed in *U.S. News & World Report*. WANTED: MARY POPPINS, added *Newsweek*. Television's freak-du-jour talk shows jumped on the subject, newspapers wrote somber editorials, and government bureaucracies that watched over the mushrooming day care industry were quick to point out that any supervision problem was not their fault.

With the nation alarmed, advice to parents came from all points—how to look past references and trust their instincts on how the au pair related to the kids, and vice versa. Reports of abuse also came from the nanny–au pair community, as some girls told how their job descriptions changed radically once they were inside a household. Instead of just taking care of a child, they were treated like live-in maids, bartenders, gofers, and sex objects by the busy mothers and fathers who thought the small salaries they paid bought unlimited privilege.

Actually, the number of working mothers with children under five years of age and using an in-home sitter or nanny had been falling for a long time. In 1965 it was fifteen percent, but by 1990 it had shrunk to only three percent. The mobile middle class had found it cheaper and more expedient to shuttle kids to day care centers than to have the intrusive presence of someone else living in their house.

Tales of child abuse at the hands of their keepers were not new. In 1983 six-month-old Elizabeth Phillips was shaken so hard by her babysitter, the blood vessels burst in the child's eyes, leaving her blind for life. The babysitter, found guilty and given a minimal sentence, had been in the midst of a sex-change operation at the time. Also in California, in 1988, five-month-old David Duncan died from abuse inflicted by a family day care provider. Ashley Snead, ten months old, was murdered in 1987 by the grandmotherly operator of a day care center who poisoned the child to keep her from crying. A police check found warm, friendly Martha Guba, who ran the center, had a string of convictions in other states, ranging from larceny and grand theft to abusing her own kids.

Senator Christopher Dodd of Connecticut complains that auto mechanics, pet shop owners, and barbers all have to pass licensing examinations, but almost anyone with a sincere look and a vacant room can go into the kid care business by meeting only minimum requirements. The result, in a society where children are farmed out to people who are not their parents, is a growing number of abuses.

There is no sign that the situation will change.

It was against this macabre backdrop that the case of Olivia Riner would be played out. For here was a nanny from a foreign country and with impeccable credentials, who stood accused of killing the baby in her care. This was not a movie, not a book, not a fictionalized exaggeration.

It was real, and it was a nightmare that wrenched the soul of Westchester County.

PART TWO

Landscapes

Chapter Eight

PLACES

THE MERE MENTION OF WESTCHESTER COUNTY IS ENOUGH TO make frustrated dwellers of New York City salivate. Imprisoned in concrete canyons, they can envision a place of rolling hills, quiet suburbs, and true tranquility. For almost three hundred years the county has been a lure to those who seek an American Dream neighborhood while still having one of the world's most important cities at their doorstep.

The land had been settled by several Mohegan Indian tribes, and it was not until the seventeenth century that its destiny began to change. A poor lad with a thirst for adventure quit his job as a carpenter with the Dutch West India Company and turned to opening new trade routes for Europe's businessmen. By the age of twenty-seven Frederick Philipse was known as the Prince of Traders. In 1676 he purchased a vast tract in the former New Amsterdam area that reached from the modern day Hudson River to the Bronx, New York.

The Dutchman's sons and grandsons continued to build in the fertile area. Communities were established and prospered.

The American Revolution changed the ownership, however, when Frederick Philipse III sided with King George of England in the dispute with the ragtag colonists. For that, the last lord of the manor was stripped of

71

all his holdings. Some 92,000 acres reaching over twenty-four miles along the banks of the majestic Hudson River were turned over to tenant farmers. It marked the start of democracy in the region, and a few years after the revolution, the New York State Legislature divided Westchester County into twenty townships. Their prosperity drew settlers from the waves of European immigrants coming to the new United States of America.

Among the townships inked onto that map was Mount Pleasant, a rather idyllic location covering twenty-eight square miles near the narrow middle of Westchester. The town was divided into the Village of Pleasantville and the abutting hamlets of Valhalla, Hawthorne, and Thornwood.

Its isolated location managed to keep the place distant from such unpleasantness as the War of 1812 with England and then the Civil War, which did little more than pump in additional money. A saw mill was established, pickle factories succeeded, as did the Kensico Dam project and the Snow Flake Lime Works, the massive marble quarry in Thornwood which produced the beautiful veined stone hauled downriver to build New York's exquisite St. Patrick's Cathedral.

Money seemed to float into Westchester, and the place bloomed with new fortunes. The most famous person to come out of Mount Pleasant was Nelson Rockefeller, whose family owned 2800 precious acres in the Pocantico Hills. He became governor of New York and vice-president of the United States.

The truly glorious years of Westchester County began in the 1920s, following the business acumen of DeWitt and Lila Acheson Wallace, who bought a hilltop in Pleasantville and set up a headquarters for their eclectic magazine, *The Reader's Digest*.

The red-brick village life in Westchester, combined with the railways extending out of New York, enticed other businesses to make the jump, creating new jobs and a tidy base of taxes. Each new mile of Interstate Highway 287, the Sprain Brook Parkway, the Saw Mill River Parkway, and the Taconic State Parkway meant more access to Westchester. Pleasantville and Mount Pleasant became quite pleasant indeed.

A promotional piece by the county called Westchester "the classic bedroom community for Manhattan's movers and shakers." General Foods, IBM, Pepsico, Texaco, Nestle, TWA, and other corporate giants moved in. Life seemed charmed.

Nothing lasts forever, and Westchester's isolation from the outside world was no exception.

Growth took its toll, and the burgs of lower Westchester began to look like a megatown. The problems of an overgrown New York City crept northward along those same routes that once brought peace and success. The trouble was quiet, but insistent as termites chewing on the foundations of a stately mansion. Once Westchester was among the three wealthiest counties in the entire nation. By 1982 it ranked eighteenth and was going down.

In 1980 Westchester had 866,599 residents, or five percent of the entire population of New York State. Ten years later the total rose to 874,806, but the mix had changed. More minorities had moved in and the white population had aged.

Black residents were 9.5 percent of the population in 1970 and 12.1 percent a decade later, a demographic alteration the Westchester Community Services Council noted as being due to "an accelerated out-migration trend for whites," governmentese for white flight. By 1990 the white population had fallen 4.9 percent from ten years earlier, while the overall nonwhite population was up a hefty 32 percent, including an Hispanic community that increased 89 percent. The language of the towns was no longer solely English, but could just as well be Korean or Haitian or Spanish or Arabic.

Alongside that shift came a severe money squeeze. Recession ate into the local economies, government budgets were stretched thin, the real estate market dried up, and the sweet taste of Westchester County turned a little sour.

For residents clinging to the idea that their land is especially blessed, one thing that is cherished is the togetherness found in the parks and the bars along the tree-lined streets that meander through beautiful countryside. Many families have been there for generations. Friends stick together and look out for each other. In the tight little thickets of population, like Thornwood, an "us against them" attitude is not far below the surface.

And Olivia Riner was an outsider, from Europe! There was no way she could be considered one of "us."

By American standards, Westchester County may be very old, but measured against Switzerland, the county is relatively young. Call us when you reach five hundred years and we will talk, say the Swiss, who are already at the eight-hundred-year mark.

Landlocked Switzerland is in the heart of Central Europe, with Italy to the south, Austria and Liechtenstein to the east, France to the west, and Germany to the north. The tiny, oval-shaped nation covers only about 16,000 square miles—just over the combined size of the American states of Connecticut, Vermont, and Rhode Island.

Its location at the flash point of so many wars, revolutions and assorted uprisings during Europe's tumultuous early centuries helped the Swiss decide the best way to survive was not to play the unstable game of politics. The various tribes of ancient Switzerland banded together in 1291 to become a single entity, and vowed to stay out of the conflicts of their neighbors, declaring neutrality as conflict raged around them.

While the Germans made cannon, the Swiss made chocolate. The French marched on Egypt, while the Swiss tinkered with precision timepieces. The Italians were crushed trying to become a military power, and the crafty Swiss became the world's best bankers. Europe was ravaged by wars while the Swiss castles and towns aged gracefully.

The borders help define the languages and customs of the Swiss who live near them. Almost seventy-four percent of the people speak German, about twenty percent speak French, some five percent speak Italian, and the rest use a rare tongue known as Raeto-Romansch.

Today, a walk through the cities will take a visitor down streets centuries old, into arcades where merchants have been showing their wares for hundreds of years and down sidewalks that have felt the tread of peasants' bare feet and the soft boots of the gentry. Statues abound, depicting everything from ogres eating children to knights battling lions. Intricate clocks toll the hours in town squares, and in the countryside, cows wearing bells as big as bowling balls nibble on emerald grass, clanging their way toward milking time. All around, the serrated teeth of some of the world's tallest mountains insulate the country.

The majestic Alps spread across about 61 percent of Switzerland, but are not the only mountain range in Switzerland.

Across an undulating plateau that forms the midlands, where most of the farms and urban centers are located, is a chain of limestone mountains known as the Jura. As those craggy crests march toward the northeast, the final large hill, known as the Lagern, is located just on the northern edge of the village of Wettingen, in the northern canton of Aargau, just across the Rhine River from Germany's Black Forest.

When Olivia Riner stepped outside the apartment block where she lived with her parents, she saw the Lagern looming over the village like a benevolent wall that kept away the outside, dangerous world.

Her hometown was steeped in history long before she came on the scene, but over time, what was once a village noted for its wine-growing ability mushroomed into a blue-collar residential suburb for metropolitan Zurich, just fifteen miles away to the south.

It is impossible to avoid the past in Switzerland. No matter how modern Wettingen, a town of some 18,000 residents might be, their past would always be reflected in the baroque Wettingen Abbey which dominates the town. Once of religious significance, it now is a school, but still features statues of abbots and monks whose names have been lost to time.

Wettingen is not truly alone. The Limmat River, angling through to the west like a giant number 7, separates it from the bustling city of Baden. As the abbey watches over Wettingen, the Stein Castle marks Baden, once the capital of the Hapsburg Empire. The Old Town, with its medieval look of stepped gables and brown roofs with dormer windows, was once a favored stop for royalty and the wealthy, who, since the time of the Romans, would seek the comforts of Baden's 118-degree hot sulfur springs.

Today, Baden is known throughout the world not for its hot baths, but as the headquarters for BBC-Brown Boveri, Ltd., a massive enterprise that does the equivalent of $25 billion a year in business globally. It ranks only behind food giant Nestle as the largest company in Switzerland.

Olivia Riner was born in the small village of Wurenlos on November 7, 1971, the year that the women of Switzerland won the right to vote. When she was only a little more than a year old, in the first month of 1973, her parents, Kurt and Marlies Riner, moved the family about ten miles to Wettingen and settled in.

Their only child, known as "Olli" to her friends, grew up as a sensitive, gentle, and friendly girl who went through her kindergarten, primary, and secondary schooling in solid but undistinguished fashion. In a land where private houses are rare, the three members of the Riner family lived in a third-floor apartment, in a block of seven such flats, at Seminarstrasse 78. Kurt, a tall, sandy-haired man with a brown mustache, worked as the civil defense chief for the town of Neuenhof and was an officer with the local volunteer fire brigade. A peculiar law in neutral Switzerland requires that every new house or apartment building have a well-stocked, up-to-date atomic bomb shelter. It was the task of Olivia's father to determine that those shelters were adequately stocked. Her mother, a slim and attractive woman with dark hair, worked across the bridge in Baden, for Diebold AG.

Wettingen offers little in the way of entertainment for young people. There is a motion picture theater and a disco, and the Riner apartment building was right next to Altenburg Stadium, which is home to the town's soccer team. Those things paled in comparison with hopping aboard a commuter train heading down through a picturesque valley to the lights of Zurich.

In many countries it is not unusual for the young people, after their compulsory schooling, to do extensive traveling before settling down. Any summer, the roads of Europe are stocked with young hitchhikers carrying only their backpacks and a sense of adventure. Youngsters from Australia and New Zealand regularly spend months abroad before returning to their isolated homelands. Switzerland is no exception. Young men and women want to get out and take a look at the world they have seen on television and read about in books.

The weather in Wettingen is bright in the summertime, but the winters are bitterly cold, with a thick layer of clouds blotting out the sun, and who needs a lifetime of that without first checking out what else may be available?

From the northern sector of Switzerland, where the German influence is heavy, many Swiss dash southeast and spend time around Geneva, near the Burgundy area of France. Many choose to summer in England.

Olivia wanted more, and the United States was a strong attraction. She had twice visited America, seeing the honky-tonk life of New Orleans and the fantasy parks of Disney World in Florida, and she liked what she saw. She knew her special skills in child care might be just the ticket abroad for an extended stay. After all, Olivia had ranked near the top of her class in the Zurich medical training school, Juventus, followed that with experience as an assistant to a pediatrician, and provided primary care for children. With those credentials, and the desire to go abroad, she was an attractive prospect for the Sweden-based E.F. Au Pair, part of a nonprofit foundation that specializes in foreign exchange positions for hundreds of teachers, tourists, students, and au pairs.

Olivia was willing to exchange her knowledge and experience for a year in the home of an American family, providing child care five days a week. She would be paid $100 a week and given room and board.

After an application, a background check, and some telephone interviews, an au pair position came through. On the first day of November 1991, four days before her twentieth birthday, Olivia Riner notified her local police that she was leaving, boarded a plane at Zurich's Kloten International Airport, and spent seven and one-half hours flying to America. She was met at New York's sprawling John F. Kennedy Airport by the people who would be her family for the coming year, Bill and Denise Fischer, and their infant daughter, Kristie Rebecca.

They drove north from New York City, where she glimpsed the spires of that metropolis, and soon were on a superhighway whisking through countryside where trees were almost barren of foliage. By the time she arrived in the community of Thornwood, Olivia knew she was far, far from home.

The neighborhood, however, seemed ordinary enough. A couple of shopping centers were nearby, and the entire place had an air of stability and safety. A house just up the street, not too unlike the one at the end of the long black driveway that the car entered, was for sale, and the asking price was $249,000.

She would learn that her new home had a somewhat confusing history. Bill Fischer, who had grown up in the area before going into the Navy and experiencing the sunny clime of San Diego, California, had returned to his roots and worked for twenty-six years at a garage founded by his grandfather. Denise was an accountant for a company called Chrysler Capital, in nearby Stamford, Connecticut.

The house, on just under an acre at 5 West Lake Drive, had existed for thirty-five years, built by Bill's in-laws. Bill had lived there for twenty-two years. When he was divorced in 1989 from his first wife, Grada Menting Fischer, who moved to Manhattan, he stayed on good terms with her and her parents and eventually bought out Grada's interest in the house. After he met and married Denise, he remodeled it. Bill's two children from his first marriage had grown up in the house. Troy, twenty-five, now lived in Manhattan; and Leah, twenty-two, still lived there.

Exhausted by her trip, Olivia was shown to her bedroom. It was on the right side of the downstairs hallway. By looking out her door, she could see right into the baby's nursery.

She was lonely that first night, but not discouraged. It had been her choice to try America, and she had known that the real world was going to be different than Disney World. She would live here for a year. She could do that, couldn't she?

Chapter Nine

MOTIVE

THE STORY, WITH TOO MANY DRAMATIC ELEMENTS TO BE KEPT under wraps, broke in the morning newspaper on December 3. Gannett's *Reporter-Dispatch* carried the headline:

THORNWOOD INFANT GIRL DIES;

NANNY FACES ARSON CHARGE

Picked up by the Associated Press, the item spread across the nation, and, from the newsrooms of New York's television stations, camera crews scrambled to Thornwood in time for the nanny's afternoon arraignment. The small corps of Swiss correspondents based in the United States received frantic telephone calls from their editors.

Olivia Riner and Bruce Johnson had both experienced bad nights. She had been unable to sleep in her small cell almost until dawn, and Johnson tossed and turned in his own bed, asking himself over and over why she would have committed such a crime. The question would haunt him for months.

He was back at the station early, standing in the hallway when Olivia was escorted into the cramped offices shared by the department's two lieutenants. She was finally allowed to speak by telephone with her father, Kurt, in Switzerland. In the communications room, the tape recorder remembered everything that was said.

Olivia was crying, almost hysterical. Kurt Riner was certain there had been some tragic mistake. Alerted hours earlier, he had telephoned the police station the previous night, while his daughter was being questioned, but was not permitted to speak with her. Shortly before three A.M. an exhausted Olivia passed up a chance to telephone her home from jail. Now her father encouraged her to steady herself and cooperate with the police. From Switzerland there was little he could do, other than dispense love and support.

Events turned darker for the young woman. Police had now jumped the arson charge from the third to the first degree and, frighteningly, had added a felony count of second degree murder.

Still woozy from the frenzy of fire, death, accusation, abandonment, and arrest, Olivia was now swept up in the legal process. Represented by Todd G. Lamond, a lawyer provided free by the Legal Aid Society, she was taken upstairs in Town Hall Plaza to a courtroom of pale wood and churchlike pews for arraignment before Justice Robert Troup. From Manhattan, an attorney named Laura Brevetti came up to represent the interests of the E.F. Foundation and make certain the nanny's rights were guarded.

The shy Olivia had begun to close in upon herself, limiting her communication. She remained silent throughout the hearing, letting Lamond take the few legal steps available in the face of the double charges of arson and murder. Troup ordered the continued lockup of the nanny, sending her off without bail to the women's detention center of the nearby Westchester County Jail in Valhalla.

Even as she was led away, still wearing the ragged jeans and throw-on sweats that Carpenter had picked out of her closet, the case had begun to mushroom beyond the tiny village.

That same morning, Mount Pleasant police decided to return the fire-wrecked house to Bill and Denise Fischer, who came by the station. In an extraordinary lapse of judgment, they decided it would be possible to gather additional evidence from the scene to support the murder and arson charges, even while allowing the owners to do whatever they deemed necessary with the property.

One well-known criminology text, *Techniques of Crime Scene Investigation* by Barry A.J. Fisher, head of the Los Angeles County Sheriff's Criminalistics Laboratory, is adamant about protecting a crime scene. It states that no one, including other investigators and superior officers, should be allowed access to a crime scene without specific permission of the senior investigating officer until all needed tests are complete.

In this case, the senior officers decided that civilians, including the Fischers, Gallagher, and workmen, could do as they pleased in the house less than twenty-four hours after the fire. Police would work around them. Experts continued visiting the house for weeks, long after the site had been trekked over and molested by countless individuals.

With Bill and Denise Fischer driving one car and Detective Johnson and Lieutenant Alagno in a second vehicle, they returned to the house, which had been kept under police guard throughout the night.

Alagno, using a handheld circular power saw, ripped out sections of the door to Leah's bedroom and unscrewed the lock on the nursery door. Both were placed in plastic bags as evidence.

In the nursery, the burned car carrier had been cut free of the carpet and now leaned against the dresser. They did not move it.

Johnson took out his video camera once again, and with daylight to help illuminate the scene, began videotaping the destruction. Bill Fischer, knowing bad weather was expected, arranged to have sheets of plywood and tarpaulins placed in the broken windows. The family gathered what they could salvage in boxes.

* * *

At 10:30 A.M. Kunjlata Ashar put her emotions on hold. As an assistant medical examiner for Westchester County and a certified pathologist, part of her duty was to perform autopsies. The native of India would get through the process by being thoroughly professional, viewing the event through a clinical prism. The job was always difficult, but even more so when the victim was an infant, such as the baby girl that now lay on the autopsy table.

Ashar got to work. She recorded the height as twenty-four inches and the weight exactly thirty pounds and five ounces. Severe burns covered 80 to 85 percent of the baby's body. She worked steadily, examining the interior of the body, all of the organs and each individual bone, as well as the exterior. Finally she came to a conclusion. The cause of death was a combination of asphyxiation, inhalation of carbon monoxide, and the horrible burns to the body.

Read another way, the autopsy's conclusion meant death was not due to broken bones, suffocation, or internal damage that may have accompanied a beating or a fall. Detective Johnson's theory that Olivia had perhaps hurt the baby and then killed her to cover up the accident vanished. The prime motive simply disappeared. The police had guessed wrong.

If things were getting tangled in Thornwood, the atmosphere was frantic on an upper floor of a glass and stone office building at the foot of the Longfellow Bridge in Cambridge, Massachusetts.

The building at 1 Memorial Drive was washed by bright morning sunshine. Out front, on the Charles River, rowing crews from Harvard and MIT glided along, and the occasional Red Line train rumbled past on its way from Harvard Square to Government Center in Boston. Located on the socially accepted "right" side of the Charles, the E.F. Foundation occupied several floors at one of the best addresses in the Boston area.

The offices were bustling with attractive young women

who helped keep the American base of the Swedish company humming along in its myriad endeavors, which included foreign travel, exchange students, cultural exchanges, and providing au pairs to clients around the world. They hurried about their business this particular morning with an extra bit of effort, and gossip filled their idle moments, tales about what was going on in the private offices.

Louise Jakobson, the chairwoman in Boston, had been in constant contact with the company's headquarters. The news from Thornwood, plastered all over the newspapers and aired on television stations, could be a dagger pointed at the corporate heart of the foundation. If Olivia were convicted of murder, the foundation would suffer extreme damage to its reputation through bad publicity and possibly would be hit with an expensive lawsuit.

The girl had been thoroughly checked out by E.F. Au Pair and had seemed a good match with the applicant family. Something had gone terribly wrong, and, like it or not, the E.F. Foundation was along for the entire ride.

That meant legal help. The girl was represented at her arraignment by a public defender. That just would not do. A decision was reached to find a top American legal talent to conduct the defense of Olivia Riner and, as a byproduct, save the reputation of the au pair agency that had placed her in charge of the baby who had died.

But which attorney should be hired? America may have a deficit in many things, but it leads the world in lawyers. The search began with telephone calls.

Chapter Ten

THE PLAYERS

"THE DOCTOR HAS BEEN SHOT."

"Who did it? "

"I did."

"Where's the gun? "

"It's in my car."

This confession, pure and simple as can be, is a no-brainer for a prosecutor. The person who committed the crime admits doing it. Police find the murder weapon almost immediately, and an extraordinary amount of witness testimony, forensic evidence, and a powerful motive surface. No doubt, the killer goes to jail. She did.

Jean Harris, the tidy headmistress of the posh Madeira School for girls in McLean, Virginia, on the night of March 10, 1980, infuriated and jealous, pumped four bullets into her former lover, Dr. Herman Tarnower, known for his popular weight-loss guide, *The Scarsdale Diet*. Harris, a fixture in the social circles of the Virginia hunt country, admitted pulling the trigger as soon as police arrived at Tarnower's New York estate in the Westchester County town of Harrison. Her trial became one of the most famous of its time. When she was convicted and sent to prison in 1982 on a fifteen-years-to-life term, a bit of fame fell to the man who put her behind bars.

After the Harris trial, when rangy young George Bolen

walked the halls of the Westchester County Court House, the court regulars knew that here was a man with a future. Only thirty-four years old, the intense media coverage had made the assistant district attorney a courtroom celebrity.

He was a product of Brooklyn, New York, the University of Pennsylvania, and the University of Virginia Law School, a combination that can tame a pit bull tenacity by making it work for the law instead of against it. Bolen graduated from UVA in 1971 with little desire to jump into the lucrative field of corporate law or private practice. He felt he was a "born prosecutor," and headed home to Brooklyn to take a salaried job with the office of District Attorney Frank Hogan. Three years later he moved north to the quieter surroundings of Westchester County and began working out of the courthouse in White Plains.

With the Harris verdict, the ramrod straight Bolen was deluged with offers from private law firms that waved ridiculous amounts of money at him. He made the jump, and went with a medical malpractice company, where he needed only three weeks to decide that the private sector was not for him.

He returned to government service, once again in his post of assistant district attorney. The tough, aggressive prosecutor was back in harness, eager to put away the bad guys and gals.

So in the last month of 1991, when District Attorney Carl Vergari was handed a dilemma, the answer was not too far away.

The newspapers were trumpeting the case, in which a Swiss was accused of murdering a Thornwood baby. New York television stations were slapping the story on the evening news. To top it off, that movie had just come out about a murderous babysitter. Those in charge of the case did not need glasses to see that it had all the earmarks of a Big One.

The two ADAs at the scene the night of the fire were

out of the question for handling the case. Maryellen Martirano was in the Domestic Violence and Child Abuse section, and this case had already been elevated to homicide. Jim McCarty, who had answered the call as a homicide specialist, was already up to his neck trying the high-profile, second degree murder of Carolyn Warmus, which was set to resume in January.

Vergari and Anthony Molea, the chief assistant district attorney, felt optimistic. The calendar indicated the assistant district attorney who happened to be the head of the trial division was available.

On the snowy morning of December 5, Vergari reached for his star. He turned the prosecution of Olivia Riner over to straight-shooter George L. Bolen.

Bolen lost no time taking action. A quick look indicated that as of three days after the alleged crime had been committed, no direct evidence existed to link the defendant with the event. The prosecutor headed for Thornwood.

En route he stopped by the police station in Mount Pleasant and interviewed Detective Johnson, and both of them drove the few miles over to 5 West Lake Drive. The fresh snow that had fallen overnight carpeted the ground and left a dusting of white on the piles of charred debris alongside the house.

They were not the only ones around. A woman from the insurance company showed up to survey the damage, and several other people were poking about. Johnson picked up his video camera again and began to shoot the area. Off camera, someone laughed. Leah Fischer and John Gallagher, wearing jeans and jackets, picked through the ruined remnants of her room, looking for a necklace he had given her. Their search was recorded by Johnson's roaming lens.

In the infant's room the burned carrier seat still sat propped against a wall. Later that day Johnson would return to the house and retrieve it, putting it into a brown plastic garbage bag for use as evidence in the arson-murder investigation. Between the evening of December 2 and the afternoon of December 5, this piece of melted plastic and charred cloth, which was to become one of the strongest pieces of evidence in the case, had stood in the room, unguarded and ignored, available for anyone moving through the house to touch or examine. Its bizarre journey to the courtroom was only beginning.

Other evidence was currently undergoing testing at the county crime lab. When the preliminary tests came in, Bolen was not pleased. Everything was inconclusive. By the end of the day he had little more than what he had started with—a case based totally upon circumstantial evidence.

For courthouse regulars the backstairs gossip was already under way. One uniformed court officer explained it this way: Vergari was nearing the end of his career and someone would eventually replace him. Since Molea, the chief assistant, had an eye on a judgeship, among the likely successors were the current star, Bolen, and the promising Jim McCarty, who was assigned to the Warmus trial. The verdicts in McCarty's murder case against Warmus and Bolen's murder-arson case against Olivia Riner could vault one of them into a favored position to eventually succeed Vergari. Bolen's victory in the Jean Harris trial was a dozen years ago in an arena where "what have you done for me lately" is an operative phrase.

While the State of New York, County of Westchester, was aligning the foundation of its prosecution of Olivia Riner by choosing a star prosecutor, the other side, the defense, also was coming together.

When the E.F. Foundation, parent company of E.F. Au Pair, narrowed its possibilities for legal representation of the accused Swiss nanny, they chose not to take the cheap route. Instead, they went to the Upper East Side of Manhattan and picked someone with an extraordinary legal background. It would cost them plenty, but the risk of a loss was too much to conceive.

The telephone call to the switchboard of the Morrison, Cohen, Singer & Weinstein law firm was answered by a receptionist on the ninth floor of a skyscraper at 750 Lexington Avenue. The entry hall where the switchboard was located was more like the wing of an exclusive art museum than a waiting room for a lawyer's office. Original works by artists such as Jonathan Waller, Jock McFadyen, Wolfgang Koethe, and John Keane hung on the walls, portraying scenes as disparate as people asleep in meadows or a bike rider lying dead before a line of soldiers. The ebb and flow of the human tide ran through the three floors of the fifty-lawyer firm.

In general practice, the firm represents companies, handles real estate transactions, watches over the sale and purchase of corporations, performs trust and estate work for millionaires and litigation work on everything from divorces to defamation. In other words, for the correct fee, this is one-stop shopping for anyone needing a lawyer.

The receptionist, in a silky voice, asked the party on the telephone to wait for just one moment, please. She punched some buttons, and in a tasteful office a woman answered the call. Laura Brevetti was about to step to the mark.

Brevetti, sitting in surroundings that bespoke elegance, was quite happy in her role as a partner in the prestigious law firm. She had skyrocketed to the top rungs of the legal profession, having gained financial security, professional reputation, and the respect of her peers during the fourteen years since she was admitted to the bar. The splendid office was a long way from the Bensonhurst section of Brooklyn where she was born forty years ago. As the youngest child, with three sisters and one brother, she learned to be rough to survive in an Italian family. Inquisitive even as a young girl, she regularly would have her head thumped by whoever's patience finally snapped when she pestered them with too many questions. All the time questions, until people would yell at her, in English and Italian, to just shut up, Laura, shut up!

From her Bath Beach neighborhood near the Verrazano Bridge, Laura Brevetti could not even see the towers of Manhattan, where she would eventually practice law in the office of a skyscraper. Her insatiable curiosity first led to a cum laude degree from Barnard College in 1973, and then a law degree from Georgetown Law School three years later. Precise and fearless in the courtroom, Brevetti worked as an assistant district attorney for four years in Kings County, New York, then stepped into the extraordinary role of attorney-in-charge of the U.S. Justice Department's Organized Crime Strike Force, going up as prosecutor against the mob back on her home turf of Brooklyn. She basked in the excitement of prosecuting money launderers, tax evaders, and corruption in labor and government. Being Italian had nothing to do with it. The Law was the Law, and Laura Brevetti was its instrument. A portrait of her and her accomplishments went nationwide when the Dewar's Scotch company featured her in a profile, although she did not drink their product. The crime bosses of New York, particularly the Bonanno family, felt the lash and were none too unhappy when, after nine years, Brevetti was lured away from the Strike Force by MCS&W to the uptown partnership with the big office and the thick carpets and the original art. She would head the firm's white-collar criminal defense group. But put a barracuda in an aquarium, and it remains a barracuda.

Tall and blond, wearing red-rimmed glasses and tailored clothes, the veteran lawyer listened to the latest pitch. The company wanted to hire her to go to Westchester County and take a look at the situation involving Olivia Riner, make sure her rights were being protected, that sort of thing. A quick job. Consultant basis.

Brevetti agreed to attend the December 3 arraignment almost as an observer, with Lamond from Legal Aid handling the actual representation of the accused nanny. It was only after she had a chance to talk with Olivia for thirty minutes in the police department's interview room that the relationship changed. Brevetti found a girl still bordering on hysteria, still pulling at the ragtag tissue given to her the previous night, and discovered she believed what Olivia had to say. In broken English that Brevetti could barely understand at times, the girl described her story and the futile telephone call for help. The young woman had no idea what was happening to her. Further, Brevetti was flabbergasted at the police performance. They had not even put up a yellow restraining ribbon around the crime scene! The reading of the Miranda rights was questionable. The fact that Olivia had not been represented by a lawyer or had an interpreter during the long interview by police bothered Brevetti deeply. From that moment the talented uptown lawyer decided to represent the Swiss girl in the great ordeal to come.

The next order of business was a felony hearing scheduled on December 6 before Justice Troup in Mount Pleasant Town Court. Olivia's parents, Kurt and Marlies Riner, had flown to the United States from Switzerland and were holding hands in the courtroom when their manacled daughter was led in. Marlies gave her an encouraging thumbs-up gesture, but Olivia could only return a nervous smile. Brevetti felt the hearing would be useless, and informed Troup that her client waived the procedure. Instead, the defense lawyer wanted to focus on something more significant—getting her client out of county jail on bail. Olivia was having a rough go of it in the Valhalla jail, and even the arrival of her parents did not seem to relieve her anxiety. She could see her lawyer and her parents during the day, but she still slept in a cell behind a locked steel door at night, alone with her nightmares. The authorities had decided to keep her by herself, in protective custody, because they felt a possible danger from other women inmates if they put a young woman accused of slaying a baby into the general jail population.

Meanwhile, the police chief of Mount Pleasant, Paul Oliva, had begun granting brief interviews with the news media about the case and maintained that his officers had developed a wide array of evidence to tie the "direct ignition" of the fires to Riner. He said the case was strong. For some reason, however, when the media asked about someone else at the scene, the police chief would not identify that person as John Gallagher, and insisted no one else was a suspect.

Police Chief Oliva's view was very different from the way Laura Brevetti saw the same situation. To her, the police should be out trying to find who really set the fire that killed little Kristie Fischer. She insisted that her client was not alone at the fire scene.

For the coming months, that would be the bottom line for both sides. The prosecution said Olivia was the only one with the opportunity to set those deadly fires inside a house that was demonstrably secure. The defense insisted that someone else did it.

Brevetti needed help. She did not doubt her courtroom ability, but in this particular case she needed a particularly high level of expertise. Back in the old days, with the Strike Force, she would have had all the support she needed—investigators, experts in arcane fields, psychologists, whoever might be needed to weld together an airtight case. Now she was going to have to do just the opposite and unravel the net that had closed around her client. Every witness, every piece of evidence, had to be thoroughly examined and turned inside out in a search for flaws that could prove Olivia Riner was innocent.

She rounded up Elan Gerstmann to be her right arm on the legal side of the ledger. Gerstmann, a sharp mind out of Columbia and the University of Buffalo Law School, would provide a second set of eyes on legal technicalities, do research, plan strategy, and track case law and testimony. More importantly, the young man was an excellent sounding board for Brevetti, whose mind would throw out a torrent of "What if we . . . " questions, just like she did back at the house in Bensonhurst. The difference was, by 1992 no one could thump her on the head.

With Gerstmann in her corner, she would be able to deal with the legal talent arrayed against them, but to counter the work being done by the police in Mount Pleasant and investigators from the District Attorney's Office, Brevetti needed a good cop of her own.

Pulling up a name from her years with the Strike Force, she called the International Security Agency in Manhattan at One Penn Plaza. By December 5 the ISA began working on the case, and by January 9, as things began to heat up and become more complex, the company decided to assign its high profile director of consulting services, Christopher Rush, to the job on a full-time basis.

It proved an uncanny linkage. The savvy, quick-study lawyer was matched with a street-smart ex-policeman schooled in patience and the dirty fingernail side of law enforcement.

Chris Rush learned hard lessons about right and wrong and the use and abuse of authority early in life, growing up as an Irish-Catholic kid in the wrong part of Belfast, that ancient battle-scarred city of Northern Ireland. When the family moved to America, with few possessions, the tenacious, burly kid got a job helping serve subpoenas, riding around New York's mean streets in a station wagon loaded with papers to drop on people whom a judge wanted see.

He enjoyed the respect that came from working on the positive side of the law, but he needed more than piecework. After a young life of insecurity, Rush longed for the certainty of a civil service job with its regular paychecks, insurance coverage, and eventual retirement benefits. On his twenty-first birthday he got the telephone call for which he had been praying—he had been hired as a New York City policeman.

For almost nine years Rush worked the streets that showed him the sour core of the Big Apple. Everything from homicides to drugs, prostitution to burglary, arson to extortion. The big young man with the quiet, determined manner was content with making a career out of the NYPD. Then came a day in the 34 [sic] Precinct when a fellow officer needed help with some bad guy who had a gun. Officer Chris Rush ran to help, and, unglamorously, stepped into a hole in the street. The fall ruptured ligaments in his right ankle, and Chris Rush eventually found himself enmeshed in a series of painful surgeries that pushed him into early retirement and out of his beloved job as a cop.

While undergoing surgery and rehabilitation, he did a stint in Brooklyn with the U.S. Marshal's service, working the first trial of suave crime boss John Gotti, the Teflon Don. Finally, Rush's years of investigative experience, his deliberate and contemplative methods, and a special knowledge of electronics made him a prime candidate for the private investigative field, particularly in the lucrative corporate security sector. Instead of chasing drug dealers, Rush found himself helping Fortune 500 companies. The poor kid from Belfast was now wearing double-breasted suits and commanding respect in boardrooms around New York. But deep in his bones Chris Rush was still a cop, who each morning proudly pinned the little green and white NYPD Honor Legion ribbon in the lapel of his stylish suit.

Brevetti's call was like a siren sounding for an old war horse. Rush had a chance to be a cop again. Brevetti had found her flatfoot.

Chapter Eleven

MOURNING

THE MOUNT PLEASANT CEMETERY RESEMBLES A LARGE CITY at rest. It has stone houses, paved roads, manicured gardens, and is close to the Bronx River Parkway and commuter rail lines. It sweeps gently upward from the expressway, crosses Commerce Street and climbs section by section along the southern flank of Stevens Avenue in the hamlet of Hawthorne, adjacent to Thornwood.

The cemetery is neatly divided into tidy areas that mirror the development of surrounding communities over the long years. In the lower sections are boxy mausoleums of weathered granite—with their decorative, hinged iron doors and carefully chiseled carvings spelling out old-line names of yesterday's gentry—marking the final resting places of such families as the Morgenthaus. Upon those lower slopes of the circular patch denoted as Section One, the trees are tall and aged. Thick, full bushes are kept trimmed just so.

The cemetery expanded beyond Section One over the years, as more people moved into the Mount Pleasant area and eventually died. Newer sections were added, slightly higher up the slope and spreading away from the center, creating a pattern that was repeated over the years. The names of the first Dutch and English families gave way to smaller markers bearing Jewish, German, and Italian surnames. Newer grave markers commemorate the latest wave of immigrants, from Asia, who are buried beneath immaculate headstones bearing the angular script of the Orient.

On December 6, the day that Olivia Riner appeared in court and her attorney waived the felony hearing, Kristie Rebecca Fischer was buried at the Mount Pleasant Cemetery. Only a few miles separated the two events.

A cortege made the sharp right turn off Commerce Street, after having moved slowly up from nearby White Plains. A quiet memorial service had been held for the infant at the Ballard Durand Funeral Home, a massive, old white structure of wood and stone with tall columns out front. A large crowd overflowed the main salon, and the double doors were opened to the room. Mourners gathered in the wide hallway and in the adjoining front room, as pale rays of sun played over thick curtains and a worn, patterned carpet.

The cars swept around Section One of the cemetery and climbed the neat roadway; turning right at the Wein Memorial, a long bench of gray stone bordered by box hedges. About a hundred yards along the top of the ridge, the vehicles stopped next to a line of struggling bushes in the newest section of the cemetery.

A crowd gathered there, too, and they stood in near-freezing temperatures on soggy ground. A chill breeze crested the hill, moving the branches of a small oak tree that had long since dropped its leaves. A tiny black and silver marker showed they were at Section 27.

Those awaiting the cars could see all the way across the highways to the trees that stood thick beside the Hudson River. Silence reigned, even the hum of distant traffic seemed muted, as the waiting crowd was joined by those from the cortege, and they shuffled among the straight and narrow walkways laid out as aisles between the grave sites. Everyone was careful not to step on the surrounding resting places, where markers showed Millers and Robbins and Hoffmans and Kleins were buried beneath the close-cut grass, or to jostle the tiny pebbles and rocks placed as special remembrances atop the newer markers.

The ceremony was short, for it does not take long to bury a baby. The little urn containing the cremated mortal remains of Kristie Fischer was buried with quiet dignity. The tiny grave, only one foot square, was on the upper right-hand side of a newly purchased two-grave family plot.

Then the family, the friends, the acquaintances, the townspeople, the police, the firemen, and the strangers all departed, going back to lives that would never be quite the same again. Winter would not officially begin for another two weeks, on December 22, but people who stood upon the windswept hillside that Friday felt they had never been so cold, never in their entire lives.

Chapter Twelve

THE COURT

BY SHEER LUCK, THE OLIVIA RINER CASE, ONCE SHE WAS bound over for trial, fell on December 9 to Judge Donald N. Silverman. In Westchester County's legal system, the assignment of cases is through a blind draw by the presiding judge. That it should have ended up on Silverman's calendar was simply a bit of irony, as if Madame Justice had peeked from beneath her blindfold and toyed with her scales enough to keep things bubbling in this odd and tragic case.

In that blind draw, Olivia Riner got a break.

Hearing her case would be a young, liberal Democrat who was born in 1947 in the Rockaway section of New York, one of those tough neighborhoods where upwardly mobile young people no longer choose to live. Silverman left the New York area to take his bachelor's degree at Boston University, and then read for the law at George Washington University, both institutions popular with New Yorkers en route to becoming lawyers.

But when he passed the bar exam in 1973 and was ready to hang out his shingle, Silverman decided against settling down and earning big bucks. A 60s idealist, he instead moved across the country, out to Medford, Oregon, a small town on the edge of the redwood forests, and began his legal career defending people who could not afford to pay. When he finally moved back to New York, it was in the same role, as a lawyer for the Legal Aid Society. (Even as a judge, Silverman would be a friend of the downtrodden, with a deep sense of conviction to make certain that any defendant before him received every single right due under the Constitution of the United States. He would bristle when police took their powers too far.)

The young lawyer, however, was also an ambitious man. While he could bypass the traditional lawyer's footrace to money, he longed to be able to do more than represent the indigent. His life was the law, and the upward track would require wearing a black robe. He had to become a judge.

To hold such an office in New York requires a political commitment as well as a legal brain. For several years Silverman compiled a stop-and-go record as he worked his way up in the Democratic party, winning some battles and losing others, but all the while solidifying his political credentials. By 1988 he was serving on the bench in an appointed capacity when he entered a race for a Westchester County judgeship.

As a candidate, he won the endorsement of the local newspaper for his record of pro bono work, and the editors wrote that his time with Legal Aid had given him a "great understanding of defendants—dry-eyed and unsentimental, but humane."

While acting as an appointed justice, Silverman had written an opinion that broke a dreadful habit of the state, in which county prisoners who had already been processed were still held in county custody weeks after the state should have taken them. Some were kept in day rooms of overcrowded local facilities, something Silverman said was a threat to both their health and safety. It was a decision that reflected his sentiments that the guilty must pay, but authority must not be allowed to establish a gulag or a dungeon.

The newspaper called him "a walking study in contrast—anything but flamboyant." His opinions, the editors claimed, were "quiet, scholarly and very learned."

They urged voters to cast their ballots for Silverman. The election for the position of Westchester County Judge was anything but easy, despite his media support.

Silverman went to sleep on election night, 1988, thinking he had lost the race, only to come out on top a month later when the Board of Elections finished counting thousands of paper ballots that had not been immediately tallied. "I won by the overwhelming majority of about two votes," he recalls.

Actually, he understates the political feat he accomplished. There were four open seats, and the first three were filled without question. In the tight race for the final position, Judge J. Radley Harold had a 2700-vote lead on election night over Chief Assistant District Attorney Anthony Molea, a Republican, and Democrat Silverman. The month-long canvass of paper ballots turned it around, installing Silverman as a winner by 1075 votes over Molea and 1220 votes over Radley. Since recounts usually tend only to increase the margin of victory for whoever is in front, Silverman's win was an astonishing turn of events.

The upset in 1988 guaranteed Silverman a judgeship for ten years. He finally had won the robe that he wanted, but faced an uphill battle with the courthouse crowd to prove that, despite his freebie work for the underclass, he could be a fair judge. It took time, but the prosecutors finally believed him. Silverman earned a reputation of being firm but fair.

It was more than just having lawyers adjust to a new judge, for something usually seems out of place in the courtroom of the Honorable Donald N. Silverman. The attorneys look appropriately serious; the court officers, in their stiff white shirts and black gun belts, are obviously officers of the law; the defendant can be easily found because of the perpetual look of concern on his or her face; the clerk and court stenographer are in their respective nests; the audience fills the pews in back, and the reporters and courtroom artists are in the front rows. The only person who looks out of place, at first glance, is the Honorable Donald N. Silverman. You want to call out, "Hey, kid, get down from there! That's where the judge sits."

Black hair, big glasses, short and tending toward a bit of pudge; gaining weight is a constant fear because of the time he spends sitting in a chair. He has the unlined face of a law school senior playing at mock court, and he sits on his perch, sometimes in a slouch, with his august black robe—the ancient symbol of his rank—unzipped and open, showing a bright red tie and a striped shirt with a white collar, or some other colorful combination. One would almost expect a wisecrack from Hizzoner, and he does not disappoint. There is a hint of someone who might want to chuck the courtroom trappings and do a summer of stand-up comedy in the nearby Catskills. He jokes with a jury to loosen them up, and throws the quickest puns in the courthouse. Some of the legal fraternity, those who wear suits and ever-serious looks, kiddingly refer to him (always out of earshot) by the acronym NJBJ—the Nice Jewish Boy Judge.

But he's a teddy bear with a steel-trap mind, a legal scholar cursed with a personality, a judge who doesn't consider humor or courtesy to be a felony, nor a courtroom to be a mausoleum. The judges of yesteryear, who peer down from paintings on the walls, frown disapproval. On one lunch break, he is on a quick errand, blue suit buttoned over a maturing midsection, trying to blend with the tight-laced business crowd hurrying through the plaza behind the courthouse. He spies a couple of reporters who know his case is scheduled to resume in fifteen minutes. "Relax," calls Silverman. "You don't have to go up until you see me come back through here. No judge, no trial."

Lawyers tend to ignore the media while in the courtroom, but Silverman will come down from the bench during a break, robe flapping, to critique a picture by a courtroom artist.

But attorneys learned a long time ago not to misread him because of his youth and buoyancy. When Silverman is in that high-backed chair, an experienced jurist is in charge of the proceedings.

By 1992, at the age of forty-five, Silverman had been a lawyer and a judge for almost half his life, and the county robe he wore was feeling a size too small for his ambition. He announced his candidacy for the Supreme Court—the equivalent of a Superior Court in other jurisdictions, and not the highest appeals court in the state—in the November 1992 election. If he made that jump successfully, the young judge would be in a position that would allow a thoughtful jurist, over time, to proceed to higher levels in the world of judgedom. Simply put, Silverman was in a dead-end job and wanted something better.

So when the Olivia Riner case was handed to him, it was a two-edged sword that could cut both ways.

Running for office requires time to campaign, time to raise money. From the start, Silverman determined to stick to his well-known pattern of putting the trial on a fast track, much to the chagrin of the opposing lawyers who wanted more time to prepare their cases. For a politician, a day lost in December, or in May, would be a day lost on the campaign in October. This particular trial could easily stretch more than a month plus a few weeks of preliminary hearings, which meant time was definitely going to be a factor. Other candidates would be out on the campaign trail, raising bucks, pressing voter flesh and printing bumper stickers, while Silverman was overseeing one of the most important trials of his career.

That, however, stood a chance of working in his behalf. High-profile criminal cases would result in headlines and television coverage, which was good, because it would be akin to free advertising for the candidate.

He would have to tread carefully. A wrong turn of phrase or an unpopular decision on a point of law might return to haunt him in coming months. Indeed, sniping began later in the trial process, as one side or the other would hint that some Silverman position had gone against them for political reasons.

In fact, Silverman would eventually give both sides just about anything they wanted, within the letter of the law. The Riner case was going to rise or fall on its own weight and evidence, and not by some quick-gavel decision by a judge who would soon have to face the voters.

The focus of the legal maneuvers and eventual trial of Olivia Riner shifted in mid-December from the village level in Mount Pleasant to the Richard J. Daronco Westchester County Government Center, a twenty-story courthouse tower at the corner of Martine Avenue and Grove Street in the middle of downtown White Plains, the county seat. On the far side of Martine is the city's sprawling Galleria Mall, and next door is the city library. An enclosed bridge extends from the courthouse tower, across Grove, to link with the blocky county office building.

The tower was opened in 1975, and in 1988 an eight-foot-high statue atop a granite block was dedicated just outside the front doors. It depicts a uniformed patrolman holding his billed hat in one hand, his other hand resting on his gun belt, and his bare head bowed in tribute to the fifty-plus law enforcement officers who have been slain in the line of duty in the county. It is one of the few places in Westchester County, and particularly around the courthouse, where one will ever see a policeman have his hat in his hand about anything.

Chapter Thirteen

BAIL

FOR OLIVIA RINER AND LAURA BREVETTI, THE MAIN GOAL IN December was to have Olivia released from the Westchester County Jail, pending her day in court. It would not be easy.

District Attorney Vergari had made it plain early in the episode, only a day after the fire, that to release Olivia under any condition was to risk having her flee the country to avoid trial. Authorities already had confiscated her passport, which would have made such a flight virtually impossible, but the district attorney shrugged that one away. "You never know."

In the event that bail was to be considered, the D.A. wanted it to be high, at least a quarter of a million dollars, because the crimes of which she stood accused were so serious.

Meanwhile, Olivia had sought to establish a routine in the women's jail, making it through each day in an orderly fashion. If she could handle one thing at a time, look forward to something happening at a specific moment on the clock, then eventually she would be allowed to leave. Her new lawyer had promised that, but cautioned that it would take time. For the month of December, Olivia Riner, in her lonely cell, had plenty of time. "It's agonizing for both her parents and her," Brevetti said after one visit to the jail.

* * *

The nanny was allowed out, under guard, on December 10, a Tuesday, for a brief appearance before Judge Silverman. Although she spoke English enough to be understood, she was not fluent enough to follow the complexities of the legal arguments that swirled about her that day, and no interpreter was present. Both Brevetti and Silverman took note of the language situation, something the authorities had dismissed from the earliest moments of the case as being inconsequential. The court would go to great lengths to find an interpreter who could keep the defendant informed of what was being said in her murder and arson trial.

During the hearing, Brevetti acknowledged the prosecution wanted strict requirements for bail and said she would need some more time to meet those standards. The bulk of the fifteen-minute hearing instead dealt with the early phases of her challenge of the crime scene and the evidence gathered there.

On one important point Silverman came down on the side of the defense. The house at 5 West Lake Drive had been given back to the Fischer family on the morning of December 3, less than a day after the fire wrecked it. Since then, family members, police looking for new evidence, investigating experts of various stripes, friends of the family, and a bevy of workers had been freely allowed to roam the property.

Meanwhile, Brevetti had tried to gain access to the property to conduct her own examination of the area. Since the police had never roped it off as a protected crime scene in the first place and had already surrendered it back to the Fischers, the local authorities were able to say, "Sorry, it's not up to us." The family was not about to cooperate with the lawyer of the woman they believed killed their baby. They said no. Without such access, the defense team would be at an extreme disadvantage in preparing its case.

On Monday, December 9, Brevetti finally filed for a

court order to allow entrance to the burned building where the alleged crime had taken place. On December 10 Silverman granted that request. Finally someone could examine the fire scene with an eye toward discovering something that might prove Olivia Riner was innocent and that the state's case against her might not be all that it seemed.

But eight days had elapsed since the fire, and countless feet had trod the ground and the carpets, and countless fingers had touched surfaces and sifted through debris. It was hardly a fair and even start, but at least it was a start. While police had been able to conduct their searches in private, any defense team member visiting would be under escort. Whatever the defense might find, in theory, would also be seen by a prosecution shepherd.

Following the hearing, Olivia, still in the custody of armed guards, was driven back to the county jail to surrender her freedom until the legal system beckoned again.

That would be nine days later, when Silverman decided the amount of bail. He obviously agreed with the prosecutors that the girl was a risk to flee the country before trial, even without her passport. After all, Canada was not far from White Plains. To leave jail, to walk the streets again, Olivia would have to post a bail of half a million American dollars. She obviously did not have that much in her purse, so, once again, was returned to jail.

Brevetti kept attacking the decision. There must be a combination of things, besides hard cash, that could be instituted to guarantee her client's presence in court, she argued. A half-millon bucks bail bond was total victory for the prosecution and almost a snub of the due process of law. The crime was without doubt horrendous, but the evidence against the person jailed was admittedly circumstantial, and sharp questions had surfaced about the quality of the police investigation that had resulted in her arrest.

As the newspaper editorial that endorsed Silverman for office had stated, he was dry-eyed and unsentimental about defendants, and he had seen women before who had killed. A half-million dollar bail was fine by him.

On Tuesday, December 24, Christmas Eve, they made a deal. The cash part of the bail was lowered to $350,000; Olivia would be fitted with an electronic monitoring device that would tether her by radio waves to a specific, nearby geographic area; she would live with her mother, Marlies, who had to surrender her own passport; she would waive her right to refuse extradition if she did flee the country, and the Swiss government pledged not to give her a new passport or immunity from U.S. law by offering her shelter in a Swiss consulate or embassy.

It was a lot to accomplish, but a somewhat happier Olivia again was returned to jail. It was as if she had been given a special gift on December 24, which in Switzerland is the day of Heiligabend, or Holy Night, the time when gifts are exchanged.

The jolly, American-style Santa Claus would be making his happy rounds during the night. But in the Swiss culture, a land of mythical ogres and strange evils from the black forests, Samichlaus was not a sympathetic figure. Instead of the jolly old man carrying presents, he was a terrifying figure, accompanied by a man with a black-smeared face who carried a large empty sack. Samichlaus would have been in cahoots with your parents and upon opening a book, would read off a list of the sins you committed during the past year. The man with the dark face would threaten to shove you into the sack and haul you away. Only after scaring the daylights out of you would you be showered with nuts and fruit and chocolate.

Throughout the U.S., Christmas Day would be a time of joy, but there was little of that for the two families entwined in this catastrophe. The Fischers, living out of cardboard boxes in a rented house, had a miserable Christmas. It should have been a time of wonder, the first Christmas for baby Kristie, but that had forever been cruelly snatched from them. And for the Riners, the holiday season was an agonizing experience because their daughter was locked in jail, charged with the death of the baby.

Christmas was cold and not the least bit merry for either family.

Brevetti plunged into the details of getting her client out from behind bars. The cash, although high, was raised, primarily through family sources in Switzerland, where low debt and thrifty, frugal spending patterns were the norm, and people saved money every month. The Swiss consulate in New York agreed with the governmental pledges, and a bail bondsman set up the unremovable monitoring device that Olivia would wear just above her ankle.

The court, however, refused to accept a cash bond in the form of an irrevocable letter of credit to be deposited in a New York branch of the United Bank of Switzerland. In a year that had seen American savings and loan associations dropping like flies, their greedy officials trotted off to prisons, and even the biggest banks in the United States teetering close to financial ruin because of bad loans, Silverman's ruling basically said he did not trust the banks in Switzerland, which has the most stable banking system in the world. He said it was not insured by the almost-bankrupt U.S. Federal Deposit Insurance Corporation. Instead, the $350,000 in cash or bond had to be posted directly with the court. So it was.

Monday, December 30, the day before the end of the year, was sunny and cold, with the temperature hovering near the freezing mark. But for Olivia it was as majestic as an early spring day. Wearing a dark coat with big brass buttons, and a three-inch anklet to link her with the law, she walked out through the tall cyclone fence that surrounds the Westchester County Jail. Her parents smothered her in hugs, and as she tossed her brown hair, it fanned out in the morning breeze and her face lit up in a broad smile. After almost a month she was out of jail.

But what lay ahead were six months of incredible strain and the crushing experience of her trial.

Chapter Fourteen

GRAND JURY

LITTLE MORE THAN A MONTH AFTER THE FIRE AT 5 WEST
Lake Drive, George Bolen took his case to a grand jury to
finalize the charges on which Olivia Riner would be tried.
Although it was a major step in the legal process, an indictment by a grand jury would not be a conviction, no
matter how damning the legal phraseology drawn up by
the District Attorney's Office.

In fact, it is difficult for a prosecutor to go before a
grand jury and not obtain the exact indictment desired. A
good lawyer should be able to persuade a grand jury to
indict almost anyone of anything.

What the prosecution was showing in this particular
case wasn't a slow buildup of hard and fast evidence
about murder and arson. They could not present it because it didn't exist. So far, the test results on Olivia's
clothing did not show that a flammable liquid had
splashed back on her; and there were no fingerprints, a
month after the crime, that would prove she had ever
even touched some of the containers of fuel and paint
thinner stored in the downstairs closet.

So the state's legal representative actually was giving
the grand jury a neat sales job, peddling not hard evidence, but an idea, a hunch, a gut feeling that this young
woman from Switzerland had committed this horrible
crime.

Don Davis

Bolen painted a picture that the two-story house at 5 West Lake Drive was an impregnable fortress. Olivia admitted—no, she had insisted—that she was alone inside the house when the conflagration began, didn't she? And the windows in the baby's room and Leah's room were locked, and Olivia couldn't explain how her own window was slightly open. Since no suspicious characters had surfaced, there could be no one else involved, therefore she did it. Anyway, if someone else would have committed the crime, the police would have arrested them instead of her, right? The beauty of this presentation was that the state did not have to prove a thing to this particular panel. In such a gauzy light, circumstantial evidence began to look real, not unlike a desert mirage that promises water where there is only barren waste.

Bolen presumably would not feel compelled to point out that the police investigation of the complex crime had started and ended with Olivia Riner in just a matter of hours, or that the car seat in which Kristie had burned to death had not yet even been taken to the crime lab for examination more than a month after the baby's awful death, or that the crime scene had been so thoroughly mishandled that finding almost any untainted evidence had become impossible.

Critics of the archaic grand jury system have belittled the importance of such proceedings for years: secret testimony, secret evidence, a careful presentation of some, not all, items of proof; no defense lawyers allowed inside, certainly not any reporters; the person being charged not even present; everyone involved sworn to absolute secrecy; the immunity from future prosecution granted to witnesses. The grand jury is hardly more than a rubber stamp for the state's case, a bit of antique legality designed to allow a group of selected citizens to determine that someone charged with a crime or crimes actually should stand trial.

Even the name of the grand jury is somewhat misleading, giving the impression that it is a high court, when the

grand part of the title only means that it can have more
people on it than the *petit,* or smaller, trial jury.

Despite the glaring holes in the prosecution's case, the
grand jury did its duty and obediently coughed up an appropriate indictment. Bearing the number 92–0001, signi-
fying that it was the very first criminal case in the
Westchester County court system for the new year, it was
returned on January 16, 1992, full of red flag words ac-
cusing the defendant of crimes most foul, and it read like
this:

COUNTY COURT : COUNTY OF WESTCHESTER
STATE OF NEW YORK

THE PEOPLE OF THE STATE OF NEW YORK
               -against-
OLIVIA RINER,

                  Defendant

FIRST COUNT   125.25/02/74
THE GRAND JURY OF THE COUNTY OF WESTCHESTER, by this
Indictment, accuses the defendant of the crime of MURDER
IN THE SECOND DEGREE, committed as follows:

The defendant, in the Town of Mount Pleasant, County
of Westchester and State of New York, on or about December 2, 1991, under circumstances evincing a depraved
indifference to human life, did recklessly engage in conduct which created a grave risk of death to Kristie Fischer,
and thereby caused the death of Kristie Fischer.

SECOND COUNT   125.25/04/90
THE GRAND JURY OF THE COUNTY OF WESTCHESTER, by this
Indictment, accuses the defendant of the crime of MURDER
IN THE SECOND DEGREE, committed as follows:

The defendant, in the Town of Mount Pleasant, County

of Westchester and State of New York, on or about December 2, 1991, under circumstances evincing a depraved indifference to human life, and being eighteen years old or more, did recklessly engage in conduct which created a grave risk of serious physical injury and death to Kristie Fischer, who was less than eleven years old, and thereby caused the death of Kristie Fischer.

THIRD COUNT   125.25/01/74

THE GRAND JURY OF THE COUNTY OF WESTCHESTER, by this Indictment, accuses the defendant of the crime of MURDER IN THE SECOND DEGREE, committed as follows:

The defendant, in the Town of Mount Pleasant, County of Westchester and State of New York, on or about December 2, 1991, with intent to cause the death of Kristie Fischer, did cause the death of Kristie Fischer.

FOURTH COUNT   125.25/03/74

THE GRAND JURY OF THE COUNTY OF WESTCHESTER, by this Indictment, accuses the defendant of the crime of MURDER IN THE SECOND DEGREE, committed as follows:

The defendant, in the Town of Mount Pleasant, County of Westchester and State of New York, on or about December 2, 1991, did commit and attempt to commit the crime of arson and, in the course of and in the furtherance of such crime, caused the death of Kristie Fischer, who was not a participant in the crime.

FIFTH COUNT   150.20/01/80

THE GRAND JURY OF THE COUNTY OF WESTCHESTER, by this Indictment, accuses the defendant of the crime of ARSON IN THE FIRST DEGREE, committed as follows:

The defendant, in the Town of Mount Pleasant, County of Westchester and State of New York, on or about December 2, 1991, intentionally damaged a building by causing a fire and when such fire caused serious physical injury to Kristie Fischer, who was not a participant in the crime, and when Kristie Fischer, who was not a participant in the crime, was present in such building at the time and the defendant knew that fact and the circumstances were such as to render the presence of Kristie Fischer therein a reasonable possibility.

All contrary to the form of the statute in such case made and provided and against the peace and dignity of the People of the State of New York.

/s/ CARL A. VERGARI

District Attorney of Westchester County

For better or for worse, there it was. Without a shred of hard evidence against her, Olivia Riner stood accused of four counts of second degree murder and one count of first degree arson. If convicted, she could face from twenty-five years to life in prison. Olivia could have just as easily been indicted for running a traffic signal or selling Scud missiles to Iraq, for just about as many facts existed to connect her with such ideas.

The actual five-count indictment was about as severe as they come. Part of it was based on a law, only passed in 1990, that accuses someone over the age of eighteen with creating a grave risk to a child under the age of eleven, and another charge claiming "depraved indifference to human life." Most of the turbulent language was mere window dressing. The prime point was the Third Count, the most simply worded one of the lot, that pointedly accused Olivia of killing Kristie. By having so many counts, perhaps one or more would stick when time came for a real jury to weigh the evidence.

Olivia, accompanied by Brevetti, was immediately arraigned on the charges before Judge Silverman. Brevetti entered the plea: not guilty to all counts. Olivia was allowed to remain free on bail pending trial.

Except for filling in a legal blank, the grand jury indictment was of little importance. The state's case against Olivia Riner was just as strong on January 16, 1992, as it would ever be, and just as weak as it was on December 2, 1991.

The grand jurors went home, their work done but not forgotten. The fact that the witnesses who appeared before them, including John Gallagher, were all automatically given immunity from prosecution, would flare again months later during the trial.

Chapter Fifteen

A TOUCH OF GERALDO

IT WAS FRIDAY EVENING, FEBRUARY 14, VALENTINE'S DAY, and the nation was firmly in the grasp of winter. Since outside activities were not too desirable, television channel clickers were settling in for a weekend of TV fare that would run the gamut from sports to comedy, from cartoons to talk shows, from local news to movies. A nation of couch potatoes, having put in a week at work and school, were ready to do what they did best—watch television. There are millions of Americans who do not read the *New York Times*, the *Washington Post*, or even their hometown newspapers. For articles of depth, they choose *People* magazine, which has plenty of pictures, and for the real scoop, they depend on the tabloid "reality" shows on TV, which purvey information in the splashiest and most sensational way possible.

Such was the fast-paced "Now It Can Be Told" show hosted by Geraldo Rivera. By its very nature, the show fed upon screams and blood and sirens and frightened people, preferably attractive young women. No one would confuse it with David Brinkley's probing Sunday morning show that tackles global issues of the day with a panel of erudite newsmakers. That is why Brinkley is on Sunday morning, when the television audience is minuscule, and Rivera does prime time on Friday night. The Olivia Riner case would never rate so much as an arched eyebrow on the sedate Brinkley show, but it was about to become fodder for Geraldo's millions of fans.

It began at seven P.M., with a breathless Rivera announcing that his team had uncovered a "key suspect" in a crime that "mirrors the terror" of the scary motion picture, *The Hand That Rocks the Cradle*. Across the nation, in living rooms where nothing was known about the tragedy in Thornwood, ears perked up and eyes were glued to the flickering screen. Hey, come look at this!

The viewers saw firefighters battling the blaze on West Lake Drive and heard a distraught young woman trying to report the fire to authorities. Rivera noted a baby had died in the incident and police had charged the girl who called them, the nanny, with murder.

Quick cut to Police Chief Oliva, who said, "We have reason to believe that she was involved in the ignition of the fires." Then Rivera appears, bushy mustache a-twitch, to ask, "Did the hand that rocked the cradle strike the match?" On the screen a handcuffed Olivia is led into the courtroom, while Geraldo concocts the strange question, "Now it can be told, home alone?"

The hook was set. Mothers in the TV audience throughout America were locked to their sofas. First, the show ran a teaser story about government officials reportedly abusing tax dollars. Then it returned to Thornwood, with correspondent Alexander Johnson taking over the excited telling of the event, while fast clips of fires, Olivia, and *The Hand that Rocks the Cradle* snapped across the screen, along with news headlines and the scratchy sound of the emergency recording playing in the background.

Brevetti is shown in her office, defending her client, carefully stoking the explosion she knows will erupt when this thing hits the airwaves. Then there is the panicked voice of Olivia, once again, as the cops call her back to say they can't find the address she has given. Then Olivia is shown, wearing manacles. "It was a rush to judgment here, for no apparent reason other than she was the convenient suspect," Brevetti says.

The case is summarized and Johnson and Rivera appear again, introducing the idea of a "mystery man" at the scene. The person in question was John Gallagher, and anyone who had followed the events already knew he had been at the house that night. But millions of Americans watching the Geraldo show did not know the story, and were waiting like sheep to be fleeced with the sensational "new" development.

In a classic bit of ambush television journalism, in which a camera and microphone are thrust in the face of an unsuspecting person in the guise of pursuing truth, Johnson is shown actually running after Gallagher, who manages to keep his face away from the camera and says repeatedly that he has no comment. Rivera immediately labels him as a "possible suspect," and Johnson calls Gallagher the "mysterious boyfriend of baby Kristie's stepsister [sic], Leah."

The two television announcers had revealed absolutely nothing new, but had done so at a frantic pace. Then the viewing audience, including authorities, sat up straight. For coming on the screen next were some clips of actual video footage that had been taken at the scene of the fire, not by a TV cameraman, but by none other than members of the Mount Pleasant Police Department. The Rivera people had gotten their hands on the police videotape of the crime scene.

It threw a shadow on the case that had not been there before. Two people identified as Leah Fischer and John Gallagher were shown walking through the ashes outside the burned home, their feet shuffling through the debris.

Incredibly, laughter is heard, and someone, at one point, makes the macabre statement, "You and I will stay at my house for a while, and we'll have barbecues." On the screen, no one is facing the camera at the time, so it was impossible to say who made the comment, but that did not stop the TV show from declaring that the words came from John Gallagher.

The "Now It Can Be Told" television crew made another attempt to question the police chief; but at the station house, a crisply uniformed Sergeant Dwyer wouldn't let them past the lobby. "The chief is not making any comments on the case at this time," the policeman said.

The camera snapped back to Brevetti, who delivers a hard punch. She says the state admits having no direct evidence linking Olivia with the crime, not even fingerprints or evidence of a flame accelerant on her clothing.

Johnson and Rivera chat for a moment about an alleged motive that Olivia was homesick enough to commit the crime, and discuss that Gallagher had dodged their camera and that the girl had been hysterical when she called the emergency line. Rivera had the last word: "I smell a rat."

The show stirred a hornet's nest. Police Chief Oliva called it "an awful thing" that should be totally disregarded. A Fischer relative said it was "garbage." It would later even become an issue in the trial.

Brevetti, of course, said nothing about the TV show. It had been a nationwide publicity coup for the defense lawyer, who in coming months would show an incredible talent for using the media, particularly television, to get her message across, to put the proper spin on whatever was happening. The prosecution, by refusing to talk to the press, left the field wide open for her to sow doubt after doubt about their case.

As dicey as the show might have been from the point of factual journalism, it accomplished something that the mainstream media had not done. It raised the issue of the crime scene having been corrupted so soon after the fire, and, with the use of the police video, placed Gallagher—whose name had been kept out of the press for months—in the middle of a spotlight that was threatening to shine on possible police incompetence.

PART THREE

Before the Storm

The charred baby seat that became a critical piece of state's evidence.
(Alan Zale, The New York Times)

Police photograph that was said to show the fire-singed eyebrow of Olivia Riner. *(Susan Harris,* The New York Times)

Judge Donald Silverman
answering media
questions.
(Mary Meenan)

Assistant District Attorney George Bolen. *(Mary Meenan)*

John Gallagher, the boyfriend of Leah Fischer. *(Mary Meenan)*

Chief Defense Investigator Christopher Rush escorts Olivia Riner into the courthouse. *(AP/Wide World Photos)*

Artist's rendition of Olivia Riner, Laura Brevetti and Judge Donald Silverman listening to the testimony of John Gallagher. *(Artwork by Ruth Pollack)*

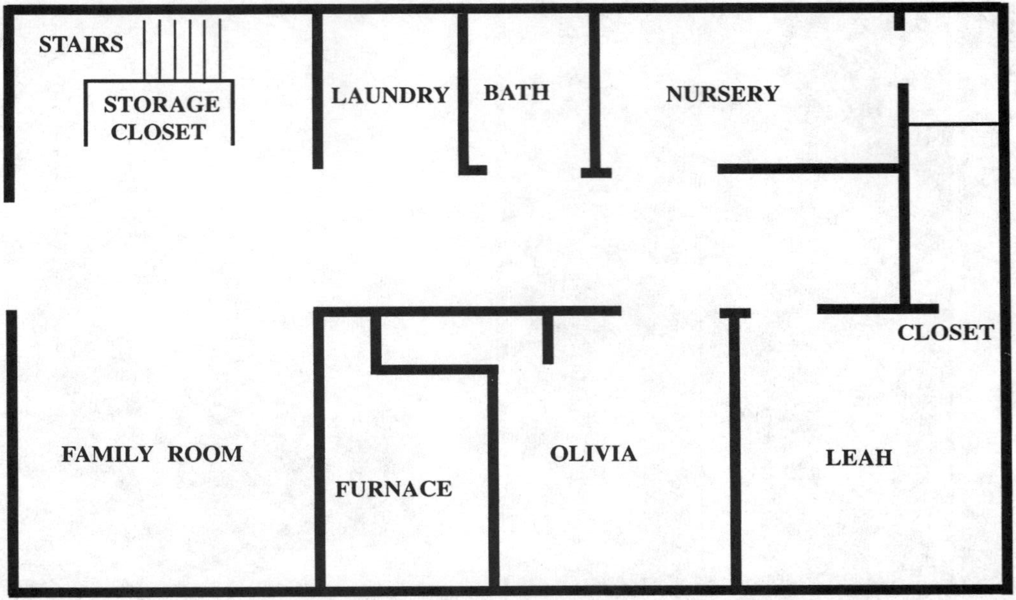

Diagram of the first floor of 5 West Lake Drive. (*Drawing by Don Davis*)

STAIRS

STORAGE CLOSET

FAMILY ROOM

LAUNDRY

BATH

FURNACE

OLIVIA

NURSERY

LEAH

CLOSET

Olivia Riner leaves the Westchester County Jail, accompanied by her parents, after being released. *(AP/Wide World Photos)*

Olivia Riner is welcomed by supporters upon her arrival in Switzerland.
(AP/Wide World photos)

Chapter Sixteen

OPENING GAMBIT

SPRING WAS COMING, BUDS SPROUTING ON WINTER-BARE TREES and flowers pushing through the soil as the weather began to warm. There was a general sense that things were beginning to move, as much in the legal system as in nature.

For both sides in the Olivia Riner case, it was time to move into the murky world of lawyerese, the peculiar and exact language of affidavits and waivers and motions.

Laura Brevetti filed papers on March 2, exactly four months after the fire, seeking to have the charges against her client dismissed. In a sweeping argument, she claimed also that some of the evidence against Olivia should be disallowed. Since there was so little evidence to begin with, the dismissal of any of it would be one less arrow in the prosecution's arsenal.

Brevetti strongly contended that her client's constitutional rights had been violated at the time of her arrest because of Olivia's confusion when Detective Johnson read her the Miranda rights. "It was clear that Olivia had little or no linguistic or conceptual understanding of either the rights read to her or the predicament she confronted," Brevetti wrote in her legal brief.

This point would play a larger role later when the tape-recorded session between Johnson and Olivia was heard in open court. Brevetti argued that since the Swiss woman did not understand the words—even the most basic term of "lawyer"—then she could not have understood the very fundamental purpose of the constitutional guarantees. Brevetti raised the question of why, at some point, the police did not think that an interpreter should have been summoned.

The defense attorney, for the first time, also formally brought the name of John Gallagher into her scenario to question why the police had eliminated him as a suspect on the spot. Since he was the only other person present at the fire, and his comments about Olivia's movements carried so much weight with the authorities, Brevetti wanted to know why he had been treated so differently. This approach would become a bedrock position in the trial as she sought to move Gallagher closer and closer to the action.

She also described how her client called for emergency help and even turned on the upstairs lights, and thoroughly cooperated with police who showed up at the scene. On the evidence trail, Brevetti criticized the police for not preserving the crime scene, and moved to suppress Olivia's diary and some of her personal photographs that had been confiscated by the investigators.

It was not likely that many of the motions she filed would succeed, but at least she would have them on the record. And since the evidence chain was obviously fragile, perhaps Judge Silverman might agree with some of her points, or the prosecution might change some of its tactics. Who knew? It was worth a shot.

The State of New York, County of Westchester fired back in two weeks, belittling Brevetti's challenge using the sort of arrogant terminology that would mark communications from the District Attorney's Office. It wasn't good enough to have clear and concise arguments in the 39-page rebuttal from Assistant District Attorney Michael Lambert; the wording bordered on insulting. When rebutting Brevetti's claim that Count Two of the indictment was unconstitutionally vague, Lambert's written reply made its point and then added, "to now state that an ordinary person would not know that such conduct was prohibited by statute goes well beyond disingenuousness. Indeed, it is absolutely absurd!"

He also defended the circumstantial nature of the case with the declaration that "it is beyond cavil that there is no innate superiority of direct evidence over circumstantial evidence." Stripped of its lawyer language, the phrase indicated that Lambert would just as soon go before a jury with a gauzy set of possibilities that might lead to a conclusion, rather than have a signed confession or a witness who could stand up and say, "She did it!" Of course, since the prosecution had neither of those things, they had no recourse but to say the vaporous trail of circumstance would be just fine.

Concerning the tape recording of the telephone calls Olivia had with the various police departments on the night of the fire, Lambert said it was of such "dubious value" that the county had no obligation to present it to the grand jury. Actually, the only dubious value of that tape would be to the prosecution side, for it clearly displayed Olivia's frantic state of mind as she broke down crying in frustration and confusion on the recorded message. Quoting the law, Lambert wrote that "the People generally enjoy wide discretion in presenting their case to the grand jury . . . and are not obligated to search for evidence favorable to the defense or to present all evidence in their possession that is favorable to the accused." In other words, justice can take a back seat to getting an indictment.

Point by point, Lambert went through Brevetti's documents, citing proper codes and defending the investigation on the night of December 2.

More papers were written and filed on both sides as the attorneys picked their way through the confused month of March, toward a decision that had been almost a foregone conclusion before the ink was dry on the first page of Brevetti's initial plea for dismissal.

On March 30 Judge Silverman denied the motion, saying the grand jury indictment had been supported by sufficient proof. The charges against Olivia remained.

While the defense team lost the battle, the war was not over yet. Things were just getting warmed up. Silverman, before upholding the indictment, threw a bone to the defense by ruling that pretrial hearings would be held on a couple of Brevetti requests.

That way, both sides could claim partial victory for the month. George Bolen's team had knocked down the dismissal attempt. Laura Brevetti would get a crack at prosecution witnesses. With such a wise set of rulings, Judge Silverman made no enemies.

Far beyond the courthouse, something was afoot in Mount Pleasant. Paul Oliva, the chief of police there since 1968, announced on March 3 that he would retire, effective April 4. The sixty-five-year-old Oliva had been on the force since 1951. After forty years and one heart attack, he was stepping down just as his department was being slammed for the way it handled one of the most important crimes ever to hit the township.

With the job of top cop now open, the town board began to look for a successor. More than three years earlier, both lieutenants on the force, Louis Alagno and Michael Mahony, had successfully passed the examination to qualify for the position. But what should have been a smooth transition would become one more element of the tangled Riner case.

Chapter Seventeen

QUEEN TAKES KNIGHT

IN THE WORLD OF CHESS, A RAMPAGING QUEEN IS BAD NEWS. As the most powerful piece on the board, she attacks anywhere, takes anything. When Laura Brevetti came into the largest courtroom on the eighteenth floor of the Westchester County Court House on Tuesday, May 12, the legal chessboard took on a new look. The Queen was at large and had fire in her eyes.

Olivia had lost weight since her incarceration. Gone was the slight roll of fat beneath her chin, and she appeared thin and small as she walked to the front of the room and sat at the desk. Judge Silverman later would guess she would hunt among the petite sizes in a dress shop. Sitting quietly, eyes down, the accused baby slayer looked more like a lost little girl, which was precisely what her lawyer wanted.

The brown hair was longer and swept back softly over her shoulders. Bangs touched her eyebrows. Her nose was sharply pointed, the eyes widely spaced, and a small gold ornament dangled from a pierced ear. Her mouth, with a short upper lip pulled down at the corners, gave her a look of perpetual minor distaste when she concentrated. Forbidden from being a fashion plate or from wearing anything outrageous, she went the other way and came into court wearing a dark blue blazer and matching pleated skirt, with a white blouse buttoned to her neck.

On her left ankle, bulging beneath the dark blue stockings, was the bulky, square electronic device that she had worn for months as a condition of her bail. With a slight smile, she took a seat at the defense table, alone.

That only lasted a moment, until the rest of the Brevetti troop filed in to surround her. Brevetti took a chair beside the girl and began shuffling a small mountain of papers, three brown boxes full of documents and black three-ring notebooks. Maya Hess, a professional translator, took a chair on the other side of Olivia. Associate counsel Elan Gerstmann moved to the end of the table. Chris Rush, dapper in a double-breasted suit, arranged paper-stuffed boxes against the wall before taking a chair. Downstairs, the burly former cop had grasped Olivia's sleeve and tucked her in close beside him as he escorted her through a phalanx of television cameras that snooped mercilessly close when they entered the courthouse.

Marlies Riner, Olivia's mother, took a place on the front pew, preparing to sit through a complicated legal hearing where she would hardly understand a word because she spoke little English. She was here to support her daughter, and with her coal-black hair, dark eyes, attractive features, and trim figure, dressed in a skirt the color of vanilla ice cream, which stopped just above the knees, she appeared almost like an older sister.

Opposite the defense table was the prosecution table, where George Bolen, the assistant district attorney, sat starkly alone, wearing a sober gray suit with tiny chalk stripes, and a maroon tie. A closed briefcase stood beside his polished black shoes.

This was Day One of the courtroom ritual, and the scene would be replayed day after day, with the only major change being the tailored, expensive outfits worn by Brevetti. For the next two weeks Olivia would wear the same blue convent school-style suit, while Brevetti's closet would yield a different combination, all suitable for a decorous courtroom, every day. Bolen wore a rotation of dark suits and power ties.

After months of getting ready, it was time to get down to business. For the rest of May, all of June, and part of July, this cast of characters would spend a lot of time together, very little of it pleasant.

The first order of business was some legal wrestling, during which Brevetti, Bolen, and Silverman picked over the evidence file and the numerous motions that had been placed before the court. The judge denied a halfhearted Brevetti attempt to gain a postponement. A potential defense witness for forensic evidence had suffered a ruptured disk in his back and a neurosurgeon was recommending surgery. The judge said he would keep the fact in mind, but that things must go forward. Silverman's reputation for running a swift trial had preceded him in this case, to the dismay of the opposing lawyers. For an attorney, there is no such thing as having too much time to prepare a case.

Then they reviewed the layout of the Fischer house and what police had taken from the various rooms, including the doorknobs, sections of Olivia's burned bedspread, glass shards from the window in Kristie's room, Olivia's passport, diary, suitcases, jewelry, a pile of fast food the Swiss girl had stashed in her room, and the clothing Olivia had been wearing when she was arrested.

The side trip to evidenceland had an unexpected payoff for Brevetti. One thing the cops seized the night of the fire was Olivia's diary, a small book with a key latch, in which she had logged descriptions of her life in America. The prosecution had liked one of the early sentences in the book, where she complained about the baby being spoiled, but the more recent entries evidencing a growing personal love for the child clearly outweighed any benefit of using it as evidence. In earlier motions, Brevetti had sought to have the diary set aside and claimed it had been taken as the result of an illegal police search. Bolen told the court he had decided not to use it after all, but he did not entirely discard it. He said that if Brevetti introduced it into evidence, he reserved the right to bring its contents forward. Therefore, the question of whether the police taking the diary without a warrant had rendered it to be, in legal jargon, "fruit from the poisoned tree," would not be answered.

While the maneuvering went on, there was a continuing low buzz from the defense table. After three other interpreters had been brought in and found inadequate for the job, Maya Hess was fitting in admirably. A New Yorker, originally from the Zurich area, she spoke the same unique Swiss-German dialect as Olivia. It was her first day on the job, but to Olivia she already seemed to be a friend. Maya was impressed, but since she was being paid by the state, the interpreter tried to maintain a sense of neutrality. The other translators simply had not been able to keep pace with the proceedings, including one woman who spoke to Olivia only on an infrequent basis, telling her what, in the translator's opinion, she should know. Silverman wanted there to be no doubt that the defendant knew what was going on around her, particularly since the language issue had already been raised. He would not allow it to become a point for future appeal. Maya proved up to the task, her eyes glued on whoever was talking, and softly translating each word into Olivia's tongue. She would keep the pace up for eight grueling weeks, only rarely having to ask for a word to be repeated. Bolen, with his rapid-fire delivery, made a conscious effort to slow down his speech pattern.

The first witness to take the stand in the case against Olivia Riner was patrolman Scott Carpenter, primarily because he was the first law enforcement officer to arrive at the December 2 fire. The officer walked in wearing a clean and pressed dark blue uniform, confident of being on the side of the law, which sets wrongs right, and settled into the witness chair as if he were a wise young Solomon. Carpenter was going to learn a mirror can cast different reflections of the same image.

Bolen walked to a wooden podium about ten feet away from the officer and began a series of methodical questions, literally walking the policeman through the night in question, recounting Carpenter's dramatic attempt to reach the baby. The witness told of how he and officer Bobby Miliambro made their way into the house, found the nursery, and, crawling on their hands and knees, discovered the burned baby in the corner, and how he thought that what he was looking at was not human at all, but a badly burned doll. There was a definite air of believability about the young man with the crew cut, and if a jury had been sitting in the box that day, instead of press people, Carpenter's simple volley of statements might have provided an emotional trigger to set a sympathetic tone for the trial. He was not talking about the defendant, Olivia Riner, he was talking about the murdered baby, Kristie Fischer.

But there was no jury, and the person most interested in him was defense counsel Laura Brevetti. She weighed his each and every word, measuring his story for its tensile strength. Backing her up on the legal points was a fast-scribbling Elan Gerstmann, while Chris Rush, taking in the testimony with a facial expression that gave away nothing, would provide Brevetti with street-cop details. This was a formidable machine.

Carpenter rolled on, explaining how he escorted Riner that night to the house of George and Helen Fries, how the ambulance personnel around her administered oxygen and checked for burns, and how, when he questioned Olivia, she just repeated, in broken English, "I don't smoke. I have no fire."

The policeman said he left the Fries home when Detective Johnson arrived and went back to the fire scene, and recalled that he later helped Johnson escort Olivia to the Town Hall Plaza police headquarters. Before his shift ended on December 2, Carpenter went back to West Lake Drive and spent two and a half hours on duty there before returning to headquarters with the change of clothes for Olivia.

It was a tight presentation. No frills. Straight out of Joe Friday and "Dragnet." Just the facts. As Bolen rested his part of the questioning, Carpenter had every right to feel good about his testimony. That would not last long.

Laura Brevetti stood up to begin her cross-examination, carrying a huge black notebook full of secrets to the podium and peering through her red-framed glasses at the big cop. This was not a woman who was intimidated at the sight of a uniform and a badge. She looked at Carpenter as if he were a frog in biology class, about to be dissected.

The style of questioning was different from the start. Where Bolen had used broad brush strokes, allowing the officer to fill in the story, Brevetti was a nitpicker. How tall are you? Five-ten. How much do you weigh? One hundred and ninety-five pounds. Describe the leather coat you were wearing that night. When did you turn off the lights of your patrol car? Where is Post Five? It was Chinese water torture, a steady drip, drip, drip of almost inconsequential questions that was driving the courtroom to distraction. Brevetti was headed somewhere, but she alone had the map.

Despite her intensity, she remained friendly to the officer, presenting absolutely no threat. She asked about the first time he talked with John Gallagher that night and how he recorded his observations in a three-by-four-inch spiral memo pad. She queried him about a typed report of four pages and a supplemental report of one page that he composed the next day. Did he remember that? Yes, he did. Routine stuff.

Brevetti, almost in a chatty mood, took Carpenter back through his two visits inside the house, but in much greater detail than Bolen. The cop told of being forced back by smoke the first time, and hearing Gallagher yelling something, and of Olivia standing in the driveway, weeping and talking about cats. He recalled the firefight-

130

ing chaos during his second trip inside, how hard it was to breathe in there, how the flashlights cut through the smoke and finally the beams pointed to the dead baby. Listeners could almost taste the acrid smoke that Carpenter described.

The policeman gingerly described how he put his face close against "what appeared to be the baby's mouth" and felt no breath coming against his cheek. The infant was charred black and the car seat was twisted and melted almost flat. He stayed in the house about three minutes. Exited alone. No, he said, he did not inspect the window in the baby's room. No, he didn't smell anything that reminded him of a combustible liquid.

He described Detective Johnson arriving and leaving Olivia with him. Brevetti pointed to the small memo book, the spelling error of "opar" for "au pair." Bolen jumped to his feet, his face a mask of indignation, and objected. The judge agreed and Brevetti waved it off. No problem, she said with a smile. Everybody makes mistakes. She moved on, having left the clear impression that the patrolman didn't know how to spell.

That light jab was just to let Carpenter know who was in control. To make sure he understood that, she followed with a powerful uppercut, asking the patrolman if he discussed with the detective what he had observed in that dramatic, heartrending moment in the baby's room. Carpenter shied like a horse facing a difficult hurdle. "I assume he saw what I saw . . . I honest to God cannot even recall the topic of discussion."

Brevetti's mouth dropped open and she slapped a black pen against her neat skirt, staring at Carpenter in clear disbelief. At great personal risk he had discovered a baby that had been burned to death, the most dramatic thing that had ever happened to him as a cop, and he did not pass the news to the detective in charge of the investigation? An uncomfortable silence enveloped the courtroom.

Okay, Brevetti continued, what did you do after leaving the Fries house at 7:10 P.M.? He said he found Gallagher standing in the driveway with Leah Fischer. It was raining and they got into the patrol car and, as the heavy drops tattooed the metal roof, Gallagher dictated a statement while Carpenter wrote in longhand. The first question was, "Why were you here? "

Brevetti introduced the statement, two pages of regular letter-sized paper, blue and unlined, into evidence. Gallagher did not answer the question at first, according to those notes, but later said he had been on his way home from work and arrived at 5:15 P.M. The questioning lawyer fell completely silent for a moment, seemingly lost in thought as she stared over the heads of the reporters, into the glare from the windows. She said absolutely nothing, and Carpenter began to fidget in the chair. This was not going the way he thought it would.

Brevetti resumed, asking why, when Gallagher was in the car, the officer didn't question him in more detail. "Why would I ask him questions? He was giving a voluntary statement." Carpenter said his job was only to gather names and addresses and keep order at the scene. It was up to the detectives, not him, to do the investigation. Brevetti snapped back with a sharp comment and Silverman cut her off, saying she was becoming argumentative. The judge said the police officer told her what he had done and it was not important whether the lawyer thought "it was stupid police work."

That was the first of many times that the defense lawyer and the judge would tap swords. Brevetti turned to her notebook and asked Carpenter what he did with the statement, the two pages of notes he had taken from Gallagher. Carpenter replied he informed Lieutenant Alagno of the interview and placed the document in his briefcase in the squad car. He did not mention it to Johnson when they rode side by side to take Olivia to the station, he mentioned it to no one while at headquarters and kept it with him when he returned to West Lake Drive for guard duty.

The only two adults who had been in the house immediately after the fire started and before authorities began to arrive were Olivia Riner and John Gallagher. The only official statement Gallagher had made was left hidden in a patrolman's briefcase during one of the most critical junctures in the case.

Unaware that the Carpenter interview with John Gallagher even existed, Detective Johnson arrested Olivia an hour and a half before the patrolman resurrected the statement from its resting place. By the time he pulled it out at midnight, at the end of his shift, the document had become almost immaterial to the developing case because a suspect had already been arrested.

So, missing from the background picture that Johnson formed through his personal interviews with Olivia was the claim by Gallagher that, upon arriving at the house, he had seen a frantic Olivia running back and forth in the hall, between the baby's room and the front door. That statement, of extreme importance, became the basis for much of the speculation that followed, even in the office of the district attorney, of how Olivia had acted that evening. In fact, when answering Brevetti's motion for dismissal, Assistant Attorney General Lambert had written that Gallagher "observed the defendant rapidly pacing back and forth." Johnson had known nothing of the statement and it had never been amplified through more intensive questioning.

Brevetti was content to leave that questionable procedure exactly where it lay for the time being, and pushed ahead to what she considered an even more important point, perhaps one of the most important elements of her case.

She wanted to show in the coming trial that the scene of the fire had been corrupted before relevant evidence was gathered, and that the ruination had its roots in the stumbling performance of a small town's police force. With a smile, she continued to coax Carpenter up the stairs toward a figurative guillotine.

Beneath her gentle probing, Carpenter admitted that,

after he had helped transport Olivia to the police station, he drove back to the house "to have a look around." He was curious about what had happened, he said.

Did you have any official function there at the time? No.

You walked in the various rooms? Yes.

"I want to be fair," the lawyer said. "You had no function there other than curiosity? "

"Yes. I was just there to look around."

Brevetti struck a pose that would have done actress Meryl Streep proud. Her left elbow was on the podium and she rested her carefully coiffed head onto an open palm, eyes flipping open wide at the tidbit of golden testimony that had just been cast before her. The first policeman at the scene of the crime had admitted that not only was the area improperly protected, but that he, a trained and uniformed officer of the law, had helped trash it!

Officer Carpenter had started the day off crisp and blue. By 4:30 P.M. he was wiping his face and pressing his palms to his forehead, brow knitted together in a nervous frown. He tried to recoup his lost turf, but only made things worse. "If someone was looking at me, they might think I was investigating. But I was just walking around."

Day One of the preliminary hearing finally came to a merciful end. Brevetti later would say that she didn't think she was being mean to the young cop. Perhaps not, but she had taken the state's first witness and hung him up like a cheap suit.

Chapter Eighteen

DETECTIVE JOHNSON

BRUCE JOHNSON CAME TO THE STAND AFTER CARPENTER WAS finally dismissed on Wednesday, May 13, and quickly became the focus of the preliminary hearing, for he was the man who had questioned, suspected, and arrested Olivia Riner. If Brevetti wanted to demonstrate that the police did not have sufficient reason to arrest her client, she would first have to crack this 225-pound walnut.

George Bolen had studied Brevetti's slashing style during the dismantling of Scott Carpenter, and, with this witness, intended to give her much less room to maneuver. He slowed his own pace and adopted some of her tactics. When Johnson sat in the witness box, he began a skein of testimony that would continue for days—actually stretch throughout the trial. The detective was the primary witness for the state in the trial to come, and this would prove to be an excellent test run. Just as drivers in the Indianapolis 500 automobile race were running time trials that week, Bolen and Johnson would use this appearance to see how his story played under pressure.

Bolen did not want a repeat of the Carpenter episode. Even today when the young officer was questioned further, he remained flustered, though a bit more aggressive. When Brevetti pushed her question on what Carpenter and Gallagher had done while talking in the car, the policeman remembered taking a cigarette from Gallagher.

He quickly added, "I didn't steal it from him." Even Olivia smiled. When Brevetti started her detail work again, asking Carpenter if he recalled walking with Olivia to the police car, Judge Silverman reached the limit of his patience with the nitpicking. "The only question here is whether there was probable cause to arrest Miss Riner," he said. "We're not going to get into whether there was probable cause involving someone else." He had no intention of allowing Brevetti to turn a preliminary hearing into a trial of John Gallagher.

With Carpenter gone and Johnson on the stand, Bolen stood, pushed his steel-framed glasses firmly onto the bridge of his nose, and began to lead Johnson through the basic information of where he had been when the call came in and how and when the detective arrived at the scene. Not unnoticed at the defense table, those innocuous early statements also revealed that Johnson knew Bill Fischer. "Not an acquaintance, but I knew who he was."

The detective said Sergeant Dwyer and Lieutenant Alagno had taken him to the broken nursery window and pointed out the "charred infant" on the floor beside the dresser, and that officer Miliambro told him an au pair had been watching the child before the fire. Johnson said that was the only information he had when he walked into the Fries house and met Olivia, who was seated, crying, at the dining room table. At six P.M. he sat down and began to talk to her.

Johnson, tall, with a full head of dark brown hair combed back on both sides, and a mustache, seemed comfortable as he told his story. Unlike Carpenter, he had been in the witness box for a big trial before. His professional air was impressive, and he was not afraid to smile. In a courtroom, professionalism goes a long way. In telling her story to the detective, Olivia said she had been in the laundry room, feeding the cats, when one ran out from her bedroom, which led to the discovery of the fire on her bed. She said she noticed her window was open, but added, "I don't open window." She described the smoke coming from beneath the nursery door and how she had found the "door locked. It never locked."

The detective carefully went through his questioning of Olivia, as if opening a folder that contained precise information. The call to authorities, the sound of the smoke alarm, how John Gallagher had suddenly shown up and yelled, "Where's Kristie?" and grabbed the fire extinguisher and kicked down the door to the baby's room. She said another man went in briefly and was forced out by the smoke.

Johnson testified he asked the important question of whether she was alone in the house, the second time he had asked it. First she said, "Yes, the only other one was Kristie," and now she confirmed that "if anyone else was in the house she would have known it." The girl had begun to calm down and her English answers were more understandable. Outside, the billowing and crackling fire raging next door and the yells of the men fighting it provided a macabre background for their conversation, which continued for an hour in its initial phase. He jotted some notes as they went along.

Then he went with Dwyer and the D.A.'s arson expert, Joe Butler, on a tour of the Fischer house, first looking at the circular burned patch on Olivia's bed, then in the nursery where the melted bottle and box of matches were observed, and finally visiting Leah's bedroom, which had been gutted.

Thirty minutes after leaving Olivia alone, he was back in the Fries residence to resume questioning. Once again, what happened? Olivia repeated her story, saying she had been playing with O.J. the cat in the living room when Oliver streaked by in terror. Johnson said he immediately noticed the discrepancy of her now saying she was in the living room instead of in the laundry room. While going through the story again, Johnson noticed the shocked parents, Bill and Denise Fischer, being taken to another room in the Fries house, and he decided it was too noisy and confusing to continue his work there. "I asked her to accompany me back to headquarters."

By eight o'clock they were in the detective's office, along with dispatcher Betsy Hoagland, and after asking Olivia if she needed anything to eat or drink, or if she needed to use the rest room—all refused—they began the questioning once again. This time they went back to the afternoon hours, when Bill Fischer had returned home for a late lunch, while she was playing with the baby in the nursery. Olivia's replies were filled with rich detail. About three P.M. Kristie had started to whimper and Olivia had fixed an eight-ounce bottle of formula and water to quiet her, then changed the child's cloth diaper. When the baby began to fall asleep in her arms, she put Kristie into the car seat, propping her lolling head against a pillow made of a rolled diaper.

Olivia started a load of laundry and went to her room to read. Bill came downstairs, looked in on the sleeping baby, then returned to work. Twenty minutes later Kristie was again awake and Olivia took her upstairs to the kitchen and put her in a swing while the nanny prepared a four-ounce bottle. That done, they went back downstairs and Olivia sat in a big chair to watch television, while feeding the milk to the hungry Kristie.

At four P.M. the propane gas delivery man walked by the front door, then back a few minutes later. The baby was nodding off, and Olivia once more changed a dirty diaper, then placed the sleepy baby in the car seat on the bedroom floor.

Olivia returned to do the laundry and put some folded clothes on the floor of the baby's room. The cats began to meow, and she opened some food for them. Oliver finished first and stalked away, only to come running back a few minutes later, and the nightmare of the fires began.

No, she said, she had not looked at Kristie's door or at the closed door to Leah's room, but instead had run upstairs through the smoke to get the fire extinguisher. Johnson wanted to know more about Leah's bedroom being closed. Olivia said she had been in there only twice during the month she had stayed at the house, once when being shown around, and once to get an ironing table. She said Leah kept the door closed to keep the cats out.

After putting out the fire on her bed, she discovered the baby's door was closed and saw smoke coming underneath it. She tried the knob and found it locked. She grabbed the slip of paper with the emergency numbers on it in her own darkened bedroom and went upstairs to the kitchen to call for help.

After the episode with the telephone, she saw Gallagher approaching the front door, gave him the extinguisher, and watched as he ran down the hall and kicked open the locked nursery door.

While she was telling her story, twisting a tissue into a wet and torn blob of paper, Johnson had spent time looking at her eyes. In the bright fluorescent light of the office, they appeared to have been singed by fire, particularly on the right side. Otherwise there were no injuries that he could detect.

The repetitive questioning at the police headquarters had continued for about two hours. As the night grew later, Johnson took a bathroom break, then resumed questioning. Olivia had not moved from her chair the entire time.

In the mind of the detective that night, Olivia had already crossed the boundary from witness into the dangerous turf of suspect. From that point, he would tread carefully before making an official charge. On and on and on they went, covering the same ground until Johnson knew the answers before he asked the questions. But nothing new was gleaned. He wanted to know if she was sexually active, had a boyfriend or was jealous of any of the Fischers. No, she replied.

At 10:30 P.M. on that chilly December night, Bruce Johnson had heard enough. He looked carefully at the girl and told her she was under arrest. Ten minutes later he slipped a new TDK sixty-minute tape into the Aiwa recorder, pressed the button to make it record, and started with Olivia once again, this time first reading her the rights to which she was entitled as a prisoner. Bolen neared the end of the careful presentation and reached into his gray briefcase to submit the tape, marked "912548 interview with Olivia Riner original," into evidence. That recording of the hour-long arrest interview would have a far-reaching effect on the trial.

The assistant district attorney rested his interview of Bruce Johnson until everyone had a chance to listen to what was actually on the cassette.

Having recorded Olivia's and Johnson's words on tape was one thing. Playing those words back in a courtroom without distortion was something else entirely. The tape recorder had been behind Johnson's back during the interview, so his words were clear. Olivia's responses were blocked from the microphone by the detective's body, and came in as faint, and at times totally inaudible, sounds. To improve the quality of the tape, Bolen had taken it to the Organized Crime Strike Force, the people for whom Brevetti had once been a star. The OCSF experts ran it through their machines to enhance it and turned out a second tape, which Bolen then placed into evidence.

To simply plunk it into a huge tape deck and jack up the volume would have been an unthinkable scenario in court, since the degree of hearing for different people, meaning the jurors, would require varying levels. The high-tech answer was unveiled on Day Three of the hearings.

On Thursday, May 14, the court of Judge Silverman took on the appearance of Mission Control or a studio band session. No jury was yet in the box, but everyone else involved in the case donned a pair of black, cushioned HyDyn HD1234 battery-powered headsets. Volume and tone were controlled by sliding a red or yellow button on the right side. When everyone in the room was ready, they pointed their faces toward a black box set against the far wall, which would transmit a radio signal to the headsets. The box was hooked to a tape deck beside Bolen's desk. At 10:15 A.M. he pushed the button to start the contraption, saying, "I hope it works."

Silence in the court but voices in the ears. Johnson asking Olivia if she wanted to say anything different than what she had already stated. A strained, quiet woman's voice—distant from the microphone—replied: "No."

Then things faded into mumbles, and finally Silverman tired of the electronic sideshow. Removing his headset and motioning for Bolen to stop the machine, the judge said what he was hearing was "very unclear" and some of the words were undecipherable. Silverman wanted a written transcript.

"I'm having difficulty understanding what she's saying . . . I'm getting some things but I'm missing a lot," the jurist said. "I do not want to make decisions on something I cannot understand."

He might as well have stuck a hot poker to Bolen's fingers. The prosecution lawyer was on his feet, saying that the tape was "the main evidence" in his case. He did not have a transcript.

Brevetti, being cagy, said, sorry, she did not have one either. Too bad, George. Would've loved to help. She cheerfully agreed with the judge, saying the tape was inaudible, but added that in her opinion a reliable transcript could not be produced from it.

Silverman was not ready to let it go that easily, but he wanted words, not sounds. Bolen slumped in his chair, as if the weight of the world was on his shoulders. "In all honesty, that transcript would have to be done by me," he said, sighing.

The judge was unmoved by either act. Both sides had had six months to come up with an understandable record of what was on that tape. He would not be thwarted. Each side, he said, should come up with a transcript, then get together to see which sections could be agreed upon. Meanwhile, Brevetti could cross-examine Johnson for the rest of Thursday and Friday, bringing him to the same point when the tape began. But when court resumed Tuesday morning, Silverman directed, the transcripts must be ready.

It was a logical decision, a perfect way around the stalemate on an important piece of Bolen's evidence. But it was going to be more difficult than the judge first imagined.

Brevetti was not about to help make her client's taped responses understandable, for to do so would be to help the prosecution incriminate her. As far as the defense team was concerned, that tape was going to be no more understandable than a rap music album recorded in Latin.

Laura Brevetti and Bruce Johnson greeted each other with extraordinary politeness. Then the games began.

Her opening points were seemingly random, just some things that she may have recalled from the lengthy testimony that the detective had given for Bolen, although the punch line was never long in arriving.

Johnson had testified that he had been a volunteer firefighter for fifteen years, ending in 1982. On the surface, that would seem to give him more expertise with such things as arson. Brevetti established that he had never been officially trained in fire investigation, so any decision on how a fire actually started would have to be the conclusion of someone else, because the policeman lacked the scientific knowledge. That tidbit would not pay off for several weeks, but pay off it would.

She questioned him about his notes. Johnson said he had taken three pages of handwritten notes during his hour-long interview with Olivia at the Fries residence and later turned them into a typed report of two pages. Notes that he took, plus his recollections of what happened at the police station from 7:00 P.M. through 1:15 A.M., were assembled in a nine-page handwritten document that he produced the following weekend on his days off. They were then given to a secretary to type and he signed off on it.

Brevetti changed course and hammered at the exact times of Johnson's movements on the night of December 2. From 6:05 until 7:00, he interviewed Olivia Riner at the Fries home; from 7:00 to 7:30 he was at the fire scene with his colleagues; at 7:30 he was back interviewing Olivia next door, and soon thereafter they left for the police station, arriving at 7:50 P.M. Two hours and fifty minutes passed, before the arrest was formally made. Where, spectators wondered, was all of this numerology leading? All of that was old information. Midnight passed, and up until 12:30 on the morning of December 3 Olivia was still insisting, "I don't light no fire."

At any point prior to that, Detective Johnson, had you asked the girl if she had started the fire? Johnson said no, he had not. Six and one-half hours had passed, the arrest had been made and follow-up interrogations had been conducted, and the detective had not asked the pointed question of "Did you do it?"

Brevetti leaned on the podium and rolled her eyes in apparent frustration. "Officer Johnson, what were you investigating? A car theft?"

Silverman scolded her again for being argumentative.

Brevetti resumed, taking Johnson back through the house again with Dwyer and Butler, having him describe to whom he had spoken and what he had seen. By the time he returned to the dining room table in the Fries house, he only knew that the baby had died in the fire and the nanny said she was alone in the house at the time.

The drumbeat of Brevetti's questions did not seem to be getting to the veteran officer as she went along, seemingly aimlessly.

They spent some time describing the construction of the bedroom windows, particularly how they were built to slide from side to side. He confirmed that the window in the baby's room, which the state had consistently claimed had been "cracked," actually contained a hole large enough for him to stick his head through.

Johnson was asked about some of his acquaintances in the tightly knit hamlets. He had already said he knew who Bill Fischer was, and now she drew from the detective that he also knew John Gallagher before the night of December 2.

As court adjourned for the day, onlookers were exchanging knowing glances. Two policemen had testified about being at the scene and both admitted knowing John Gallagher. The point was so obvious that Brevetti had not bothered to jump on it at all.

That brought them to where Johnson had turned on the tape recorder. Things could go no further without the tape, which had already been determined by the judge to be unacceptable in its present form. Although it was only 12:30 P.M., Silverman adjourned court for the day.

The pretrial session had begun on Tuesday. Now it was Friday, May 15, and the case seemed to be evolving into a different shape.

George Bolen had gone into the most famous case of his career, trying socialite Jean Harris, with a total confession, having only to determine the matter of degree, not the issue of actual guilt. This one was going to be an uphill battle all the way, and Laura Brevetti wasn't going to give an inch. One witness had already been destroyed, and his main man, Johnson, was clearly having some problems. And the trial had not even started!

Johnson was back on the stand Friday morning, Brevetti putting him through the hoops again, just as the detective had badgered Olivia during the evening hours of December 2, covering the same ground again and again, looking for wrinkles and discrepancies.

He supplied a description of his escorted visit through the fire scene and the observations of Dwyer and Butler, the arson specialist, who had declared the fires were "not accidental, not incendiary, not electrical" in origin. So when Johnson walked back to the Fries residence, he testified, Olivia was still only "my best witness."

Silverman: "Did you believe at 7:30 that there was probable cause that she started the fire?"

Johnson: "No."

That idea did not really come to him until 8:45 P.M. at the station, when he came across another variation of her story. At first she had told him she had been feeding the cats, then changed to say that she had been playing with them.

At eight P.M. Johnson had taken the telephone call from Dwyer, who said the baby's diaper had been doused with paint thinner and that cans of paint thinner had been discovered in a downstairs closet. Johnson said that Olivia continued to insist she was home alone. Suspicion grew.

Brevetti: "She was the best suspect you had."

Johnson: "No. She was a witness. I had my own suspicions that there was an arson involved."

Silverman: "At six o'clock, she wasn't a suspect. At 7:30, she was?"

Johnson nodded in affirmation. Just a moment earlier he had said he did not believe probable cause existed at that time, and now he was admitting that he considered Olivia to be a suspect, even before they left for the police station.

If Olivia's story had holes in it, so did Johnson's.

At headquarters more people got involved in questioning the girl at the desk in the detectives' office. Lieutenant Alagno joined in about 10:30 P.M., but remained silent while the tape was rolling. Dwyer arrived after midnight. From 12:15 until 1:30 A.M. Police Chief Paul Oliva led the interrogation. Then Johnson and Dwyer took it up until 2:45 A.M. and its merciful end.

Throughout the pounding, Olivia Riner repeated her story with startling consistency. Her nervousness was focused upon her hands as she shredded the tiny piece of tissue paper. Because she stared at her busy fingers, Johnson "gently lifted her face" with his hand in order to get

145

answers to his questions. And every time he looked at those singed eyelashes, he believed the slight burning had happened not while she was trying to extinguish the fire, but while she was starting it.

From the moment the first cop arrived at 5 West Lake Drive and started asking her questions, Olivia had kept to the same story, working in an unfamiliar language while undergoing intense questioning for a prolonged period of hours. She steadfastly insisted that no one else was in the house, although by saying so, she was casting herself as a suspect. The variations of her tale were minor—living room or laundry room, playing with or feeding the cats, standing at the foot or the side of her bed when she put out the fire—and above all, there was not a hint of a motive for the crime.

The police obviously still had some questions. They asked if she was covering up for someone, and both Dwyer and Johnson mentioned John Gallagher by name. Olivia said no, she was not.

Johnson had explained in court that his own feeling that night was that the baby had been harmed, or perhaps choked, and the fire was started to cover up the accident. He was wrong. "The next day, we learned the baby died of smoke inhalation," he said.

Something strange was bubbling to the surface as Johnson's testimony came to a close. The question hung over the court of why things had moved in such a hurry on the night in question, why didn't police wait for forensic evidence to be developed? Why, in only five hours of interviewing only one person, someone who consistently denied guilt, had a single detective been allowed to unilaterally make the arrest on an arson charge in a case involving a baby's death, without a conference and significant counsel from his superior officers, without being given all of the pertinent information already available, and without even consulting with the chief of police or the two assistant district attorneys who had driven to the scene?

No time had been taken to carefully test and weigh the

evidence, no time to question other people in the neighborhood, no time for reflection, no time to wonder what the future of this particularly cruel crime would be, based upon what was at hand. But there had been plenty of time for mistakes.

Chapter Nineteen

THE TAPE

LAURA BREVETTI WAS NOT AMUSED. THE AFTERNOON SESSION began at two P.M., and the cranky air-conditioning in the court finally decided to work, refrigerating the room enough to store meat. She took her associate counsel's dark suit coat and threw it over her shoulders; pearls, blue skirt, striped blue blouse, and a man's coat much too large for her. Judge Silverman couldn't resist, and commented that the usually impeccable Brevetti now "looks like early bag lady."

The pretrial session was drawing to a close.

Lieutenant Louis Alagno, a man of medium build with soft dark hair, walked to the witness stand, the single gold bars of his rank glittering on the collar of his white shirt. As senior police officer at the fire scene on the night of December 2, he had overall supervision of the police there.

Alagno, like almost everyone else, had been alerted at his home by a call from Sergeant Gardner, and arrived at 5 West Lake Drive between 5:30 and 6:00 P.M. It did not take long for him to get there, since he lived only two houses away. Alagno found no fires burning, and uniformed officer Carpenter and off-duty sergeant Brian Dwyer, acting as a volunteer firefighter, already there.

The lieutenant described how he went into the home of his friends George and Kathryn Fries at one point and

148

saw Olivia seated alone at the dining table, and then went back into the den to speak with the distraught Fischers.

He said that during the evening, he authorized Dwyer to go on overtime to help with the investigation and instructed Carpenter to fetch clean clothing for Miss Riner, who had been standing in the rain when the lieutenant arrived.

Back at police headquarters, Alagno said he recalled the conversation with Detective Johnson about 10:30 P.M. concerning the detective's decision to place the nanny under arrest. "I would have stopped him if I disagreed. I did not disagree," he testified.

Johnson had told his boss that his decision was based upon what he had observed at the scene of the fire; the physical layout of the relatively small house; that three separate fires had been set; that Miss Riner had been the only one in the house at the time, and that she stated she had seen no one else. "That led us to believe she was the one who started the fire," said the lieutenant. He made no notes during that night, he said.

At 2:30 P.M., after only thirty minutes on the stand, the lieutenant was allowed to walk out of the courtroom. He had been a professional witness, exuding an air of confident authority. On the afternoon of Friday, May 15, 1992, Lieutenant Lewis Alagno gave the impression of an officer of the law who was an experienced leader, a man who would leave no stone unturned in the investigation of such serious crimes as arson and murder.

Less than a month later, after Wednesday, June 10, there would be a different impression. By then Alagno had already been passed over for promotion to become chief of the Mount Pleasant Police Department, and a dark question of possible favoritism had clouded some police actions on the night in question.

Brevetti had not played her trump card of Lieutenant Alagno's relationship with a possible suspect. It was too good to waste in a preliminary hearing. She wanted the jury present when she laid it on the table.

If others involved in the investigation seemed to have some loose edges, there was none of that where Sergeant Brian Dwyer was concerned. All hard angles and business was the lanky Dwyer, with twenty-three years on the police force and twenty-five with the volunteer fire department. Black hair swept low across his right forehead, and, unlike many in the department, he was clean-shaven. When he settled into the witness chair, Dwyer exuded confidence. He knew both of his jobs cold, and when he was asked a question, he would answer in the cop monotone voice made famous by television detective Joe Friday on "Dragnet." For Dwyer, his responses would be just the facts.

He had a surprising recall of details. From the early moments of his testimony, observers got the feeling this man had a photographic memory. He knew what was in a room that he had entered six months ago, was able to filter facts through the chaos of firefighting, and could precisely estimate distances between objects that he had seen only at a glance.

He had arrived on the first fire engine to respond, observed the dead baby in the nursery room, and checked the charred area of the nanny's bed, his exacting eyes taking in details.

When Dwyer went outside, he was already able to report to Lieutenant Alagno that a baby lay dead inside the house, and the two charred areas he had observed appeared to have been caused by a flammable liquid. And when Detective Johnson arrived, Dwyer led the small expedition to the window of the baby's room, where, as Johnson peered inside, Dwyer told him the fire looked to be of suspicious origin.

The third fire then erupted, and Dwyer donned his fireman's hat again. When it was out, he, Alagno, and a representative from the medical examiner's office went to the room and took 35mm and Polaroid photographs, with Dwyer switching once again into being a policeman.

Joe Butler arrived, and his evaluation agreed with Dwyer's: the fires had been intentionally set with a flammable liquid, which they could not exactly identify. Dwyer fetched Johnson from next door about 7:00 P.M., and he and Butler gave the detective a walk-through.

When the medical examiner first checked the infant corpse in the sergeant's presence, Dwyer said he did not smell any pungent odors of the sort a flammable liquid would emit. Instead, he only detected the horrible odor of burned human flesh, the "burnt skin of the baby." It was only later, when the little body was removed, that the diaper fell back into the car seat and Dwyer recovered it, discovering the strong odor he guessed was paint thinner.

Upon cross-examination by Brevetti, Dwyer said he recalled seeing John Gallagher at the scene that night, but did not feel that it was significant. Moments later he admitted that when he had returned to police headquarters and was questioning Olivia, she was asked if she was covering up for Gallagher and she denied it.

Even those seemingly opposite statements did little to dissuade anyone from questioning the reliability of Sergeant Dwyer's testimony. Here was a taciturn man who allowed no room for error. When Dwyer said something, you could take it to the bank. The prosecution was betting on that appearance. No mistakes where Dwyer was concerned.

So, a month later, when the no-nonsense sergeant blew himself right out of the water on the witness stand, he almost took the whole case down with him. For now, however, when he walked out of the courtroom, people were impressed.

The pretrial hearings entered their second and final week in a small courtroom on the fourteenth floor. It had one bench along the wall at the rear for spectators, a few chairs, and only one judge's picture on the wall. It seemed more suited for a racquetball game than a murder trial.

Brevetti entered in a fire-engine-red suit, Olivia still

wearing convent blue, Bolen in gray. It was to be a big day, the day that the taped interview would be played.

Hoping against hope, Judge Silverman asked if the transcript he wanted was ready. Bolen had given a copy of his version to Brevetti on Sunday, then she listened to it and put stripes of highlight marker onto sections with which she disagreed. There were many such areas of conflict in the forty-two page, double-spaced document. Laura Brevetti was not about to let this vital piece of evidence get in without a fight.

But for the time being, Silverman said, they would go with what they had. This hearing had to move forward, because there was a long trial ahead. The clock was ticking.

The padded headphones went back on, Bolen clicked the start button at 10:40 A.M., and the voices of Bruce Johnson, Betsy Hoagland, and Olivia Riner once again came into the ears of the people in the tight courtroom. There was a field of static and, along with the distance between Olivia and the microphone on December 2, many words still could not be understood.

BRUCE JOHNSON: Nineteen ninety-one, 10:40 P.M. We're located in the detectives' office of the Mount Pleasant Police Department with myself, Detective Bruce Johnson, and civilian dispatcher Betsy Hoagland.

OLIVIA RINER: What?

BETSY HOAGLAND: He's telling you who I am.

O.R.: Oh.

B.J.: Um, your name is Olivia Riner [Reiner]; correct?

O.R.: Yes, Olivia Riner.

B.J.: Say what?

O.R.: Riner, but you can pronounce it Riner [Reiner], it's all right.

B.J.: Riner [Riener]. Okay, uh, what is your date of birth?

OR: November 5, 1971.

B.J.: You're employed by the Fischers at Five West Lake Drive, Thornwood, New York?

O.R.: Uh-huh.

B.J.: I am just going to read a couple of questions to you and then we are going to go on from there. You have the right to remain silent. Anything you say can, and will be used against you in a court of law. You have the right to talk to a lawyer and have him present with you while you are being questioned. If you cannot afford to hire a lawyer, one will be appointed to represent you before any questioning, if you wish. You can decide at any time to exercise these rights and not answer any questions or make any statements. Do you understand each of these rights that I have explained to you?

O.R.: Some I don't.

B.J.: Which—What don't you understand?

O.R.: Some words.

B.J.: What words don't you understand?

O.R.: [Inaudible] What's remain?

HOAGLAND: Be quiet. You can just be quiet.

O.R.: What's court of law?

B.J.: That is the, ah, the American judicial system.

O.R.: The lawyer?

B.J.: The lawyer is someone who can, ah, represent you for legal purposes.

O.R.: [Inaudible]

B.J.: Which you are entitled to have, if you wish. Now with you reading these, do you understand these now?

O.R.: [Inaudible] Can I?

B.J.: Sure.

O.R.: What's afford—to hire?

B.J.: If you don't have money, the court will appoint an attorney to you.

O.R.: Oh.

B.J.: If you have money and you want to hire your own attorney . . .

O.R.: Yes.

B.J.: You may do so.

O.R.: Oh. Decide?

B.J.: Decide.

O.R.: Yes.

B.J.: It's a yes or no. It's up to you whether you . . . you can decide to stop or to . . . answer questions or not answer the questions.

O.R.: That's all?

B.J.: Yes. On this side here, do—do you understand all—all those?

O.R.: I think I do, yes.

B.J.: Okay. Um—Having explained these to you, these rights to you, do you wish to still talk to me? I'm going to ask you the same questions I have been asking you since I've seen you.

O.R.: I can't say anything different.

B.J.: You can't say anything different.

O.R.: No.

B.J.: So you wish to still, ah, discuss it with me?

O.R.: I can talk, but I can't say anything different.

B.J.: Okay, okay. You can talk, but you're not going to say anything different, right?

O.R.: Yes.

From that stumbling start in which Olivia was advised of her rights, the tape wound on. Her voice is heard as strained and tearful, even when she acknowledged that she had not been mistreated. To actually *hear* the tape was a shocking realization that the suspect being questioned had little understanding of what was happening to her. It was the voice not of a competent young woman, but of a frightened girl.

Johnson slowly started questioning again from the moment Bill Fischer had come home for lunch. The conversation went on in a stop-and-start fashion, with Olivia working her answers out in broken English, willingly giving the inquisitive detective precise details, down to the amount of ounces of milk she fed the baby. When she did not understand a question, Johnson would try to rephrase it.

Her voice would break now and then and she was obviously weary after five hours of questioning, but she was absolutely unchanged from her earlier stories. Nothing had altered, except the tale was now on a tape recording.

When it was done, Judge Silverman, observing that he still had plenty of time before the lunch break, instructed Bolen to replay the Miranda rights section over again, paying particular attention to Johnson's twenty-three-second reading of the little card and the obvious confusion of the girl who had been listening to him. Lawyer? Appoint? Decide? For Silverman, the former Legal Aid attorney, a clear understanding of those rights was of paramount importance.

Brevetti argued the tape could not be understood at critical points and that instead of hearing Olivia's voice at such times, the tape only picked up the definitions being given by Johnson. Bolen countered that the tape was "basically audible" and that if a person listens to it two or three times, "you get a knack" for the way the defendant says things.

Silverman made a ruling that had been expected. He would not allow the case to be wrecked just by a sloppy tape recording. He might have serious questions about the content, but declared that the tape itself was of sufficient clarity to be understood. "I feel I can get the meaning of everything that is said," the judge ruled.

Bruce Johnson returned to the stand to take up his testimony where it had left off with his recording of the interview. He was not kept long. Everyone by this time had a firm idea of the story of Olivia Riner and Bruce Johnson on December 2.

Bolen elicited that Johnson had actually handed the plastic Miranda card, a yellowed little document with one corner missing, to Olivia so she could read it to ensure her understanding. In the past few months, however, Johnson had thrown it out and gotten a replacement. The replacement, not the original card, would go into evidence.

The detective said that in the later hours, no one had yelled at Olivia, made no promises or threats, and that he was not told during his questioning that telephone calls had come in both from the E.F. Foundation and her father in Switzerland.

Brevetti had a few questions. Johnson acknowledged he was not familiar with the metric system, had no knowledge of the German language, and had not sought an interpreter. When Brevetti asked, the detective denied he warned Olivia that she was a nice person but was going to be transferred to a place where people were not as nice as her. That final piece of information had been given to the lawyer by Olivia herself, who claimed her interrogators had threatened her that night.

Long after the trial, a police procedures expert would wonder why the Mount Pleasant questioners had only recorded the one-hour-long interview. He said such tapes normally are kept running throughout the questioning period, no matter how long it is, to both ensure that all of the defendant's rights are being observed and, more importantly, to catch any confession that may pop up during intensive probing.

It made no difference. For now the evidence was done for the pretrial hearings. Closing arguments would be heard the next day.

Chapter Twenty

MAY 20

THERE WAS A SENSE OF TENSION ON THE FOURTEENTH FLOOR at eleven Wednesday morning, when the handful of observers directly interested in the *People of New York* v. *Riner* once again shoehorned themselves into the tiny courtroom.

The excitement stemmed not from the tight confines of Courtroom 1403, but from the fact that this was going to be decision day. Silverman had met with Brevetti and Bolen the previous afternoon in his office on the seventeenth floor and given them an idea of which way he was leaning. Gossip in the hallways predicted Bolen would win every point, from the probable cause to the admissability of Johnson's tape recording.

Marlies Riner was back in court, something that should have been taken as an ordinary appearance but had become a major headache. The U.S. Immigration and Naturalization Service had discovered that she was in the United States on a temporary visa, and chose to make an issue of the fact. Despite the pressure from almost everyone involved, including Judge Silverman, who is married to an immigration attorney, the federal bureaucracy would not budge. Thousands of illegal immigrants might cross the Texas and California borders every night, but the government had found out that Marlies Riner's approved time in this country was up, and she had to leave.

157

No deal could possibly be worked out, said the bureaucrats in Washington. Law's the law, you know. Out she goes. It did not matter that her daughter was on trial for murder.

So Marlies Riner had to leave on Friday, spend an INS-enforced weekend beyond the United States' borders, and return after a few days. The INS had been generous, speeding up the paperwork needed to give her a new visa. Even Bill Fischer was amazed by the lack of feeling demonstrated by the federal government, telling friends that allowing Olivia's mother to stay in the country would have been a decent thing to do. Eventually, after Washington had flexed its muscle and was satisfied that it had won the fight, she was allowed back in the courtroom to support her daughter. She brought a gift from Switzerland for the lawyer, and Brevetti, Olivia, Marlies, and Maya giggled like schoolgirls.

That would be the last light moment of the day, for the legal work was about to take a sharp and unexpected turn.

Brevetti painted a picture of an hysterical young woman, fresh to this country, isolated in her role as a nanny for a suburban family, and faced with a horrible tragedy that was compounded by intense police questioning. Brevetti's first attack was on the actual time Riner had been taken into custody, for if she could prove that Olivia had been intentionally detained before that tape recording was made, then an argument could be put forth that the arrest was illegal, since the Miranda rights were not promptly administered.

According to the defense, Olivia was a Swiss citizen, accustomed to obeying police officers, more so than Americans might be, and she was never specifically told by Johnson or Carpenter that she was free to leave the interview. "I argue that she was in custody as of 7:30 P.M.," Brevetti said, referring to the moment Johnson had returned to her after touring the fire scene.

Brevetti said Johnson had been told by brother officers

at the burned Fischer house that the fires had been intentionally set, and therefore knew a crime had been committed. "He felt before 7:30 that he had sufficient probable cause to arrest her," the lawyer stated. But instead Johnson just resumed questioning her "to see if her story changed and if she would give incriminating answers."

Silverman interrupted, pointing out that a person does not have a constitutional right to be arrested. "Just because you have probable cause to make an arrest doesn't mean you will make an arrest," the judge said; further questioning might develop more information.

Brevetti pushed ahead, saying Johnson was trying to isolate Olivia, to get her into a one-on-one situation where the large policeman could confront the petite Swiss girl. Silverman was not buying that either.

"Like you and me right now," the judge observed. "We're one-on-one and you're not in custody."

Brevetti waggled a handful of papers at her side before realizing it was just another of the judge's little jokes. "I have a couple of friends around me," she countered.

"Point taken," replied Silverman.

Bolen turned in his chair and looked up. "Including me."

Brevetti bowed. "Thank you."

The verbal duel resumed. "When Detective Johnson could not sustain that one-on-one situation at the Fries home, he decided to move to the police station," she charged. "He could not maintain that sort of isolation when more and more people came into the Fries residence."

Because of that isolation factor, the lawyer claimed Olivia's "freedom of movement was curtailed" and the detective planned to re-create the sense of isolation behind the doors of the police station. Brevetti challenged the wording Johnson would use later on the tape, when Olivia acknowledged freely accompanying him to Town Hall Plaza. "The last place on earth she would have wanted to go was the police station," Brevetti said, contending that by the time her client got into the detective's car, she had been "bled dry" of information. "She had told him everything."

Brevetti played a strong card when she recalled that the detective chucked Olivia beneath the chin to lift her face during questioning. The idea of a cop touching a woman prisoner in any way is a dicey one. Brevetti made no hint that the touch was a sexual caress, but claimed it carried a sense of power over the suspect. She interpreted it to mean, "You're not going to look where you want to look, you're going to look where I want you to look."

On a stride now, Brevetti criticized Johnson for not investigating anyone else at the scene, even though later that night Olivia would be asked repeatedly if she was covering up for someone, was jealous of a Fischer family member, was having sex with anyone or participating in some sort of conspiracy.

She became bitter in attacking the fact that Olivia was made to strip naked in the detectives' room, instead of being taken to the privacy of the women's rest room.

She also pointed out that no new information was gathered by the police, despite the repeated questions. Further, the time before the arrest blended seamlessly into the time after it. "There was nothing to show this girl that something was different," Brevetti said, "that the situation had changed."

The defense attorney now prepared to rub salt into any wounds she may have made in the prosecution case. She assaulted the detective's use of the Miranda card. "He read it in continuous paragraph form," she said. "There was no pause to see if she understood" each of the five separate rights to which she was entitled. A careful officer, she said, citing another case, would have explained each of the five points as he went along. Instead, she claimed that Johnson plowed through the important legal chore, giving his own definitions and allowing the civilian dispatcher to join in, while a confused Olivia stumbled over even so basic a concept as "a court of law."

When Johnson defined the court as being "the American judicial system," it was perhaps obvious to him, but it was Greek to the girl from the other side of the world.

"Detective Johnson's explanations, to say the least, were woefully inadequate."

At times Laura Brevetti knows when to shut up. This was such a time, so she did.

For by slamming away on Miranda, she knew she had punched Silverman right in his heart. His years of representing the indigent had left him with a deep conviction that all of the legal rights of a prisoner must be firmly protected. He had thrown out a confession before because the administration of those rights had come up short, and he wouldn't hesitate to do so again.

With a comment that seemed almost an aside, Silverman jolted the court. He wanted a tape recorder, a headset, and a copy of that Miranda tape delivered to his office immediately. He planned to listen to it, probably several times, during the luncheon break.

The judge had some concerns!

Suddenly, at twenty minutes after noon, less than two hours after the opening summons for the day, the routineness of the preliminary hearing was shattered. Silverman called a ten-minute recess and left a roomful of people trying to figure out just what in the world was happening.

What should have been just a footnote to the coming trial had taken on a life force of its own, and time was running out.

This was no time for stoicism. Indeed, Assistant District Attorney George Bolen was galvanized into action by Silverman's unexpected action. The judge now wanted to carefully comb through the Miranda tape recording. Brevetti had also made a good case that Olivia may have been in police custody for three hours prior to being officially placed under arrest.

Having had only a few minutes' respite to digest what had happened, Bolen began his remarks precisely at 12:30 P.M. Only yesterday afternoon the judge had indicated that he was favoring the state's position on all counts. But something had changed as Silverman listened to Brevetti. She had made points!

Bolen, who had remained unflappable at the prosecution table, where he sat alone in his characteristic slouched position and with his back to the opposing side, was undergoing a transformation. In fact, as his calm demeanor fled, he became more animated than at any point so far in the legal proceedings.

Normally, his questioning and presentation had been of the matter-of-fact variety, almost cold in precision and certainty. Now Bolen was in constant motion, moving with dancelike steps behind his chair, the polished shoes sliding on the tan carpet while his fingers poked holes in the air. The back of his normally well-groomed hair was tousled from the careless hand that had been run through it. He was delivering a virtual torrent of words. It was as if someone had fallen out of the lifeboat and was grasping for a handhold before being swept away by a surging ocean.

The custody issue was as important to him as the Miranda question. For if Silverman ruled in favor of the defense on that matter, agreeing that Olivia had been under actual police jurisdiction prior to her arrest, then the entire case would be endangered because of an illegal detention.

"That's the whole ball game!" thundered Bolen, throwing up his hands in dismay. Olivia Riner, he insisted, was clearly not under federal or state custody until 10:30 P.M., when Johnson read those rights to her.

Judge Silverman was obviously taken aback by the vehemence of Bolen's rebuttal. "George scared him," a courtroom observer would say later. The judge hurriedly said that he was not giving a yes or no decision at that point, but felt that even if he did rule in Brevetti's favor, the prosecution would still have "substantial" statements and other evidence that could be used in the case.

No dice, thought Bolen. He wasn't buying half a loaf. The judge's comment was akin to saying that if you chop off one leg of a dog, he still has three others, so what's the big deal? In this case, such an amputation could well mean the death of the dog.

Should the judge grant any part of the Brevetti motions, the state's case would be substantially weakened, possibly fatally flawed, because there was so little there anyway. The entire episode had unfolded within a matter of a few hours, and even the least subtraction of events could wreck a case that was totally circumstantial.

Bolen was nervous, but conceded that there were a number of significant comments on the tape. Unspoken, but hanging in the court like a thundercloud, was the question of what would happen if the judge decided to throw out the Miranda warning too.

Bolen said the detective was questioning Olivia simply because, at the time he arrived, she was just the best witness that police had found.

Silverman threw another heart-skipping question, noting that even after Johnson observed the singed right eyelash and learned from Dwyer that paint thinner may have been the cause of the fire, the continued questioning of Olivia Riner did not seem to add much to what the police already knew. This was not a good omen to the prosecuting attorney. Bolen actually did a quick little box step, as if waltzing alone, as he ticked off the points of argument on his long fingers.

Off to the right, the interpreter was cooking with her translation. Maya's forehead rested on a hand, and she leaned forward and stared at Bolen's mouth, trying to catch his every word. Her comments to Olivia, seated beside her, gave a low, buzzing undertone to the proceedings. Bolen glanced over in annoyance at the source of the noise several times.

Silverman would have had to be blind to miss the

quirky actions of the assistant district attorney prancing before him. The judge threw a lifeline, saying he expected to hear Bolen argue that Johnson was conducting a "noncustodial interrogation" that involved a transfer of the parties from the Fries house to the police station.

He "expected to hear"? It was an astounding moment. The judge had interrupted to make a vital point that had not been made by the state's prosecuting attorney, almost as if he had come down from the bench to whisper, "Hey, don't forget to mention this. . . ."

It was instantly clear to everyone that the judge was once again firmly in the prosecution corner. He did not think Olivia was under arrest at 7:30 P.M. Observers wondered what would have happened on December 2 if, at any early point, the Swiss nanny had risen from her chair and attempted to walk away. But she had not, staying instead to cooperate with the police, so the point was moot.

Bolen caught the judge's broad hint and his body language began to relax, his pacing slowed, his voice louder, his bearing returning to military ramrod normal. Confidence flooded back.

He emphasized there was never a hint of forcing Olivia to talk, and she cooperated throughout the long hours of interviewing. Her recorded answers to the detective's questions proved that.

Bolen dismissed the use of two officers to transport the girl as a commonsense thing to do "the way things are today." The presence of Carpenter in the car would prevent even the appearance of anything "untoward" happening—meaning no sexual hanky-panky or off-the-record deals. Johnson simply was taking no chances, the lawyer said. He also held that the change of location was insignificant because the detective had every right to continue his investigation.

The Miranda reading, a troubling subject, was next. Bolen said it didn't come off as cleanly as it usually does on television shows because "we live in an imperfect world" and things, well, happen. The bottom line was that the suspect was given her rights and the detective tried his best to explain any point or word that she did not understand. "Finally, she was reading the card itself."

When Johnson had asked if she understood what was happening, the girl nodded affirmatively. "You don't need to be a law student to understand those rights," Bolen said. He belittled the language problems obvious on the tape recording, saying Olivia had a sufficient command of the language and a reasonable intelligence that could comprehend the words on the little plastic card.

Bolen recited his main points and concluded quickly, having felt the tide change in his favor, at least putting him back into the lifeboat. He had explained the shift of venues for questioning, and defended the awkward Miranda incident to his satisfaction. Anyway, Silverman had already tipped his hand in public. Sewn together, the elements of the state's case could stand. "There was no illegal detention, either at the Fries house or at the police station," Bolen declared and sat down.

That was that. Silverman backtracked on his earlier plan to announce his rulings immediately after the arguments. He had points to review, wanted to put on the headset and crank up the tape recording of the Miranda reading and close the door to his office. "I am influenced by the arguments from counsel," said the young jurist, adding that he wanted time to rethink some earlier positions.

As he exited through the side door by the bench, the opposing sides emptied into the hallway. Neither rejection nor elation could be read in the faces of Bolen or Brevetti. Like everyone else, they were unsure exactly what would happen. The judge seemed to be waffling, leaning one way and then the other. It was as if the whole crazy case had slipped through a momentary time warp. Nothing looked quite the same anymore. No bets were being made on the decision that would come down the next day.

MAY 21

The flap that Vice President Dan Quayle made by criticizing the popular "Murphy Brown" television character for having an out-of-wedlock baby was the talk of the coffee shop as the lobby crowd waited patiently for the wheezing elevators of the Westchester County Court House. People seemed to treat the vice-president's remarks and the elevators with the same degree of seriousness. Some things in life just had to be endured.

Thursday was supposed to have been an off day, but the little courtroom quickly filled, then waited twenty-four minutes past the scheduled 9:30 A.M. starting time before Silverman hurried in and took his seat. He may have been running a bit late, but was now wasting no time.

The judge looked out at the people before him and announced that his formal, written opinions on the law would come later. For the moment he would cut to the chase.

He said he had spent Wednesday afternoon concentrating on two points that he considered critical, and listening numerous times to the Miranda tape and the questioning that followed. Bolen and Brevetti did not look at him. They stared at the white legal pads on the tables before them, ready to scribble when the judge made his points.

The tape. Silverman had been quite concerned about portions that seemed inaudible, and wondered how important those parts actually were, whether they meant Olivia had not understood the constitutional guarantees. "I don't find them [the garbled portions in question] significant," he said. "It is audible in every material respect."

Score one for the prosecution. Bolen didn't even look up. This was a win, but it was only one. Other issues still threatened his case.

Silverman then spoke of Olivia's ability to understand the English language, and therefore her ability to know what was being said concerning her rights and her understanding of the Miranda warning. The judge concluded that the Swiss girl was not fluent in English, but possessed language skills that were "perfectly functional," and a "fairly good vocabulary." Her accent was not a problem. Her answers and the continued verbal cooperation indicated that she was responsive. In other words, by answering the police questions, Olivia had demonstrated she could speak English well enough to know what was going on at the Fries house and at the station later.

And that meant that she knew what was going on when Detective Johnson read her all important rights. "It is the court's finding that the Miranda rights were properly given. They were understood by the defendant. The defendant waived her rights under Miranda."

Another big win for the state. The possibility of an improper reading of the rights was not going to shield Olivia from going before a jury.

The judge turned to the "custodial interrogation," as if there was any question of this ruling, after he had coached Bolen that it should be argued. He rushed on, without a flicker of indecision, the lawyers writing rapidly to keep up with him.

Silverman provided some suspenseful buildup, saying he had given a great deal of consideration to the arguments of the defense on whether a "police atmosphere" existed and whether Olivia had been illegally deprived of her liberty. Brevetti sipped a glass of water and Bolen took off his glasses, squaring them neatly on the legal pad, while the judge rambled on.

In the court's opinion, Olivia Riner, throughout the night of December 2 and into the morning of December 3, "was of a mind to cooperate fully with the authorities." That could mean one of two things—either she was innocent and had nothing to hide, or she was guilty and wanted to give the appearance of cooperation.

By giving her full range of help, not seeking outside advice, and never once making a move to leave the questioning area—indeed hardly ever moving from her chair—her actions led the judge to believe that she had stayed there voluntarily. She was not chained to the floor, and could have walked at any moment. "The court finds, in the final analysis, that it was not custodial in any respect," he said.

It was still another win for Bolen. Three for three. Probable cause was the only thing left. Yes, Silverman said, that was the easiest call of the bunch. There was probable cause for the arrest.

"The defense motions are denied in every respect," Silverman ruled.

Game, set, match. It was a clean sweep for the State of New York's representatives. Their case was clean, unsullied by Brevetti's allegations that the law had been unfairly applied in arresting Olivia Riner. At 10:07 A.M., only thirteen minutes after court began for the day, Bolen walked out with a victory on all fronts.

Brevetti had not truly expected to win, but as Chris Rush escorted Olivia to the waiting limousine that would whisk them back to Manhattan while Brevetti talked to a ring of reporters, there was clearly some disappointment. "We must move on," she said about Silverman's decisions. "We can't look back. We have to live with it and deal with it."

The defeat had been total. She had tried everything in the book to get a legal break to loosen the case that could send Olivia to prison, perhaps for the rest of her life, and nothing had worked. They would have one final shot, a chance to move the case beyond the reach of one judge and into the hands of twelve jurors.

Playtime was over. This case was ready for trial.

PART FOUR

Trial

Chapter Twenty-One

"I'M NO SHERLOCK HOLMES"

THE FINAL WEEK OF MAY WAS SET ASIDE FOR SELECTION OF A twelve-person jury with four alternates. Based upon the complexity of the case and the intense examination expected from the two determined lawyers, it was anticipated that every minute of the available time would be needed, and that Silverman would have to push hard to get things done.

The work of jury selection had actually started the preceding Thursday, after the judge ruled on the preliminary motions. Silverman, Brevetti, and Bolen had huddled in the judge's chambers to process special questionnaires five legal pages in length, filled out by some 250 prospective jurors.

The twenty-seven questions asked for not only the name, marital status, and job description of the person, but the occupations of their father, mother, and spouse, even if deceased. The names and jobs of all children were sought, as well as whether the prospective juror had ever been a victim of, charged with, or convicted of a crime.

The meat of the questions came in the middle.

Have you or your children or anyone close to you and their children ever been the victim of child abuse, child molestation, or child mistreatment?

Have you or has anyone close to you ever left your child in the care of someone else on a regular basis (for example, babysitting or day care)?

Have you or has anyone close to you ever had any problems leaving your child in the care of someone else?

Have you personally or has anyone close to you ever been investigated or charged with child abuse, child endangerment, child molestation, or anything dealing with the improper treatment of children?

It also queried whether the potential jury member had read, heard, or seen anything about the case or had formed any opinion on whether Olivia Riner was guilty or innocent.

By the time a hot and sultry Friday afternoon came, with people rushing out for the Memorial Day weekend, only to run into a traffic jam seven miles long at the Tappan Zee Bridge north of White Plains, the opposing lawyers in the Riner case had solidified their ideas of who should serve. In most trials the questioning of prospective jury members can be a tedious process of the hunt-and-peck variety, as lawyers seek information from the men and women before them. They try to get a handle on how one particular person might react to the stress of judging a criminal case, and whether that person might harm the defense or the prosecution. In the Riner case, much of that work would be done through reviewing the long documents filled out by the jurors.

When court convened on Tuesday morning, May 26, the weather had changed from scalding to cold and rainy, and the Riner case was displaying the same sort of instability. Silverman called the unusually high number of jurors because many would be automatically excused, unable to commit to a trial that could last for an expected month and a half.

Without warning, Silverman banned the news reporters and the public from the courtroom while the screening was done. Only those behind the closed doors would hear the important selection process. That decision brought a halt to the sunny courtship between the judge and the press and hung a veil of secrecy around a procedure that normally is an open part of any trial.

On Tuesday about eighty people were winnowed from the pool of possible jurors, and the rest were asked to return on Wednesday. The press was allowed back inside as Brevetti and Bolen combined their study of the questionnaires with gut feelings. The lawyers kept their comments general.

Olivia finally emerged in a new outfit, a pearl-gray suit with white pumps and pleated skirt. The colors made her skin seem more fair than usual, and her hair took on a more golden hue instead of flat brown. It was the first time in three weeks of open court she had worn something other than the blue blazer that made her look like a student in a Catholic boarding school.

Bolen and Brevetti did the lawyers' minuet, explaining what the prosecution had to prove for a guilty verdict and what the defense must do to demonstrate innocence. Bolen promised grisly photographs would not be bandied about the court. He was a total gentleman with the jurors, granting even a rare smile as his hands fluttered, clasped, and opened to emphasize points.

Brevetti countered that perhaps such photos might be kept hidden, but some things were bound to emerge that might offend the sensibility of a normal person, and she added, "I may not make it so easy." She wanted to know how many of them owned pets, particularly cats; who had been to foreign countries or had contact with recent arrivals in America; and whether they could understand that different people might act in different ways when faced with an identical situation.

She paused a moment, then unfurled a red flag, only to get a surprising answer. "Let's get it out in the open," she said to the jurors. "Is everyone familiar with the movie *The Hand That Rocks the Cradle*?" Almost every head in the jury box shook side to side in a negative response. Only one woman raised her hand out of the sixteen sitting there. Generally an older group of middle-class white people, they obviously did not frequent movie theaters. Brevetti was pleasantly surprised, and slammed that particular subject closed. "It has nothing to do with this case! Bingo! Out!" she boomed.

Her presentation was softer than Bolen's, using more eye contact and remembering names of individuals without having to look at her notes. She modestly played on her own vulnerability as a lawyer. "I'm not Perry Mason or Matlock or Jessica Fletcher," she said, comparing herself unfavorably to several popular television lawyers and mystery solvers. "I'm no Sherlock Holmes."

The jurors grinned among themselves. With her class New York lawyer act and flashy wardrobe, she might not be a famous TV attorney, but she certainly looked the part.

A brief recess was called. There were still some 170 people in the jury pool, and not a single juror had been selected by the middle of the week. It was shaping up to be a long process.

Things changed rapidly. Before the luncheon recess was called, no less than six jurors had been chosen! The three men and three women were immediately sworn in, with the first person chosen, Shanet Yancy, named foreperson of the jury.

Another sixteen were empaneled for examination, and Brevetti and Bolen repeated their routines. Immediately after lunch six were chosen from that group of sixteen. After a long time of idleness, the selection process had leapt forward and named all twelve jurors for the trial. All were told to return for duty on Tuesday morning.

A final twenty-five people were summoned and four alternate jurors picked in short order. By 3:30 P.M. on Wednesday, it was done. Silverman commented that when two good lawyers decide they want to do something, they can deal with a matter quickly.

Both attorneys were confident. Bolen was certain of a guilty verdict, Brevetti equally certain that her client would be set free.

One was wrong and just didn't know it yet.

That same day, attention had shifted to the seventeenth floor, where Carolyn Warmus was finally convicted of second degree murder for gunning down her lover's wife. Her first trial, totally based upon circumstantial evidence, had ended in a hung jury. The second trial featured new evidence, a ten-dollar pair of black knit gloves that linked Warmus to the murder scene. Prosecutors Jim McCarty and Douglas FitzMorris could finally move on to other things.

Chapter Twenty-Two

ANGEL FACE

THE DOORS TO COURTROOM 1400, A SPACIOUS LEGAL ARENA, opened promptly at 9:30 A.M. on the morning of Tuesday, June 2. Clerk Sarah Tully was in her position just below the judge's bench, and court reporter Steve Sacripanti was in an adjacent cubicle, his black BaronData transcripter at the ready. In the four corners of the big room, to keep the peace, were uniformed court officers Sergeant John King, Jim Skehan, Mark Sweeny, and Mike Benevento. Like the balky elevators that reluctantly hauled people to the upper floors of the courthouse, the room had a wilted air about it. Brown water spots mottled some of the ceiling tiles, and the woodlike wallpaper was peeling away at various panels. The portrait of a judge hung beside a faded American flag. The Bible used to put people under oath rested in a dusty plastic holder on the rail of the witness stand.

Every seat in the audience rows had been taken, and press representatives, including a number of correspondents from Swiss newspapers and magazines, filled the front three rows on the right side. Since cameras were not allowed, a group of artists working in paints, watercolors, ink, and chalk were spread out across the first row. Television reporters fussed with their makeup.

George Bolen, as always, was alone at the prosecution table. A wheeled cart marked DISTRICT ATTORNEY NO. 11

was parked beside him, loaded with papers. At his feet was a cardboard box filled with potential evidence, including a red fire extinguisher that stuck above the rim like a crimson-stained thumb. He wore a charcoal-gray suit and a subdued red tie.

The three women and one man at the defense table were in conservative wardrobe. Laura Brevetti checked in with a tailored suit of navy-blue, a single strand of pearls over her white blouse. Olivia was again in her familiar blue outfit; translator Maya Hess wore a black skirt and purple blouse; and associate counsel Elan Gerstmann's suit was dark blue. Olivia was trying to regain her composure after running a gauntlet of television cameras to enter the building. Chris Rush had taken her by the wrist, clearing a path through the cameramen.

Outside, the morning weather was warm and eventually would climb into the upper eighties, putting a strain on the cranky air-conditioning system in the jammed courtroom. News headlines in the morning papers noted the end of the election primary season for Bill Clinton and President George Bush, and the unexpected surging popularity of possible candidate Ross Perot, the Texas billionaire. But the biggest story was from Long Island, New York, in which a seventeen-year-old girl allegedly stalked and shot the wife of a thirty-eight-year-old man the teenager claimed was her lover.

Judge Silverman brought his court to order at 9:40 A.M., and after disposing of a minor housekeeping dispute between Brevetti and Bolen, had the jury of seven men and five women, and the alternates, brought in at 9:58. Everyone at the defense table stood, as they would throughout the trial whenever the jury entered or left the room. Bolen remained in his chair, as he would throughout each and every jury movement. The jurors' eyes locked on the girl with long brown hair seated on the far side of the room. It was their first look at Olivia Riner.

Silverman gave the jury some preliminary instructions and told them to rely on their own common sense while listening to what the lawyers and witnesses had to say. He warned them to keep their opinions to themselves until it came time to deliberate, not to read or listen to news reports, and not to "try to play detective" by going out to the crime scene. The judge instilled in them the gravity of the situation. The men and women in the jury box were holding the fate of a human being in their hands.

Opening arguments in a case are designed to give the jury an overview of what is coming. The prosecution tries to establish in the minds of the jurors that the person charged is obviously guilty. The defense will say the defendant is as innocent as a lamb.

Bolen began to pace before the jury box as he launched a two-hour opening statement. He quickly got to the point by reading the grand jury indictment and ticking off the counts of second degree murder against Olivia Riner, whom, he said, had "intentionally, knowingly, and willfully" killed Kristie Fischer on the night of December 2, 1991.

But he acknowledged that exactly what happened on that horrible evening remained a mystery, so much so that all of the evidence to be presented would be of only a circumstantial nature and the state might not even be able to demonstrate a precise motive for the murder. On this important point, he wanted the jury to understand that they could still convict a suspect. Some things just remain unknown.

"Some offenses are so askew of humanity, so devoid of rationality, that it is exceedingly difficult to imagine what could have possibly motivated them to kill," he said.

"Because the motive is not apparent does not mean that the person accused did not do the crime . . . Sometimes the reasons for people's actions can never be determined. But the maxim holds true: actions speak louder than words."

While George Bolen carefully painted in details that he meant to cover, there was one thing in particular that he wanted to impress upon the jury, something that could overshadow everything else. The jury was being asked to believe that the petite young woman sitting over there at the defense table, the girl with the fair skin and long brown hair and blue eyes, was a cold-blooded killer. He did not want them swayed into believing she was hardly more than a teenage babysitter.

"With her angelic face, you have to ask yourselves: Why? Who could have done this? It couldn't possibly have been her." But the prosecutor told the jury that indeed it had been her. Appearances can be deceiving, he said, summoning a German phrase to emphasize his point, *Kleider machen nicht leute*, which was translated loosely to mean clothes do not make the person. Don't be fooled, said Bolen, there was a streak of evil beneath the neat and polite exterior, because that girl dumped flammable paint thinner on that baby and then set a match to it.

He emphasized his theory that the house was locked tight that night, a virtual fortress against intruders. "No one tossed . . . a Molotov cocktail through the window," the assistant district attorney said. There would be "no signs of forced entry in this case: no doorjambs jimmied, no tool marks, no broken windows—zilch, *de nada*." Therefore, the jurors would be left with the singular conclusion that, since no one else could have gained entry to 5 West Lake Drive, Olivia Riner was the only logical suspect, the only person who possibly could have committed the crime. And Olivia had insisted throughout that no one could have been in the house without her knowing about it. She was alone. She did it!

John Gallagher had told police that when he arrived, he saw Olivia pacing back and forth in the family room. According to Bolen, that meant that she knew there was no use in trying to save the child in the nursery. "The baby was already dead before she made that first call," he said.

Bolen had worked the jury well, ending his presentation at 12:27 P.M., just after disclosing that Olivia had told Bill Fischer, during "an unguarded moment" while standing in the driveway, that she had closed the door to the baby's room. As Bolen returned to his chair, he glanced at the jury box. Two solid rows of serious faces looked back at him.

They were almost ready to vote a guilty verdict on the spot.

Agatha Christie's wise Miss Jane Marple said, "Nothing is ever as it seems" and "Beware your first impression."

Laura Brevetti had already distanced herself from the fictional lawyers and detectives of televisionland, but she well may have reflected upon the famed mystery writer's words. For as Brevetti rose to her feet at 1:19 P.M., her job was to convince the jury that something happened at 5 West Lake Drive on the tragic night of December 2 that was entirely different from what the prosecuting attorney had led them to believe. She had to persuade them that they were just at Chapter One of a true mystery, and by the time they reached the end of the story, they would learn that the persuasive assistant district attorney's conclusions were just flat wrong.

Speaking in slow, schoolteacher cadences, she told the jurors the trial "will not answer who done it. The only thing that will be answered in this trial is who *did not* do it." And she emphasized that Olivia, under the laws of this nation, was not guilty of anything at all until the state actually proved a case against her, beyond a reasonable doubt. Just because the assistant district attorney said something was true did not make it so.

Facts, she said. Base your judgment on facts. Be inquisitive. Question what the witnesses, even the experts and policemen, said. Question the explanation of every piece of evidence and how it was gathered. Do not be led around blind by the state's arguments.

"From the first hour, the first minute, the police department set out, not to solve this crime, but to build a case against Olivia Riner," Brevetti said. Therefore the web of circumstantial evidence did not include some items that lay right at their feet. "The police conclusion was that she did it and they didn't have to look further. What they found was just too perfect."

As for the motive for the murder, she asked the question of them. Why would Olivia, an experienced young woman trained in handling babies, have done such a cruel thing and have not even made up some story, something like having seen a suspicious shadow outside, to create a decent alibi?

"She said to police, 'I didn't hear anything, I didn't see anything.' Are these the words of someone who has just committed a crime? " Brevetti asked. "For what reasons? And then leave everything behind for the police to find? It doesn't make sense."

She interpreted the circumstantial evidence angle differently than did Bolen, saying that, in reality, it meant there was nothing at all to directly link the crime to her client. Rebutting the state's case, point by point, she spent her two hours of opening arguments giving the jury a fascinating first look at the crime from Olivia's side of the fence.

Brevetti had one cautionary strategy in the back of her mind. At this point in the trial she did not seriously challenge Bolen's argument that the house at 5 West Lake Drive had been locked up tight. That was the state's argument, and not only did Brevetti not want to tear it down, she wanted Bolen to bear down on that point even more. She and her investigator, Chris Rush, wanted the state to make the point as strongly as possible, that the house was not a suburban house at all, but a castle of stone with parapets and maybe even a moat, solidly built so no intruder could possibly enter. Locked doors, locked windows. They wanted the state to plant solidly in the minds of the jurors that, beyond the shadow of a doubt, 5 West Lake Drive stood ready to repel any invader on that dreadful night six months ago.

Meanwhile, there were other items that Brevetti did

want to attack in her opening statement. On the critical point of why Olivia did not try harder to bash down the baby's door on December 2, the lawyer urged the jurors to transplant themselves back to the confusion that rained around Olivia that night, and not automatically think that the situation should have been handled differently. "Don't be Monday morning quarterbacks with twenty-twenty hindsight. Put yourself in her shoes. You need to live that night," she said.

"A terrible tragedy occurred on December second. A number of lives will never be the same," she said in closing. "You are the only people left to prevent the commission of another crime—the conviction of Olivia Riner for a crime she did not commit."

Chapter Twenty-Three

BILL FISCHER

THE FIRST WITNESS CALLED WAS NONE OTHER THAN BILL Fischer, patriarch of the clan. His appearance brought a hush to the courtroom on that second day of June, exactly six months to the day from the time of the fire. There was an ineffable sadness about the sandy-haired man who walked in through the swinging doors, a visible reminder that this was not some academic exercise for the legal profession, but a trial of someone accused of the murder of a baby—this man's child. The blue suit and maroon tie with white stripes gave away nothing, nor did the trim shape with muscular shoulders and flat stomach. The hair was swept left to right, and he wore a thick brown mustache. It was his eyes that caught the crowd, eyes filled with loss and a pain so real and deep that it seemed to wash through the courtroom like a cold, rising tide.

The effect was not lost on the jury. They had been strongly moved by Bolen's opening presentation, then had question marks dancing in their heads after Brevetti's statements. But that had all been theory and legalistic hocus-pocus. Now, sitting in the square witness box in front of them, was the man around whom the hurricane had swirled. Bill Fischer was a man carrying a heavy load of sorrow on his slumping shoulders, and the jurors were ready to help lift his burden.

For the next ninety minutes they would hear Fischer talk about his family, his life, and elements of the tragedy in a slow, quiet monotone. As he spoke, the case would become a tangible, personal thing for the men and women in the jury box, for few witnesses could have been as sympathetic as Bill Fischer on that warm June afternoon.

From the defense table Olivia Riner watched him without expression. He did not so much as glance in her direction.

Bolen began slowly, doing no more than putting the ball in play, letting the jury get a feel for one of his prime witnesses. He had Fischer describe his son and daughter by a previous marriage. Troy, an industrial designer, lived in Manhattan and worked in Mount Vernon; and Leah, who still lived at the family home, currently a receptionist for an auto dealership and taking classes three nights a week at Pace University.

He described his own occupation as partner, with his brother Robert, in Fischer's Garage, where he had worked for twenty-six years. The shop, built in 1929, was in its third generation of Fischers. He owned a 1980 Chevrolet Blazer, his wife Denise had a 1986 Honda Civic, and Leah drove a 1989 Toyota Corolla.

He had lived for twenty-two years in the house at 5 West Lake Drive in Thornwood, and Troy and Leah had grown up there. The house itself was thirty-five years old. There were four cats—Kabuki, Fleetwood, Oliver, and O.J.—and one dog, Snuffy.

His words tended to drift off, and Bolen had to ask him to speak into the microphone and raise his voice. Fischer leaned forward on his elbows. He described his neighbors and said he had known George and Katie Fries since he had first moved into the house.

Bolen then had Fischer describe the house. Fischer verbally toured the property, from the well-worn blacktop driveway that ended at an open-sided carport; the metal shed with sliding doors in the backyard, where he kept the lawnmower, gasoline, and garden tools; the canoe that rested upside down along the rear deck; the 275-gallon oil tank on the right beside the propane tank; the bushes and trees on both sides; and the flagstone patio at the front door, bordered by five hip-high shrubs. There were two entryways, at the front and side, on the second-level deck, but only one way in and out on the ground floor, through the front door.

Inside were white cathedral ceilings on the upper floor, with five skylights that allowed in sunshine, even during the winter.

Bolen skipped to Fischer's personal regimen. He usually got to work about 7:30 A.M. and was home about 6:00 P.M., making the twelve- to fifteen-minute drive in the Blazer with Snuffy on the seat next to him. He liked to get up early. On Sunday night, December 1, he had found the propane supply was low and decided to call Suburban Propane on Monday to fill the tank. Denise would have known about it, but not Olivia.

Then the prosecuting attorney jumped back and had Fischer describe the interior of the house. It was a bit awkward, moving from the family to the house to personal traits and back to the house. Considered to be a glitch in questioning his first witness, those sudden shifts of topic would become Bolen's trademark over the coming weeks of interrogation. Instead of treading a straight line of inquiry, as he had done well during the preliminary hearings, Bolen would bounce from place to place in the story. "You think he confused you? He confused me, too, and I was on his side," one witness observed after the trial.

But for the time being Fischer's soft voice was more than carrying the day. The jury didn't care about skipping over details. They were just enthralled by the presence of Fischer, for what he was describing was a typical home in a typical Westchester County suburb. A sense of personal empathy was sprouting, binding them together.

There were three television sets in the house, one upstairs in the master bedroom, one in Leah's bedroom downstairs, and one in the downstairs family room. The front door, which entered the family room, was glass in a wood frame, and flanked by three equally tall glass panes.

Fischer described how the propane delivery man would leave a receipt slip either in the mailbox or stuffed into a joint of the door. Yes, as you approach the front door, you can see inside.

There were no screens on the bedroom windows in December, and the locks on those sliding windows were located on the center posts. Sliding doors were kept closed and locked by blocks of wood in the metal tracks. Details began to pour out in a confusing fashion as the afternoon session neared its close.

The kitchen had a Formica counter. Fire extinguishers were in Leah's closet, in a kitchen cabinet, and in the family room storage closet. They were made by Sears. An audio monitor was in the baby's room above the crib. Fischer said he had met his current wife through his business when she had brought her car in for repair. In the fall of 1991 she was working as a tax accountant in Stamford, Connecticut.

The first phase of Fischer's testimony came to a rather merciful end as it trailed off into trivia and Silverman called a halt for the day.

In what would become almost a custom, a useful one for the defense, television crews were waiting in the courthouse lobby for an interview. Bolen never spoke to the press, and cameras and tape recorders were not allowed in the courtroom, thus leaving the propaganda field wide open for Brevetti, who did not hesitate to give the day's happenings a little spin in favor of the defense. She became adept at dropping pearls of wisdom in carefully crafted bites of sound that the TV stations would dutifully report, no matter what actually had happened in court that day. The reporters, nice-looking young men and women, spent little time in court and therefore were easily conned. Brevetti sheared them like a flock of sheep.

At the end of that first day of testimony, she simply ignored the emotional appearance of Fischer and turned the evening news story into her own version of what had happened, pointing a finger at both John Gallagher and the investigating police. She said the cops had repeatedly questioned Olivia about whether she was covering up for someone. It did not matter if it were "John Gallagher, John Doe, or Jim Smith," the police thought there was someone else involved, she declared. The television crews took off to report that the big news was that the defense attorney claimed her client was innocent.

On Wednesday the Earth Summit was getting under way in Brazil, the Danes voted against joining Europe's Economic Union, President Bush and Bill Clinton had nailed big primary victories, and Laura Brevetti finally wore a piece of clothing for a second time, a diamond-patterned, gray-green jacket. Olivia appeared in a white outfit of identical cut with her familiar blue suit.

Fischer resumed his testimony at 10:40 A.M., and Bolen immediately elicited another blizzard of details about the house at 5 West Lake Drive. Fischer's voice was so soft that the judge handed him two thick law books to place beneath the microphone, lifting it closer to his mouth.

Bolen was having the jury examine the house through a microscope. Schematic drawings of the interior of both floors, mounted on heavy cardboard, were displayed on skinny aluminum tripods to help the jurors follow the action.

The window in the laundry room opened outward, like an awning, when cranked from inside. A similar window in the bathroom was broken and could only be pushed open. Screens were on both windows. The location of heating vents was examined, as was the fact that an extra audio monitor had been rigged from the baby's room to the room of the au pair. A linen closet was at the end of the vinyl-tiled hallway that divided the downstairs area, and a partition of thin drywall separated Leah's closet from the baby's nursery. Just before Thanksgiving, he had put a new door on the baby's nursery, using a circular saw to cut the door to fit a slightly askew frame. Like the other doors, it had a knob with a center lock. A small exterior hole, through which a nail could be pushed as an emergency key, was on the outside of the handle.

Fischer, his face a map of heavy lines, was proving to be an excellent witness, totally knowledgeable about the house and its structural components. That gave him a solid image as a truthful man in the eyes of the jury.

He described the nursery: enter the doorway from the hall, and there was an open playpen behind the door and a dresser on the left, a basket filled with toys beside it. Tie-back curtains and sheers hanging from a café rod at the middle almost covered the windows. A dressing table was to the right of the door, and on the far wall was the crib and the doorless closet that contained shelves. There was an area rug on the floor, extending about a foot from the walls.

After fitting the door, Fischer had stood it up in the family room while he applied three coats of clear sealer, using paint thinner that he kept in the storage closet to clean the brushes.

When Bolen handed him a set of color photographs taken by Denise Fischer, depicting the inside of the au pair's room, Fischer mentioned the name of the defendant for the first time, saying they showed "Olivia's room." Jurors glanced over at her and saw not a movement.

As Bolen introduced photos of the house into evidence, a racket erupted outside the windows of the fourteenth floor courtroom and a window-washer's scaffold clattered downward. "Perhaps Geraldo," mugged Silverman, referring to the sensationalist television show. He got a laugh.

On and on came the details: the yellow Formica in the kitchen, the twenty steps in the stairwell, the fishing tackle stored in the closet, and identification of the red fire extinguisher. It was an avalanche of evidence for the jury to consume, but none of it was a direct link between Olivia and the crime.

Fischer confirmed that the house had been returned to him by the police on December 3 and that he had carpenters replace the windows with sheets of plywood. Upstairs windows, he said, in the bedroom and the kitchen above Kristie's window, had been cracked.

In describing the previous Thanksgiving dinner, Fischer noted that his former mother-in-law and her new husband, a German-speaking au pair Denise had invited, Olivia, the baby Kristie, Denise, and he were in attendance. Photographs showed Olivia with a big smile for the event. Leah dined at John Gallagher's house.

Detail, detail, detail, detail. Olivia sometimes wore her hair in a French braid. Bill maintained contact with his former in-laws and had periodic contact with his ex-wife. Bolen coaxed Fischer upstairs in the house to describe a bookcase cabinet beside the fireplace. As usual, he was precise. The cabinet had a door hinged at the bottom, and a black knob was grasped to pull it out and down. Bolen picked up a plastic Baggie and the black knob was entered into evidence.

Bolen wanted a description of boxes of matches that Fischer kept in the cabinet. The witness said he kept four boxes of Diamond brand stick matches in the cabinet, using the long ten-inch ones to light the water heater. Two days after the December 2 fire, he discovered the water heater had gone out, went to the cabinet to get the matches and counted only three boxes—two boxes of long matches and one box of short matches.

As the court took a lunch break, everyone focused on the missing box of matches. Missing matches. A deadly fire. One plus one equals two.

After lunch, Fischer resumed. There were three interior locks on the glass jalousied door of the kitchen, and the doors on the second-level patio were never used.

Finally Bolen moved his witness to talk about the baby.

Kristie, he testified, originally had slept in a bassinet in the master bedroom, but eventually was placed in the nursery crib. The door would be closed at night to keep the cats away, for they had a tendency to cuddle against the baby at nights. The Fischers kept an ear peeled to the monitor, which would alert them if the baby cried. The baby preferred to take naps inclined in the car seat with the polka dot upholstery.

Fischer discussed the eating habits of the cats, the various containers of paint thinner, gum turpentine, charcoal lighter fluid, propane gas, and mineral spirits kept in the storage closet.

Seemingly embarrassed, Bolen said he had to ask Fischer, just to make the record complete, if he had a physical relationship with Olivia? "No sir. Never," came the reply.

"Did you take out any life insurance on the infant, Kristie?"

"No."

"Do you have a will?"

"Yes."

"Any changes in that will after Kristie was born?"

"No, no changes."

Bolen elicited that smoking was not allowed in the house, and although Leah would not admit it, she did smoke, but not in the house. Olivia did not use tobacco.

Bolen pressed now on the marriage. The relationship was "very good" between Denise and himself, Bill Fischer said. Denise and Leah got along "fairly well," although there were occasional disagreements between them. Leah was "very happy" about the prospect of having a little half sister, and even gave Kristie one of her favorite stuffed bears.

Bolen had Fischer describe the application process to E.F. Au Pair that brought Olivia into their household, and how her educational background, familiarity with English, and recent visits to America were factors in their decision to hire her. She was a "fairly intelligent" girl and a prolific reader of paperback books, many of them in German, and inquisitive enough to ask the meaning of English words she didn't understand.

Bill Fischer described his relationship with John Gallagher as "very good."

But then, just as things seemed to flow solidly for the prosecution, a wheel fell off of George Bolen's wagon, as he had Fischer tell of returning home on December 2, arriving unexpectedly for lunch.

Fischer said he parked his Blazer beneath the carport and entered through the unlocked front door into the family room. Seeing no one there, he went to the baby's room and found Olivia sitting with her back to the door, folding clothes, oblivious to his presence. The baby was on the floor, playing with a little set of plastic rings, and Bill Fischer spoke to his three-month-old daughter. His voice breaking as he related the incident, he said, "She recognized my voice. She gave me a big smile." Fischer stayed in the room a few minutes, then went upstairs to the kitchen and had lunch while reading the newspaper. The baby fussed a little bit at one point, then quieted.

Forty-five minutes later Fischer returned downstairs to go back to work. He saw the baby asleep in the car seat on the floor of the nursery. Across the hall Olivia was sitting in a chair in her room, reading, with her back to the doorway. She didn't see him approach. "I said I was leaving, see you later." Then he departed to return to work.

Lawyers and court watchers knew what had just happened, and more than a few deep breaths were inhaled in surprise. Bolen cranked into a higher gear to push through the error, quickly having the emotional Fischer describe the call for help from Olivia later that afternoon. Milking the moment, Bolen had Fischer identify a photograph of the baby girl alive and happy in the car seat. The father examined it with strain evident in every feature of his face.

He told of rushing back home, and, with every eye in the jury box on him, described finding the house on fire

and being stopped from entering to get his baby. He said
Olivia told him about feeding the cats, closing the door to
the baby's room, finding a fire on her bed, and the remaining details of that horrible evening.

At 3:55 P.M., amid a thundering silence in the courtroom, Bolen said he was through with his direct examination. Bill Fischer, his face red and his emotions twisted
almost to the point of tears, was dismissed from the stand
for the day.

Brevetti was immediately on her feet, attempting to
block the photo of Kristie in the car seat from being
placed into evidence. She said it would inflame the jury
and be prejudicial to her client. Silverman, as he would
throughout the trial, would not allow the photo to be introduced. He would not let the jury become emotionally
tangled by viewing such things as pictures of babies. Ac-
knowledging that it was "a lovely picture" of the baby, he
said no, it would not go to the jury. The fact that the
burned car seat would be used as evidence should be
enough.

Bolen countered with an attempt to introduce an in-
structional film from IBM on how fires spread and the
types of damage they cause, particularly how heated window frames shatter. He contended the film would demonstrate the difference between a "classic thermal break"
and a hole punched with a blunt object.

The judge, puzzled, said he thought the window in the
baby's room was closed and locked. Bolen replied that
there was a "crack" in the left-hand pane and he had to
anticipate that the defense was going to say a "homemade
self-detonating device" was thrown into the room.
Silverman discussed the IBM film, said it went far beyond
the scope of what happened in the room on the night in
question and would be of overall questionable value. No,
he would not allow it. Bolen would have to rely on an expert witness to explain how heat affects a window.

When the day was done and the prosecution rested,
Bolen could count a few important victories. There was

the impression that Bill Fischer had made upon the jury, and the detailed description of the house, which pointed out the missing matches and the access that Olivia Riner had to a stack of flammable liquids stored downstairs in the family room.

Weighed against that, however, were the dual rulings by Silverman that neither the emotion-tugging picture of Kristie nor the boiling fire depicted on the IBM film would be seen by the jury.

But in retrospect the day would be remembered for the remarkable moment when Bill Fischer's testimony began to erode the prosecution's carefully built theory of 5 West Lake Drive as an impregnable fortress. The police, grand jury, and District Attorney's Office all firmly believed Olivia's statement that no one else could have been in the house without her knowledge. That statement had helped get her arrested and charged with four counts of murder.

Now Bill Fischer had demonstrated that Olivia was totally wrong on that point, because he had surprised her twice on December 2. When he came home for lunch and when he left to go back to work, he had to speak to Olivia before she knew he was behind her.

Far from being able to know if anyone else was in the house, Olivia, who had a habit of intense concentration when involved in a task such as reading or folding clothes, obviously could not even tell when someone drove up the driveway in a big truck and walked right through the front door.

Chapter Twenty-Four

CROSS-EXAMINATION

BILL FISCHER WAS THE STRONGEST AND MOST SYMPATHETIC witness who would testify at the trial of Olivia Riner. That did not mean he would get a free ride.

The tilt of the trial had definitely been toward the prosecutor, and the state had gained an edge when court adjourned after Bolen's questioning of Fischer. The father of the dead infant had been on the stand for almost two days, and the jury had gone home two straight nights with him on their minds.

The adjournment on Wednesday, however, would prove to be a sword with two edges. While it gave the jurors time to linger on Fischer's testimony, it also gave the defense team time to comb through that same testimony line by line, hunting for inconsistencies. Laura Brevetti, Chris Rush, and Elan Gerstmann showed up for court on Thursday morning looking a bit worn, not really caring that the U.S. Postal Service had just chosen the final version of the new Elvis Presley 29-cent postage stamp to be the slim, young rocker instead of the old, fat guy. The defense team had been up all night, blue-penciling grand jury minutes and the court stenographer's record of Fischer's testimony. They went through it all, word by word. With the brief delay in the testimony, they had come up with questions.

Brevetti walked a tightrope. She did not want to

alienate the jury by appearing to pick on Fischer, who, after all, was only telling what he knew of the tragedy that had engulfed his family. At the same time, she had to show there were holes in his story. Everyone already knew that the Norman Rockwell–style all-American family no longer existed in Thornwood or anywhere else. Every family has secrets. Brevetti wanted to gently push aside the curtain and let some light in on the house at 5 West Lake Drive.

She was not blindfolded in this, for in addition to the top-notch assistants backing her up, she had a secret weapon in the form of Olivia Riner, who had lived among the Fischers. She saw things. She heard things. She told it all to Brevetti.

Brevetti followed some of the same ground that Bolen had when she opened her cross-examination at 10:45 A.M., having Fischer describe more about the house, in particular how he nailed shut the window in the downstairs bathroom during the winter. The house was secure. Then he admitted there were two extra house keys kept on a cross beam of the carport, and that the downstairs front door remained unlocked as long as someone was home. Maybe the house wasn't secure. Conflict.

Under Brevetti's prodding, he discussed the application to E.F. Au Pair to obtain a European nanny because "we felt they were more conscientious people" who were mature and serious-minded. He said Olivia was shy when she first arrived, had no dates, few friends, and occasionally would take a walk to a shopping center about a mile away. Most of her conversations were with Denise, and he observed that "the times I did see her with the baby, I didn't see any problem." Fischer felt there were no problems between the three women in the house—Denise, Leah, and Olivia.

Fischer said that upon her arrival, Olivia had been given a detailed tour of the house, and Denise wrote out the list of necessary telephone numbers, heading it, "Emergency, dial O." Olivia kept that in her bedroom.

He activated the smoke alarms so she would know how they sounded, and he testified that Denise told Olivia that in case of fire, the primary responsibility would be to "get the baby out of the house." He added that a small screwdriver was kept in the laundry room to use in opening the locks on the doors by punching it through the little hole in the knobs. Olivia was not told it was there or how to use it.

Having conducted the cautious verbal walk through the house, Brevetti was ready to dig deeper. She had been polite, even solicitous, and the jury no longer saw her as a threat to this witness whom they liked and believed. So she had him talk about the history of the house, and the family itself, and some strange images emerged.

The house had been built by the parents of Fischer's first wife, and when his in-laws divorced, Bill and his wife moved in to share the house with her mother. His wife left the house in 1987 and in the ensuing divorce, Bill bought out her interest in it and continued to live there with his adult children until Troy moved to New York. Leah stayed.

Denise came on the scene in the spring of 1988, when she drove her car into Fischer's Garage one day to have some work done. She and Bill fell in love, and after Bill's divorce became final in 1989, Denise moved in with him at 5 West Lake Drive in the summer of 1990. They were married on July 12, 1991. Kristie was born on September 11 of that same year.

Whoa, thought the jurors, doing some quick arithmetic. It takes nine months for a human baby to gestate. Bill and Denise had been living together for a year, but were married a shade less than two months prior to the birth of their baby daughter. Nothing wrong with that, but it was not the normal run of things, either.

Brevetti moved to some of Bill Fischer's specific testimony. She asked if he was certain about his earlier comments concerning the cabinet where the matches were kept upstairs, with the little black knob that was used to pull down the cabinet cover. Yes, he replied. Brevetti, as if performing a magic trick, held up a plastic evidence Baggie that contained the black knob.

Through court motions, she had eventually received a copy of the grand jury transcript, and she now turned to page 34, where Fischer said "there is a little white knob you have to pull down," and later, "the cabinet was dark, the knob was white."

Bingo. White is not black. Gently, she said, "You had a failure to recollect and were in error." Fischer sat there stoically, while the jurors wondered, could he be wrong about other things, too?

She went ahead, questioning Fischer's testimony to the court that he had noticed a box of matches was missing from their usual place in that cabinet.

"Isn't it a fact, sir, that you didn't notice there was a box missing?"

"I did notice there was a box missing," Fischer replied.

Brevetti flipped her notebook to a page marked with a small yellow sticker and read aloud his earlier testimony before the grand jury.

"No. They're there. I didn't notice anything missing."

The turnabout in sworn testimony did not go unnoticed in the jury box.

Fischer had also testified for Bolen, in his direct examination, that Leah slept at John's house on the night of December 1, but the grand jury minutes had him saying first that she slept at home that night and second that he was not sure where she was at the time. Up and down the rows of jurors some looks of skepticism began to appear. They saw that Leah's father could not attest to her location on Sunday night, December 1.

Brevetti pressed forward with one of the more unusual slants to the case. Bill Fischer testified, insisted, that when John Gallagher slept over at 5 West Lake Drive, as he had done frequently throughout the long time he had dated Leah, he always slept on the sofa downstairs in the family room. He slept at the front of the house and Leah slept in the rear, in her room. Even that strange arrangement came to a halt, on Denise's insistence, with the arrival of Olivia, the Swiss nanny. After that, Gallagher no longer slept over at all.

Then Brevetti elicited testimony showing that Leah had "a problem" with John in November and had "come home upset and angry." Although she would sometimes confide in Denise, the two of them were "different types of people," and this time Leah talked things over with her father. She and Gallagher quickly resolved their difference.

Brevetti followed these points of conflicting testimony with a long and detailed examination of how much liquid remained in the various containers stored in the closet. In one instance Fischer had testified a container was three-quarters full, but had originally told police the same container held only a quarter or less of its contents. "Did anybody suggest to you that it would be better for this case if there was more liquid in that container? " she asked.

"No, they did not," was the reply.

The entire complex episode involving liters, quarts and containers left jurors' eyes glazed. All they really knew at this point was that Bill Fischer's original testimony was not as seamless as first thought, nor his family more ideal than anyone else's. Brevetti had accomplished her goal— not alienating the jury, but throwing Fischer's testimony into question. Because of the acknowledged inconsistencies, the jury would probably now question everything he had said.

After his three days on the stand, Bill Fischer entered the elevator to leave just as another court was letting out. He was crushed against the back wall. A woman acquaintance silently looked at him, raised her eyebrows. He shook his head slowly from side to side in reply, looking like a man who had just tangled with trouble.

* * *

After lunch George Bolen played the audio tape of Olivia's emergency call on the night of December 2. It was the first time the jurors had heard the voice of the defendant, who maintained a Sphinxlike silence in public and within the courtroom.

It did not take long, but it clearly depicted a young woman on the edge of panic, pleading with reluctant authorities that a fire was consuming the house at 5 West Lake Drive, and at the end wailing, "The baby's in the room!" The jurors, wearing the padded headsets, watched her intently as they heard her frantic words.

For the first and only time during the long trial, Olivia Riner's stoic reserve broke and she began to cry while listening to her own voice bringing back the memories of that horrible night. With tears streaming down her pale face, the Swiss nanny was led from the courtroom by Brevetti. "It was just too much," the lawyer said. "She's been trying to maintain her composure, but she was overcome with emotion."

Eventually Olivia returned to her seat and her murder trial resumed. Two witnesses later, the day was over and she was hastily bundled into the limousine for the ride back to New York. In the privacy of the car she broke down again, the tears flowing freely as she bent her head to her knees, shoulders shaking in torment. A woman passenger tried to console her, but Olivia's mother sensed the tears were a release of pent-up sorrow. "No," she said to the friend. "Let her cry. She needs to cry." Olivia wept all the way home.

Chapter Twenty-Five

ALIBI

HENRY FLAVIN TOOK THE WITNESS STAND FOLLOWING THE emotional audio tape that had shattered Olivia's reserve. His appearance was a welcome one in the serious courtroom, for Flavin is a jolly, bearlike man who watches the world from behind big horn-rimmed glasses and an easy smile. Known and respected throughout the county as a teacher of firefighting methods at the Westchester County Fire Services training center, he is stopped for quick chats by the firefighters and police officers who have learned beneath his gentle tutelage.

Flavin was not on the stand that afternoon for his personal recollections of the night of December 2. His contribution was the videotape he had made that night, showing firefighters in action.

Even as he spoke to describe the origin of the video recording, all eyes kept drifting to a television set that had been rolled to the center of the courtroom, its bright blue screen flickering in readiness for a technician to turn it on. Dust covered its top. Court officers, jurors, and spectators wrestled a few moments with dangling cords at the side of the room to close the twenty-foot-high vertical blinds. As the room darkened, George Bolen went to the far end of the jury box, while Laura Brevetti came to the near end and sat on a carpeted stair. Marlies Riner and other spectators from the left side of the room shifted to the right, standing in the aisle and along the wall for a view of the screen. Judge Silverman, black robe trailing open behind him, took station behind the witness box. Only Olivia and Maya, her interpreter, stayed put on the far side of the room.

The show began, and fire was finally brought into the court. For the first time, jurors actually *saw* something that might move the situation to a personal level. On the screen, firefighters with oxygen tanks strapped to their backs and broad fluorescent stripes around their heavy coats milled about in a haze of smoke, their flashlights drilling holes in the darkness. The sounds of approaching sirens mixed with yells and a general undercurrent of noise. "Hey, we got a fire in here," called one firefighter, his hand on the side of the house. "Must be in the walls!"

Suddenly, as the camera recorded the scene, waves of bright orange-red-yellow flames flashed upward from the window of Leah's bedroom and the firefighters leapt backward. They regrouped and the sounds of breaking glass could be heard as they smashed windows to vent the smoke. Axes bit into wood and smoke poured out in a solid column of dirty air. A hose was brought up and a fan of high-powered water swept out toward the fire. An emergency generator growled to life somewhere off camera, and big lights snapped on to pierce the smoky veil. The firefighters appeared in silhouette, as if dark ghosts were stalking about West Lake Drive.

For twenty minutes the tape continued and the courtroom remained silent. The fire dominated the room. As quickly as the videotape began, it ended. No doubt it was a powerful show, but it remained somewhat abstract and two-dimensional, not truly a gut-wrenching experience for jurors who have, through the years, become used to watching monster fires on television and in the movies. It had impact, but lacked immediacy. It might as well have been an "Eyewitness News Team" report of a fire in Toledo or Tampa, instead of Thornwood.

The entire video was shot at night, and it did not show

Olivia Riner, nor the baby, nor Bill Fischer, nor even the house in any recognizable detail. Just a bunch of firefighters putting out a blaze. Just what did it mean? Everyone had already conceded that a fire had taken place that night, so the videotape that was supposed to be a vital piece of evidence showed little beyond the fact that Henry Flavin took his video cam to a fire.

For Bolen, however, it was still one more brick of evidence that would be placed atop all of the other pieces of evidence he would produce, until the sheer weight of it all could not be ignored and jurors would find Olivia Riner guilty of four counts of second degree murder and one count of first degree arson.

Brevetti, Rush, and Gerstmann remained impassive throughout the television show, carefully masking their own emotions, but biting their lips in nervousness. Did Bolen and the police see it? Was Flavin going to leave the stand with only the testimony that he had given? Were more details going to emerge from that videotape? No? That was it?

As everyone returned to their seats, the defense team tried to look busy, even harried. They were not about to give away the fact that prosecutor George Bolen, the Thornwood police, and all of the expert help available to the District Attorney's Office had just missed the single most important piece of evidence in the entire case.

Arthur Causey came into and went out of court just as quickly as he had visited 5 West Lake Drive on the afternoon of December 2. The Mount Kisco resident, employed by Suburban Propane for more than thirteen years, added nothing to solve the mystery. He recalled that on that Monday he had backed his big truck loaded with 2500 gallons of propane up the long driveway at 4:20 P.M., stuck a ticket in the meter to register the delivery, then walked around to the right side of the house to reach the propane tank. He filled it, rolled up the hose, and punched the ticket a second time to record the amount of gas he delivered. The front door of the house was closed, so he stuck the ticket into a crack beside it, then drove away.

Except for remembering that he had seen a television set playing in the front room, Causey neither saw nor heard anything else—no cats, no nanny with a sleepy babe in her arms, no suspicious person lurking about in the thick bushes.

Bolen wanted the jury to see that the unexpected appearance by the delivery truck driver proved that there was no one else around the house, no suspicious vehicles at the curb in the hour immediately before the fire. However, Causey would not have known in any case which automobiles were familiar to the neighborhood at any given time.

From the start, Olivia had told police she had seen the propane delivery man walk by the front door twice. Causey simply confirmed that he was there when she said he was, actually bolstering her statement, rather than attacking her credibility.

In order to prove that John Gallagher was nowhere near the crime scene when the fires erupted, it was necessary for Detective Bruce Johnson to pick up the young man's time card from the auto shop where Gallagher worked as a mechanic. When the policeman examined the rectangular slip of stiff manila paper, he was puzzled by what he saw. According to the imprint of the mechanical time clock, Gallagher had not been at work that day at all—not that day, not that month, not even that year! The time slip that was supposed to prove John Gallagher was working on Monday, December 2, 1991, actually bore the date of November 1, 1989.

Bolen put Gallagher's boss on the stand to explain how the employees of the Big Dee Auto Sales—White Plains Jaguar shop punched in and out each workday. A tortured trail of questions and answers followed, which primarily demonstrated the repair facility specializing in tuning some of the finest motor cars on the road could not keep their own time clock working right.

Cornelius James Westbrook, the service department manager, is a tall, muscular man who prefers informal attire and glasses with wire rims. To explain why the clock was off by two years, Westbrook said the machine had a built-in stamp to mark the years, and while the days, hours, and minutes can be manually adjusted, only the manufacturing Simplex company could open the mechanism and change the number of the year. To do so, the firm needs the clock back and a check for $200 or more, Westbrook said. Therefore, to save money and effort, it was not unusual for a customer just to skip that process. Westbrook said his company had not replaced the yearly imprint from the time they had bought the clock, and the workers simply continued to use the same year, over and over. Every year was 1989 to the time clock at the automobile shop.

The explanation for the wrong month appearing on the time card was just as bizarre. The clock turns a cycle of thirty-one days to a month, then resets automatically to start with the first day of a new month. It is the duty of Westbrook or his shop foreman to open the clock and reset it at the end of any month containing less than thirty-one days. Such as November, which has only thirty days.

The clock should have been reset to a new month at the end of November 30, but was not. It continued to tick on its thirty-one day cycle, giving November an extra day before starting over on its own accord, beginning the following month one day late. The month marker also had not been changed, so the month registered on the cards continued to be November.

The time card the prosecution was submitting to verify Gallagher's workday was not worth the paper on which it was printed. Truth be told, there would have been multiple time cards under John Gallagher's name that would have borne the exact same date of November 1, 1989, including one that was supposed to represent December 2, 1991.

The jury was already confused with such a screwy timekeeping system, then Westbrook made it even more complicated. The clock was not measured on a gauge of sixty minutes to an hour, but by one hundred units, to better count the precise amount of time consumed in doing work under warranty. So even if Gallagher's card did have a specific time on it, although the year, month, and day were acknowledged to be incorrect, it did not even have a scale of minutes. That wasn't all. Westbrook proceeded to describe a separate "incentive" time card that was also used by the mechanics for warranty work.

When all was said and done, it was agreed that John Gallagher reported for work on the day in question at 8:04 A.M., punched out for lunch at 12:15 P.M., returned to work at 1:27 P.M., and clocked out for the day at 4:42 P.M.

Brevetti sat quietly throughout Westbrook's testimony. The witness was destroying his own credibility very nicely without any help from her. When her turn finally came, she managed to uncover one nugget. Detective Johnson did not pick up Gallagher's time card until at least December 6, a full four days after Johnson had arrested Olivia Riner and questioned whether she had acted in cahoots with Leah's boyfriend. The only reason to pick up the card at all was to prove Gallagher's claim of when he got off work on the evening in question. It did not do that.

So Bolen had to go a step further to establish exactly where Gallagher was when the fires began. On Friday morning the prosecutor called to the stand a fellow mechanic from White Plains Jaguar. John Sunseri, a small and dark-eyed man, had worked there for six months prior to December 1991.

Wearing neat white jeans and a black shirt as dark as his thinning hair, Sunseri testified that Ronnie Ball, a friend of his for the past eighteen years and one of the four mechanics in the shop, had spent the day of December 2 attending a Jaguar mechanics' training class in New Jersey. Ball had finished the class, driven back to Westchester County, and arrived back at the shop about 4:45 P.M. He drove straight onto the rails of a hydraulic lift to give his car a quick checkup.

Sunseri said he spoke briefly to Ball, then, when John Gallagher approached and joined the conversation, Sunseri drifted away to clean his tools. The time, he estimated, was two or three minutes before five P.M.

With a deep, strong voice, Sunseri gave the impression of a man of precision, just the kind of attitude needed to tune an expensive vehicle.

Laura Brevetti sat at the defense table wrapped in a cloak of pain. An old kidney problem had struck again, and she had felt its first warning signs while Westbrook was finishing up. By the time Sunseri was called as a witness, Brevetti was running a fever and a rampaging infection was getting worse. But she considered Sunseri to be a crucial witness, because he might establish the time Gallagher left work that day.

When she began to question him, there was nothing visible to indicate she was uncomfortable in the slightest. It was an extraordinary display of the mind's power over pain. She was casual in her approach, not wanting the jury to consider Sunseri to be a threat.

Her goal was to emphasize that the witness did not actually see John Gallagher leave work that day. She determined from him that Sunseri and Gallagher had known each other for several years, and Sunseri had met Leah Fischer.

Brevetti asked if the men in the shop regularly work with solvents in cleaning their tools, and whether their clothing became greasy from the machines on which they worked. He replied with a slight smirk that yes, they did, as if that was a woman's question, because obviously a man working around cars brushed against grease.

At that point the jury was measuring in their minds whether Gallagher could have left the garage around five o'clock and made it to the Fischer home in time to be involved with setting the fires. They had settled back in their cushioned chairs, having reached the conclusion that such a thing would have been impossible. The time allowance wouldn't work.

Brevetti stuck to the line about the grimy side of the business, particularly the cleaning of tools, for Sunseri had testified on direct examination that, when Gallagher and Ball began to talk, he had gone off to clean his tools. Sunseri had said he left the shop at ten minutes after five P.M., although he admitted punching out earlier on the time clock.

The defense attorney, almost casually, queried if it was normal for him to clean his tools on company time. Sunseri replied that it was.

The jury was therefore left with a major inconsistency. Sunseri was saying that after cleaning his tools on company time, he punched out at 4:53 P.M. If he was accurate on that point, then he could not have left Ball and Gallagher to chat while he cleaned his tools moments before five P.M., as he had testified earlier. And if he had been busy doing the cleanup on company time, before 4:53 P.M., he would not have been in position to pinpoint exactly when Gallagher departed.

The jurors began revising their mental notes of time and travel distance between the shop and the house on West Lake Drive. Brevetti had added an extra five or ten minutes to the Gallagher scenario, which would have allowed him to arrive earlier than previously reported. Sunseri's mushy recollection of times had resulted in a significant stumble.

Bolen would never be able to pin that time down firmly for the jurors. No managers other than Westbrook, who only discussed the strange time clock, were called to testify, and Ronnie Ball was not brought in as a witness.

Therefore, no one from White Plains Jaguar ever verified in court that Gallagher left the shop at a certain time.

Brevetti asked Sunseri to comment on John's style of driving. Sunseri laughed. "As a matter of fact, we make fun of him at times. He drives like Grandpa." A couple of jurors could not suppress smiles.

Brevetti had enough. Her energy level was wilting and her eyes beginning to water. When she returned to her seat, she felt as if she were about to collapse.

George Bolen leaped to his feet as Brevetti ended her questioning. He knew where she was going with that information, and he knew that John Gallagher didn't always drive like an elderly gentleman out for a Sunday ride. Better the jury should hear it from the prosecution side rather than let Brevetti spring it on them.

John Sunseri testified on Bolen's re-cross-examination that Gallagher was part owner of a race car and had been a veteran competition driver on the area's stock-car tracks. Sunseri kept his smile in place, proud of his friend's accomplishments.

He explained that his earlier answers about the poky driving style had been based upon the normal way John drove on the streets around Mount Pleasant. "We were not talking about track," he told Bolen. "We're talking track, we're talking different."

Chapter Twenty-Six

GALLAGHER

THE FIRST WEEK OF THE MURDER TRIAL OF OLIVIA RINER
came to a crashing close on Friday afternoon when a tall,
gangly young man in a gray suit with a patterned tie,
white swirls on black, walked into the courtroom. He
was John Philip Gallagher III, the man the defense team
sought to cast as an alternate suspect, the boyfriend who
suddenly showed up at 5 West Lake Drive moments after
it had been set afire, the guy who was so well-connected
to the Mount Pleasant police that they hardly gave him a
second look on the night of the murder.

A lot would be riding on the testimony of the twenty-
six-year-old Gallagher, who wore his red hair combed
back from a wide forehead. As a mechanic, he might
wear oil-stained coveralls at work, but in this particular
court, John Gallagher appeared somber, polite, and as
neat as a young stockbroker. He could be, perhaps, the
most potent witness in the prosecution's arsenal, and a
weakened Laura Brevetti was physically unable to meet
the challenge.

She had felt that "there was someone on my shoulder"
giving her strength during the Sunseri interrogation, but
now she was simply running out of gas. Her mates on the
defense team saw her growing weaker almost by the minute.

Meanwhile, George Bolen was going to bet a lot of

chips on this key witness, a particularly risky strategy, since throughout the testimony of John Gallagher, explosions were never too far below the surface. The first detonation came quickly. His family had been in Mount Pleasant for generations before moving two and a half years ago to the community of Mahopac in neighboring Putnam County. During his childhood, from the ages of eight to ten, Gallagher had been on the Mechanics Hills Swim Team, coached by Louis Alagno, the man who was now a lieutenant of police and the senior officer at 5 West Lake Drive on the night of the crime.

This was the first direct testimony that the jurors had heard linking Gallagher to the Mount Pleasant police, but it would not be the last.

Bolen let that one crackle for only a moment before he questioned his witness about various vehicles. Gallagher said he owned a pickup truck, an old Dodge Dart that was a rebuilding project, and a half share of a 1989 Ford Mustang. He confirmed he had spent time behind the wheel at some stock-car races.

The prosecutor, seemingly to get all of the bad news out of the way in a hurry, asked Gallagher about his high school career. "I was asked to leave," he replied with an impish grin. He said he was expelled at the age of seventeen for cutting a few classes.

In his first moments on the stand, one of the prosecution's main witnesses admitted to being buddies with the senior cop on the fire scene that night, a race car driver, and kicked out of high school before graduation. Jurors might wonder about where this would lead after such a rocky start. Bolen, however, knew that investigator Chris Rush and Laura Brevetti had done their homework on Gallagher, and that if he didn't lay the questionable material on the table, the defense would make a stink about it. Anyway, Gallagher testified that he had never been arrested. Bolen wanted to point the jury and Gallagher toward the small time frame of December 2. That's what was important, not some blemished high school record almost ten years old.

Gallagher said he had started work at White Plains Jaguar in June 1991 after various other automotive repair jobs. He lived with his parents and siblings, and had met Leah Fischer in 1987 through the introduction of a friend. Except for a seven-month breakup, which was patched up in August 1988, they had dated steadily. He nodded vigorously in the affirmative when Bolen asked if they had a "serious relationship."

The witness said Leah owned a 1989 Toyota Corolla with a stick shift and was a "decent driver."

During overnight visits to 5 West Lake Drive, Gallagher said he always slept downstairs in the family room at the front of the house. His truck would be parked half on the grass at about the midpoint of the long driveway.

A photo of the lime-green and cream-colored truck was produced for evidence, and when Brevetti was given the usual opportunity to examine it, her hands were shaking so much that even Bolen became concerned. "Are you all right?" he asked. She gave a weak nod in reply and returned to her seat.

Bolen resumed questioning Gallagher, asking if he had gone to the Fischer residence on Sunday, December 1. Yes, John said. He had left with Leah and gone to his parents' home, driving Leah's car and leaving the truck behind in its usual place. The next morning, Monday, they arrived back at the Fischer place "about 6:45 or seven" in the morning so Leah could get dressed and Gallagher could retrieve his truck. He said he did not go inside the house, but jumped in the truck and went "right to work" at White Plains Jaguar. During the afternoon, just before leaving, he said he talked with fellow mechanic Ronnie Ball at the shop.

Bolen asked him how he drove from White Plains Jaguar to 5 West Lake Drive. Since John Gallagher had lived in the small community most of his life, he knew the back roads and shortcuts that would avoid lights and stop signs. He said he would get on Old Tarrytown Road in Greenburgh, go right at the stop sign, left on Hillside to Legion Drive, then shoot down Columbus all the way to Nanny Hagen. He said it would take ten to fifteen minutes to make the drive.

On that day, he punched out about twenty minutes before five o'clock in the afternoon, chatted with John Sunseri for a while, and then talked to Ronnie Ball when he pulled into the shop. He took his normal quick route over to West Lake Drive because he planned to see Leah that night.

The prosecutor set Gallagher on course for describing what happened next, and let him go. The jurors were transfixed.

When he turned into the driveway, Gallagher testified, a bag of automobile parts that was on the seat beside him tipped over and the metal pieces fell to the floor. He said that as he reached down to retrieve them, he glimpsed a "bright light" that looked like fire, just as he heard the shrill whine of the smoke detectors going off inside the house. He ran to the house, and his movement activated the motion-sensitive floodlight. Gallagher saw Olivia Riner "somewhere between the hall and the family room," clutching a fire extinguisher. When he got to the front door, she threw it open and cried, "It's in the room! It's in the room!"

Gallagher said he grabbed the fire extinguisher, ran down the hallway and twisted the knob, finding the door to the baby's room closed and locked. He braced himself and kicked the nursery door open. He yelled at the nanny, asking if she had locked the door or why she had locked it. He could not hear her reply, and by then it didn't matter because the door flew open and Gallagher saw a terrible sight that drove everything else from his mind. "The baby was on the floor in front of me, on fire," he said.

Propping the door open with his left foot, Gallagher triggered short bursts from the fire extinguisher into the smoke-filled room. Using his hands to help describe the action, his deep voice falling even lower, Gallagher said flames were burning around the car seat, climbing the curtains and the walls, and "coming right off the child."

"I put the fire out," he said. "I started to bend down to see if it was all right. But I knew it was too late."

Bolen played the emotion card. "Why did you leave the room?"

"Because of the smoke and the smell of the burned baby," replied Gallagher.

Bolen asked if Gallagher, acting by himself, with his girlfriend Leah Fischer, or with anyone else, had anything to do with the fire or anything that happened to the baby that day.

Gallagher turned his face directly toward the lawyer. "No," he said.

It was only 12:27 P.M., a convenient time for the usual lunch break, but it was the end of the line for Laura Brevetti. Feverish and with pain shooting through her back, there was no possibility of her continuing. Judge Silverman ended the first week of trial a bit early.

It was easy to prove that Brevetti's illness was not feigned. No defense lawyer with an option would have chosen to let the jurors go home for the long weekend, which was going to be extended an extra day because of Brevetti's ailment, with the case twisting on Gallagher's closing statements. Escorted by Chris Rush, who brushed away reporters, Brevetti went down a side escalator to an underground parking garage to be driven home. She did not know which hurt worse, her back or the knowledge that the jurors would have several days to dwell on Gallagher's testimony that he was forced out of that tragic room by the smell of a baby on fire.

Brevetti was rushed to a hospital and passed out on a gurney. For four hours she was pumped with antibiotics to block the growing infection. Then, incredibly, she got up and went back to work. In a compromise with herself, a woozy Brevetti went to bed, but refused to sleep until she completed making her daily notes on the trial.

Chapter Twenty-Seven

UNCLE TONY

THE SECOND WEEK OF TRIAL WOULD BE AN ABBREVIATED ONE, beginning Wednesday morning, June 10. A silent reminder that the clock was ticking toward election was exhibited in the parking garage, where the first campaign stickers for the fall's judicial races began to appear on automobile bumpers. None bore Silverman's name.

The clock also gave some solace to the harried defense team. Brevetti's illness may have been painful, but it bought a bit of time to prepare their attack on the credibility of John Gallagher. Under Rush's direction, the campaign had taken on an almost military style. No more working out of the offices in Manhattan and having early conferences before a chartered limousine ride through traffic to White Plains. Time was critical! The eighteen- to twenty-hour workdays were routine, and there was no such thing as a day off. Brevetti set the tone, reading and mentally preparing while she was sick, just as Chris Rush had ignored a painful injury in April to stay on the case.

Olivia and her family would continue living in the brownstone townhouse of the Swiss Benevolent Society on the Upper West Side of Manhattan. While TV cameras hurried up from New York City each day to chase her at the courthouse, she could have the final laugh. Every morning, she was picked up at the apartment between Central Park and Columbus Avenue, near the ABC Network headquarters, for her trip to White Plains. The pushy TV types could not find her, even though she was right beneath their noses the whole time.

But the defense team moved out of the city and set up shop in the posh La Reserve Hotel in White Plains. Hotel rooms were reserved, as were a separate conference room and a special, tight-security "war room" to which only approved people were admitted. Paper shredders were installed to turn used documents into confetti. Telephones were checked for electronic taps. They would take no chances on their carefully gathered material falling into the wrong hands. Like the prosecution, they would turn over to the opposition only what the court absolutely required. No more. Too much was at stake. Within this bastion, Brevetti would discard her immaculate wardrobe in favor of a sloppy sweatsuit, poke a pencil into her hair, light a cigarette, grab a cup of strong coffee and bear down on the case.

Bolstered by her quiet walk on Sunday morning through the stillness of White Plains, and pills to keep the pain at bay, Brevetti was able to be back in court on Wednesday morning to confront John Gallagher. She was not at one hundred percent, but she and her team had created a map for the coming ordeal. She knew exactly where she was going.

Gallagher had been able to bask over the long weekend in the knowledge that his time on the witness stand had dealt a severe blow against the high-priced defense team that had lined up before Olivia Riner. He was now practiced in the witness game. Standing six feet, two inches tall, but weighing only 155 pounds, he came forward to face Brevetti's interrogation with an almost cocky bounce to his step.

If he was wearing a mask of contention, Brevetti was wearing one of utter contempt. She simply did not like the young man seated before her, and her body language, her acid politeness and habit of not looking directly at him—as if he weren't really worth looking at—all came through loud and clear to the jury.

Just as George Bolen had questioned Gallagher about some peculiar items in his past, so did Brevetti. But where Bolen had used a feather duster, to indicate the information was not significant, Brevetti used a sledgehammer. To her, it was all very important, and she was not going to let it be swept beneath the rug.

She started with Gallagher's statement of the past week that he had graduated from West Lake High School, although he had later couched that by saying he had been asked to leave. Brevetti asked why he was expelled from school and why he'd said he had graduated. Gallagher replied the comment had been "a mistake on my part" and that he had been forced to leave high school in his senior year simply because he had cut classes four or five times. Brevetti didn't believe that for a moment. A student just doesn't get thrown out of school shortly before graduation for missing a few classes. Chris Rush would soon drop a subpoena on the school to find out whether something more serious was the cause. For the moment, however, Brevetti could chalk up a small inconsistency from Gallagher. Once again the jury was discovering that what was said by a prosecution witness might not be the whole truth.

Okay, Brevetti said, let's change the subject and talk about your truck for a while, that Ford pickup you testified last week that you had owned for about a year and a half "and drove slowly, like Grandpa" (as noted by Sunseri). In answering a sweep of pointed questions that jerked the jurors wide-awake, Gallagher admitted the registration and insurance on the truck were not in his name, but in the name of his girlfriend, Leah Fischer.

"Because you couldn't get insurance?" the lawyer asked.

"That's correct," he replied.

She introduced a two-page insurance application into evidence that asked for prior traffic convictions, a section that had been left vacant, although when Brevetti read off Gallagher's driving record, it included violations for speeding, driving without a license, running stop signs, violating a restricted and suspended license. She wondered aloud about the insurance application statement that all responses should be "complete and truthful." The squeeze on the truck was not over yet. A photo of the truck showed a commercial license plate, but Gallagher confirmed that Leah did not have her own business and the truck was not used for business.

Only moments before, John Gallagher had reveled in the role of a knight in shining armor, but jurors were beginning to wiggle in their seats, watching a warrior fall off his horse. By recanting, by omission, by not telling the whole truth, Gallagher was leaving the clear impression that he was not above telling a lie.

Brevetti spent some time on the four-and-a-half-year relationship between Gallagher and Leah Fischer, and in doing so, had Gallagher admit that he was familiar with the layout of the Fischer house, which he frequently visited and where he began spending the night in 1989. He would stay at 5 West Lake Drive three nights a week, and Leah would stay at his family's house for three; so, he confirmed, they spent five or six nights together every week.

Bill Fischer had imposed the rule that Gallagher had to sleep on the family room sofa during those nights at 5 West Lake Drive, although he was allowed to keep work clothes and shoes in Leah's closet. He confirmed that when they slept over at his house, Leah would "sometimes" sleep in his bed.

Carefully, Brevetti broached the subject of the entry of Denise Fischer into that equation. Gallagher said he had no recollection of Denise objecting to his overnight presence, but that it was "possible" that Leah and Denise had argued about it.

"Isn't it true that Leah Fischer and Denise Fischer

didn't see eye to eye about your relationship with her and your staying overnight at the Fischer home?"

"I don't recall."

"Is it fair to say you don't have a good relationship with Denise Fischer?"

"It wasn't a great relationship, but I got along with her."

Brevetti asked about his argument with Leah in November, to which he was evasive until Brevetti read his Friday comments from the court record, where he admitted such a spat. Gallagher seemed to have caught a touch of amnesia, replying more than thirty times with remarks such as "I don't recall" or "I don't remember."

Court observers were aware that, with such replies, John Gallagher, the high school dropout, actually believed he could outwit Laura Brevetti, the smart lawyer from Manhattan. Gallagher was one of the few who did not realize it was an enormous mismatch. His mother sat in a back row twisting a handkerchief.

Brevetti pressed ahead on the personal relationship with Leah. "Yes, it is possible" that he was not allowed to stay overnight at her house before the arrival of the au pair, he said. Then he reversed himself and insisted that he was allowed to sleep overnight during the week and even on the weekend, but chose not to do so. "I believe they didn't want Olivia to feel uncomfortable with me sleeping on the couch," he testified. The final analysis of the conflicting, meandering answers was that hardly anyone in the court now did not think Gallagher had been told that his overnight privileges at 5 West Lake Drive had been terminated.

Brevetti moved directly to Sunday, December 1, and had Gallagher testify that he arrived about two P.M. to pick Leah up at her house because they were going out for brunch. He saw no one else at home when he walked through the unlocked front door and found Leah in her bedroom. Two hours later they left in her Toyota for the twenty-four-mile trip to his home in Mahopac, skipping the lunch idea.

The next morning, he said, they went back to Thornwood and Leah went inside to shower and dress. Gallagher, contradicting himself, admitted he "probably" went inside with her, past the doors to the baby's nursery and Olivia's bedroom, straight to Leah's bedroom. He left before she got into the shower.

Brevetti picked up the court record from Friday and read Gallagher's direct testimony that he had not entered the house, just exchanged cars and gone straight to work. To explain the difference, Gallagher said that "usually I go to the house, stay in the house for a couple of minutes" before leaving. Zap. Another dent appeared in his suit of armor.

John Gallagher was backpedaling from so much of his earlier testimony that it was getting difficult to keep track of how his story actually should read. Whether he did one thing or another depended on who asked him the question.

The scene shifted to the night of the death of Kristie Fischer. Gallagher confirmed his earlier testimony that when he arrived he saw some brightness from the corner of his eye. Brevetti asked about an interview the following day, December 3, when he told Detective Johnson at police headquarters that when he arrived, he saw smoke and flames before he got out of the truck. Gallagher paused. "It's possible I told him that."

He said he ran up the center of the yard, across the patio and into the family room, where the hanging light was shining. Brevetti fished out the Scott Carpenter interview where Gallagher said only a night-light was on. Gallagher said that meant only in the baby's room. Brevetti asked if he might be inaccurate on that point, too. "Possibly!" snapped the witness.

Having brought him to this particular segment of the story and having shaken his confidence, Brevetti rolled out a hot series of questions. Gallagher replied that when he came to the front door, he could hear the smoke alarm, and through the glass saw Olivia standing about ten feet away in the family room, moving "like she was confused." Using body movements of her own, Brevetti asked for more detail. Was she standing like this? Was she walking, like this? What exactly was she doing, Mr. Gallagher? "She was moving like she was confused," he replied, she was standing in one spot, shifting her weight back and forth.

Laura Brevetti, at that moment, was very pleased with the prosecution witness. He had already compromised his integrity, and now he had steamrolled his own most important statement to police. She reached again for the interview Gallagher had given to Carpenter, and read that, while smoking a cigarette with his friend the policeman, Gallagher had said that Olivia "was running back and forth between the baby's room to the front door in a confused state."

Voices rose. Sharp. Loud.

Gallagher said he didn't know just where Olivia had come from.

Brevetti hammered. You didn't actually see her running back and forth at all, did you?

"No," said John Gallagher. "I couldn't see if it was from the baby's door . . . the general area."

"You had no way of knowing that! You did not see that!"

"No," he answered again.

Still, Brevetti pressed him, and he testified that he had seen the nanny moving "more like a jog. It wasn't running."

Negative, said Brevetti. Oh no, you don't. She was not about to let this point slip through. "She was in the living room the entire time you saw her."

When that particular segment was done, the prosecution's witness had challenged his own earlier statement to the police that he had seen Olivia pacing back and forth in the family room instead of trying to save the baby. He had not really seen what he had told Carpenter and Johnson. The alleged fact, which now lay in tatters, had been one of the most important points used by the District Attorney's Office in deciding to charge the nanny with murder.

The clash was not yet over. Brevetti found more discrepancies between Gallagher's police interviews and what he now claimed he saw and said and did. Did she scream "Door, door" or "Fire, fire"? He had said both. Did he have to grab the fire extinguisher away from her, did she give it to him, or was it a combination of her giving and you grabbing?

Gallagher acknowledged that perhaps using the word "grab" had been "a bit much."

"A bit of exaggeration?" asked Brevetti.

And the door to the baby's room, you said you twisted the knob back and forth, but did you *push* on the door? she queried. No, he didn't recall doing that, Gallagher said.

She questioned about the remarks he made while he battered down the door. Did he ask, "Why is the door locked?" as he had said in court, or, "Why did you lock the door?" as he told Scott Carpenter. Two different questions, Brevetti said. Two different versions, one implying that maybe someone else had locked it.

Gallagher said he might have told Carpenter something different than what he told Bolen in court.

Even Judge Silverman was having some serious questions about this witness. "Were you sure back then?" the judge asked.

"Yes. It just happened."

"Now, you're not positive."

Brevetti drilled Gallagher a while longer on the details of how he put out the fire in the nursery, and pointed out a few more inconsistencies in his story, then decided to open up one final can of worms before letting him leave the stand. The man who was supposed to have been a critical witness for the prosecution had been turned into a wonderful witness for the defense. He turned out to be flat wrong on a number of points, admitted trying to defraud an insurance company, and personally had uprooted the prosecution's important declaration—that Olivia Riner had been pacing back and forth, doing nothing, while Kristie Fischer burned in an adjacent room.

But first, Brevetti wanted Gallagher to describe whether he had any personal knowledge of any of the cops on the Mount Pleasant police force.

Gallagher said he knew patrolman Scott Carpenter. He said he knew Lewis Alagno. He said he "knew of" Detective Bruce Johnson and Sergeant Brian Dwyer. He insisted he did not personally know Police Chief Paul Oliva, although the chief was an old friend of Gallagher's grandfather.

After Oliva retired, town officials bypassed the two lieutenants in order to come up with a candidate who had not been tainted by the happenings of December 2. They had named Sergeant Anthony Provenzano to be acting chief. Gallagher said that yes, he knew Provenzano, too.

Knew him well, in fact. So well that to John Gallagher, Acting Police Chief Provenzano was known as "Uncle Tony."

The next morning, *New York Newsday* came out with a blistering column by Carole Agus, in which she likened the events of December 2 to "old home week at the crime scene." She wrote that Gallagher had been considered "one of the guys" because "he knew all the cops."

"They couldn't have treated Gallagher any better if he was their own brother," she snapped. "He was never even thought of as a suspect, not for a minute."

The *Reporter-Dispatch* in White Plains headlined their story: GALLAGHER FRIENDS WITH SEVERAL MT. PLEASANT COPS, 'UNCLE TONY.' The story said Provenzano, when asked about the extraordinary testimony, said he had no comment.

* * *

The remainder of Wednesday was given over to the testimony of three firefighters—Thornwood assistant chiefs Joe Rod and Jim Lawrence, and firefighter Richard R. Carroll. They described the actual three hours of operations that went into quelling the blaze that erupted from Leah's room on December 2. George Bolen, still working on his fortress simulation, had Carroll describe the difficulty he had trying to open the windows in the laundry and bathroom, and Rod testified that, in contrast to Olivia's statement, he found the windows in her room closed. He said that when the fire was over, he could not tell if the window in the nursery had been broken due to heat or some other cause.

Brevetti was as easy on them as she had been tough on Gallagher, ending her cross-examination swiftly so court could adjourn. It had been a tiring and exhausting day for her, but she wanted to get word out about what had happened. The jury would not hear what she had to say, but the messages would be heard loud and clear in the community, and public opinion could be useful. If Bolen wanted to yield the public forum, Brevetti would certainly take advantage of it.

Gathering her flock of television cameras in the lobby, Brevetti said the inconsistencies of Gallagher's version of what happened on December 2 clearly showed police ineptitude. She said policemen have a difficult job and have to operate under pressure, but in this case they moved too fast. "The blame was shifted to my client at the scene by a combination of exaggerations, innuendos, and inferences," she declared. "Not through solid evidence."

Chapter Twenty-Eight

"I MADE A MISTAKE"

PROSECUTOR BOLEN HAD TO DECIDE WHETHER TO PUT OFFIcer Scott Carpenter on the stand. As the first policeman at the scene, his recollections could carry great weight because things were still unfolding at 5 West Lake Drive when Carpenter had arrived. But after having seen him sliced and diced by Laura Brevetti two weeks earlier, Bolen was reluctant to serve him up before the jury.

Carpenter had interviewed his friend John Gallagher, had not turned his notes over to the investigating detective, and admitted poking around the crime scene because he was curious, perhaps tainting evidence in the process. The officer's dramatic tale of finding the burned baby weighed in his favor, simply because of the emotional impact it would carry.

The risk was too great. Bolen instead called officer Robert Miliambro, the second cop to arrive at the fire scene. The youthful-looking Miliambro, with large eyes and a square jaw, wore his summer uniform, with the badge and honor ribbons on the light blue shirt. In five years as a cop, he had never testified at a trial.

He told of arriving at the smoke-shrouded house at 5:25 P.M., locating Carpenter, and how the two of them went into the nursery, where "I took a look and saw what we had was a dead infant." That was far from the touching scene that had been described a few weeks earlier by Carpenter, who thought he had found a scorched doll.

Miliambro described how he asked firefighters to keep the nursery door closed in order to secure the room, and returning later with Sergeant Dwyer, discovered the knob was locked. Miliambro said he took a ballpoint pen from his shirt pocket, unscrewed the cap and removed the narrow ink cartridge. He inserted it into a hole in the knob, tripping the mechanism. The policeman knew how to do that because "occasionally my son locks himself in the bathroom and that's how I get him out."

So far, so good. Miliambro precisely explained finding the melted beverage bottle at the edge of the burned area. Oops. He did not say he saw a box of matches. Bolen sprinted past the mistake, planning to try again later.

Miliambro stood outside the house for about an hour, as firefighters dealt with the inferno from Leah's room, and returned to the nursery at 7:45 P.M., accompanied by Dwyer. When the medical examiner lifted the infant from its car seat, Dwyer picked up the burned diaper that fell off. "He handed it to me and said, 'What does that smell like?' I said, 'Paint thinner.' "

Bolen retraced to the matches and the officer finally confirmed there was such a box on the floor. Although the prosecution hoped to prove a match from that box ignited the paint thinner, Miliambro twice had walked past without noticing, obviously not attaching much importance to it.

Miliambro further testified that he and Dwyer had put the burned diaper, melted bottle, charred matches, and burned section of Olivia's bed into individual plain metal containers. Bolen entered each of the five-gallon cans into evidence. The jury did not know that more evidence containers of the same kind had not been available the night of the crime, possibly limiting the collection of evidence. The silver cans made nice bricks in Bolen's growing wall of circumstances. Miliambro's testimony of finding containers of flammable fluids in the family room storage closet also pointed toward Olivia Riner having access to them.

Brevetti used her brief time with Miliambro to make the police investigation look rather silly. When she asked about the evidence taken from the nursery, Brevetti pinpointed the burned car seat. "It was left behind in the nursery that evening," said Miliambro.

She asked if he secured the various rooms to protect evidence. "It was not my responsibility," replied the officer.

"Whose responsibility was it?"

"I don't know."

Brevetti wanted to know how intensive the investigation had been. The cop admitted that no investigators came in to dust the house for fingerprints, take hair or blood samples, or photograph the contents of the family room storage closet before the cans of liquids were removed.

She concluded with his discovery of the red fire extinguisher. It had been in the kitchen closet when Olivia first grabbed it; she gave it to John Gallagher, who apparently dropped it on the floor of the family room. Miliambro found it about 10:15 P.M., outside on the wet front lawn, where it had been handled by various firefighters. Although it passed through many hands, he carefully held it by the edge of the black plastic handle to preserve it for fingerprinting. The people listening in court felt that was too little, too late.

While George Bolen was understandably wary of placing young patrolmen under Brevetti's microscope, there was little worry that the man coming up the aisle could carry the freight without problem. The curtain was going up on Laura Brevetti vs. Sergeant Brian Dwyer, Part II.

The forty-seven-year-old Dwyer was his same taciturn self when he took the oath with his hand on the Bible and sat down, supremely confident that his professionalism would carry the day. He was the one witness in the preliminary hearings who had not been raked over the coals by the defense lawyer. He could do it again.

The story unfolded in its now familiar pattern. How he arrived on the first fire truck to reach the house, at 5:21 P.M., in his role as a volunteer firefighter, and went inside the structure with Chief Wind to find "a baby had been severely burned and expired." Expired. Cop talk. Just the facts. To confirm what he had seen, he collared Miliambro and went to view the baby again. He spoke of taking Detective Johnson to the side of the house and looking in the baby's room, where "the window was cracked and glass was inside."

You could almost hear Laura Brevetti, Elan Gerstmann, and Chris Rush hiccup. They couldn't believe he had said that.

The prosecution witness, in his calm, determined, matter-of-fact way, just ripped the heart out of Bolen's theory that the heat from the fire in the baby's room had cracked the window, sending glass shards flying outside onto the ground. Dwyer now testified under oath that he had personally seen chunks of glass on the inside of the room, just where they would have landed had someone knocked a hole in the pane of glass! It was an almost unbelievable stroke of good fortune for the defense.

A marked change overcame Bolen, and he moved about the courtroom in a balletlike series of pivots and strides. This business of his own witnesses backfiring on him was getting tiresome.

In a private conference the judge had warned that the state had not laid the groundwork for Dwyer to testify as an expert in how heat affects glass. Bolen swiftly did so, with Dwyer confirming he saw a "crack in the window" when he went into the nursery with Miliambro. Bolen drew out the fact that Dwyer had conducted dozens of fire investigations where a window would break when in contact with high heat.

The prosecutor asked the question: Which way would glass go in such a scenario? "Away from the fire," replied

Dwyer. That meant that if fire had caused the break, the glass would have been found outside on the ground, rather than inside, where the careful police sergeant had already testified it was found.

Then, Bolen's case was saved by the bell, as court was adjourned for the day.

The next morning's newspapers told what had happened on the stand in their headlines. IN AU PAIR TRIAL, POLICE TESTIMONY PROVES HELPFUL TO THE DEFENSE, said the *New York Times*. The local *Reporter-Dispatch* wrote, WINDOW GLASS WAS FOUND IN NURSERY, OFFICER TESTIFIES. Similar reports were on television and radio news stations.

Laura Brevetti and her team had been up until four A.M., figuring ways to capitalize on Dwyer's error. Ironically, they had to take the same elevator as Dwyer on Friday morning, June 12, the seventh day of the trial. They did not acknowledge each other.

Bolen resumed questioning Dwyer, and again the policeman was the solid witness, with crisp answers and military bearing. But, instead of relying only on the spoken word, the prosecutor could now play a trump card to regain some momentum. From a large brown trash bag, he pulled out the charred remains of the car seat in which Kristie Fischer had died. The hideously burned seat that had melted into a square of the nursery carpet was placed on the floor of the courtroom, the remainder of the carrying handle poking up at a fifteen-degree angle. Dwyer testified the carrier was "basically in the same condition as when I first went into the room."

With a dramatic flair, Bolen entered the burned car carrier into evidence as People's Exhibit Number 1, and Silverman allowed the jurors to take a stroll around it for closer examination. The car seat that had been ignored for so long at the scene of the crime had been elevated to Number 1 on the prosecution's list of evidence.

Dwyer gave additional testimony about the "crack" in the nursery window. He described it as almost like a circle, about one foot wide and one foot deep. To listeners, the so-called crack sounded more like a gaping hole.

After lunch, Brevetti began her cross-examination, and soon had Dwyer define that the crack was large enough for Bruce Johnson to stick his head through. Bolen took off his glasses and closed his eyes, as if to doze and signal the jury that what they were hearing was unimportant.

Dwyer testified he did not personally know if the nursery window was in a locked position, although he had been standing right beside it, looking in. Then Brevetti had him confirm that most of the glass in the nursery had shattered to the inside when he popped the window with a ladder to get at the flames eating through the closet. He said he took no notes at the scene.

Brevetti then had Dwyer confirm that he saw no one dust for prints on the night of December 2 and that no search was made for, nor notice taken of, any bloodstains.

Brevetti sat down, content with Dwyer, since he had testified that glass shards were found in the baby's room.

Bolen then asked Dwyer if the scene was chaotic that night, and Dwyer said it was. The sergeant replied that a firefighter had lacerated a finger on a piece of broken glass.

As his testimony drew to a close, Dwyer tried to change his earlier statements. With access to newspapers, electronic media, and his professional associates overnight, there was little doubt he was aware of the important gaffe.

He asked Silverman if he could say something. Sure, said the judge. Dwyer then told the jury that those pieces of glass he talked about yesterday actually were also outside on the ground, and not just inside the baby's room. It was a significant change.

Brevetti bolted to her feet and viciously snapped at Dwyer, "Who or what refreshed your memory?"

"When I walked out at the recess, it dawned on me what I said, and I knew I was wrong."

"Did it dawn on you because you realized the significance of what you had said, that it was not a heat break because the glass came inside? Is that what dawned on you?"

"No. It dawned on me that I made a mistake."

By changing his testimony, Sergeant Dwyer had tripped. The jurors had expected total accuracy from this iron cop. They didn't get it.

Chapter Twenty-Nine

THE EXPERT

A WITNESS CAN TESTIFY ONLY TO WHAT SHE OR HE ACTUALLY saw, experienced or gathered with their five senses. They are not allowed to draw conclusions. If a thing happened to them or in their presence, they have direct knowledge of it and may say so. There is an exception. A highly trained person or one who has acquired specialized knowledge over the years can testify about things they did not actually experience, but know for a fact exist. Enter the expert witness.

MY ... NAME ... IS ... JOSEPH ... A ... BUTLER ... JUNIOR!

The introduction, very loud and perfectly enunciated, sounded like a clap of thunder. Previous witnesses had spoken in whispers or away from the microphone, but Butler was a court veteran and made certain his voice carried. "I think we all heard that," quipped Judge Silverman.

Joe Butler. A little man with a big reputation. Officially, his job is arson investigator for the Westchester County District Attorney's Office. Unofficially, he is a legend in the sleuthing realm of how fires begin. He is an older gentleman, with wrinkles creasing his brow and deep bags beneath eyes that constantly smile. A fringe of silver hair haloes his bald head, and sitting on his ample stomach is a belt buckle in the shape of an antique fire truck.

He started playing with fire as a young man who dropped out of college in the Great Depression and got a job with the New York Fire Department, a position he held for twenty years. Then he spent eight years as a special agent sifting through suspicious fires for various insurance companies. Twenty-one years ago, he came aboard the Westchester D.A.'s Office.

Butler took courses in arson investigation and related subjects at ten universities; instructed thousands of firefighters at home and overseas; lectured FBI agents; testified in hundreds of trials; was a member of an alphabet soup of professional organizations, and had examined thousands of fire scenes in New York, New Jersey, and Connecticut.

By the time George Bolen had eased Butler through a recitation of his credentials, the jury was clearly impressed. Somewhat amused by the fat little man's loud, precise speech, they still recognized an expert when they saw one. Bolen had finally brought out a witness who seemed sent by the gods to put this case right. Who could argue with forty-nine years of experience?

Butler would spend almost three days delivering a cascade of technical information about arson and fires. From the moment he arrived at 5 West Lake Drive at seven P.M. on December 2, until he left at midnight, Butler toured the building while rain poured down "in sheets," talked to police and firefighters, and pieced together a picture of the genesis of the deadly flames.

He testified that "three separate, distinct, and individual fires" burned in the house that night, with the one that devoured Leah's bedroom "very severe and intense." He could not, however, determine the sequence in which they began.

The second week of trial ended on that note, and a long summer weekend punctuated by thundershowers followed. When court resumed on Tuesday, June 15, Butler was back on the stand, his technical knowledge over-whelming and instructive.

He said that in the localized burn on Olivia's bed, a protected area was in the center, shielded by a visible spot in the middle of the burn. Bolen, his voice rising, asked if it could have been caused by a folded diaper, and Butler confirmed it could.

While Brevetti took notes as swiftly as an eager college freshman, Butler described the scene in Leah's room and how he believed the fire's horseshoe pattern around the bed proved flammable liquid was poured around it. He said it burned across the ceiling, ate through the closet door, and flashed into the baby's room. Bolen asked if Butler was certain "to a reasonable degree of scientific certainty" that the main fire had been deliberately set. Yes, Butler replied, the damage was too severe to be consistent with the contents of the room, even if everything had been burning at once. Definitely, flammable fuel was present.

In supervising the fire department's cleanup of Leah's room as he searched for clues, Butler testified he ordered the rubble and debris thrown out through the window and told firefighters to knock out the center vertical rod so the destroyed mattress could be shoved through. As the room was cleared, his investigation proceeded.

The lecturelike presentation grew tiresome, and jurors swapped looks of amusement as Butler continued his long narratives that lapsed into boredom. As hours passed, they picked at their eyebrows, cleaned their glasses, and studied their hands. Both Bolen and Silverman tried to keep him on track, persuade him to shorten his answers, but Butler continued the rambling discourses, almost like an elderly grandfather drifting off into tales of past glory.

Bolen had him describe returning to the house on December 16, two weeks after the blaze, to conduct a further investigation with other experts. Butler testified that "various pieces of glass which were lying on the earth" outside the nursery window were picked up, along with shards from the frame of the window. The prosecutor, again urging his witness to be brief, asked about the effect of heat on glass and which way it would topple if broken. Butler finally delivered one of the lines he had been brought in to give: "In most instances, glass affected by heat coming from a room basically will fall outward."

That matched with Sergeant Dwyer's revised testimony, strengthening the idea that heat burst the window in Kristie's room and the big hole in the pane had not been caused by an intruder.

On they went, with Butler giving long answers to the simplest questions. As columnist Nancy Q. Keefe wrote in the *Reporter-Dispatch*, "Bolen would sit down at the side of the jury box while Butler went on in numbing detail, then saying, 'in other words,' and finishing with, 'to simplify,' never using 10 words where 100 would do."

The disease was catching, and after the prosecutor let one of his own questions go rambling astray, he stopped and muttered, "Bolenspeak. The bumbling prosecutor at it again."

Despite the torrent of words, Butler had been an impressive witness, even though he lost the jury on many of his answers. He conveyed that all three fires were intentionally set by someone inside the house.

It had been hard work, but when Bolen rested his questioning of the expert witness, he had scored some points.

At three P.M. on Tuesday, Brevetti rose for cross-examination, carrying to the podium an armload of notebooks and the *Fire Sciences Dictionary*. "I guess this means you're going to be a while," observed Silverman. Indeed she was. Prior to December 2, Laura Brevetti knew nothing about arson. So she bought every major text on the subject, and by the time the trial started, she could use terms like "pyrolize" with the best of them. For the next two days she would put her new knowledge to the test against Joe Butler's half century of experience.

On Wednesday, as Silverman observed that the case

was becoming as convoluted as the quirky television drama "Twin Peaks," Brevetti countered one of Bolen's significant points. She asked Butler if the forensic scientist who collected the glass shards also took some from inside the nursery. "That is correct," Butler replied. Once again the specter of an intruder rose.

For the remainder of the day, Brevetti painted an alternate possibility for the start of the fire that destroyed Leah's room. In her scenario, it could have begun in the closed closet where John Gallagher's greasy shop boots and clothing were stored. From there, in her outline, it spread to the bed, melted the plastic foam in the mattress, which dropped to the floor to leave the suspicious U-shaped burn pattern, then spread to the window and the door. Such a scene would allow a juror to believe someone threw a flammable device onto the bed from the window, or that an incendiary bomb could have been planted in the closet. Either way, it disputed Butler's own ideas. Butler admitted some of her hypothesis might be accurate, but clung to his own version—that it started in a flammable liquid poured around Leah's bed.

In Olivia's room, Brevetti asked almost in afterthought, could Butler see in a photograph she presented if there was an object beside the bed? Butler looked at the photo. "I see a white object that may be a cloth," he replied. Where Bolen had wanted to say a car seat similar to the one the baby died in may have been in place on Olivia's bed when the fire began there, Brevetti wanted to introduce the prospect that an unknown object was possibly tossed from the window, ignited the bed, and then fell beneath it when firefighters tumbled through looking for hot spots. Again an alternate image for jurors to examine.

But all of those points were almost incidental. Brevetti had done her job with Butler in the first few minutes of questioning, when she led him to admit that throughout his investigation, he took not a single note, made not a single measurement, recorded not a single word. The elderly gentleman who said he had been to thousands of fires over the course of an extraordinary career was claiming he was able to remember every detail of this one particular incident.

"Your report was based totally on your recollections, and nothing else?"

"Yes ma'am, it was."

"Did you take any photographs?"

"I did not."

Pushed a bit further, his credibility cracked wide open. "As far as fire scene analysis, I had nothing in writing. It was all in my mind."

After that it became plain that the jury liked Joe Butler, but felt sorry for him. Brevetti confided later that even she had some guilty feelings, for, by the end of his testimony, Butler was breathing hard through his mouth in nervousness and beginning to fall apart under her relentless pressure. But sympathy has no place in a murder trial, particularly for a witness trying to send your client to prison.

As news reports emerged of the strange testimony Butler gave, combined with previous slips from other witnesses, a strange phenomenon took place on the streets of Thornwood and Mount Pleasant. When investigator Chris Rush had first begun pounding the pavement months before, looking for answers, trying to reconstruct what happened and gain background information on witnesses, he had run into a solid wall of resentment. "People were saying, 'How dare you defend that girl? She killed a baby,'" he recalled. "Now those same people came up to me in the street and said, 'I'm sorry. We didn't know. I'm so sorry.'"

Chapter Thirty

NOSEDIVE

FOLLOWING BUTLER'S RAMBLING TESTIMONY, THE TRIAL TOOK on a quickened dimension, as the prosecution brought on a firefighter and three technical witnesses. There was a sense that time was running out for the state's case. So far, little had surfaced of strategic value, and witness after witness had stumbled over facts. As he shared an elevator Wednesday afternoon with some of the jurors, George Bolen punched the 3 button for the floor where his office was located and tapped another button to take them to the lobby. A juror noticed the elevator operator was their distinguished prosecutor and cracked, "See, you've been demoted already."

Firefighter Thomas Kelsey followed Butler to the stand, with Bolen planning to show that a mysterious bloodstain found at the scene was not, as the defense wanted to portray it, a signal that an intruder entered the house.

The twenty-seven-year-old Kelsey testified that two hours after his arrival on the scene, he lost his thick gloves and worked the rest of the evening bare-handed. He was part of a three-person hose team standing near the nursery window when the big fire erupted through the back closet. While directing water onto the flames, he gashed the middle finger of his left hand. Medics wrapped it in gauze, he went back to duty and helped throw burned material out of the baby's room. During that time, he said, blood continued to ooze through the bandage.

Brevetti, on cross-examination, underlined the finger was slashed while Kelsey was outside the house, not inside. While Butler conducted his investigation, Kelsey said he looked through the house because he was "curious." He added that no police officer asked him about the injury between the time of the fire and the end of the year 1991.

In short, his testimony showed only that Kelsey cut his finger, not that it was his blood splashed on the door frame in Kristie Fischer's room.

Next was John C. Peters, a fingerprint expert for twenty-one years who was rated by the FBI as a senior crime scene analyst. From the twelfth week of gestation, a human fetus develops a pattern of ridges on the fingertips, soles of the feet, and toes, that will be unique to that person until their corpse turns to dust. A print left by such patterns is as certain a form of identification as a badge that spells out a name in big, bright letters.

But in the Riner trial, Peters explained that fingerprints were fragile things and usually do not turn up in a criminal case. The slim, intense Peters spoke so rapidly that he had to be asked to slow down so court stenographer Steve Sacripanti and interpreter Maya Hess could keep up with him. The speed of delivery did not cover the lack of substance.

He tested the evidence found at the scene and found "no latent prints of value." The big plastic bottle and the box of matches found on the nursery floor were blanks. No fingerprints were found on the knob of the cabinet where the matches were kept. Nothing was on the charred brass doorknobs. The state wanted the jury to assume that, since no fingerprints were found, there was nothing to indicate an outsider had been in the house on December 2. A more natural assumption might be that no fingerprints connected Olivia Riner with any piece of offered evidence.

Brevetti spent only five minutes in cross-examination. Since glass was among the best surfaces to hold prints, did Peters dust the glass surfaces at 5 West Lake Drive? No, he replied. Did someone submit glass fragments from the nursery window to be tested for prints? No, he said. Was Peters aware that a special response team of the New York State Office of Fire Prevention was available to rush to fires and lend their expertise? No, he said.

Silverman inquired whether Peters had found any fingerprints that would match members of the Fischer family, who had lived in the house for years. No, he said, he had not come up with enough of a print to determine the pattern of even a single finger.

The fingerprint expert had come up with a big, fat zero.

Mary Eustace was brought to the stand to solve the mystery of the bloodstain. The forensic scientist testified that five days before Christmas she received an envelope containing a tiny wooden stick topped with a bit of discolored cotton. She was instructed to determine if it was blood. Eustace put several drops of a chemical onto the stain, waited ten seconds, and noted it turned from dirty red to greenish-blue. The test was positive. The stain was blood, but she could not tell if it was from a human or an animal. Brevetti, on cross, determined the test had not been run until a full four days after the cotton swab was rubbed onto the old bloodstain, almost a full three weeks after the fire. Then Brevetti questioned the fate of the cotton swab, which the defense did not have an opportunity to submit to its own experts.

"You threw the evidence out?"

"I threw the swab out."

"In the garbage?"

"Yes."

The state contended the stain came from the slashed

finger of a firefighter. But Eustace could not even tell whether it had come from a human or a horse.

Before leaving the stand, Eustace added she also tested the articles of clothing worn by Olivia for traces of blood, semen, or saliva—the purple shirt, black pants, a pair of black panties, a bra, and a white camisole. She found nothing.

On December 16, fourteen days after the fire, a full team of experts was dispatched to 5 West Lake Drive. Two weeks had passed, and an unknown number of people had been through the house in the meantime, but the state still put three forensic scientists, arson investigator Joe Butler, Detective Bruce Johnson, and Assistant District Attorney George Bolen into the house in still another attempt to find some hard evidence. Chris Chany of the county crime lab was part of the group.

As a final expert witness, Chany said that on that day, he collected twenty-five pieces of glass out of the window frame in the baby's room, put them into a paper bag, wrote his initials on the sack, and took it back to the lab for extensive tests. Other material was also tested.

Using a gas chromatograph, Chany reported the diaper, the melted bottle, and Kristie's T-shirt all contained substances "consistent with paint thinner," but he could not directly link the substance with the containers that had been taken into evidence. In tests on Olivia's clothing, he found not a trace of hydrocarbons, meaning there were no signs of paint thinner on her clothes.

On cross-examination he said the baby's car seat was tested in the lab on January 22, almost two months after the fire, and "nothing of significance was noted." The item that had eventually become People's Exhibit Number 1 had been so mistreated before being tested that the crime lab just gave it a visual examination and let it go.

Chany said that prior to arriving at the house on December 16, he was unaware a bloodstain had been discovered, but once it was found, he took a cotton swab from his crime scene kit and procured the single sample later tested by Eustace.

Then Brevetti turned to the shards of glass that Chany collected. He said he could only tell the inside of the glass from the outside on three pieces of seven tested.

Then the expert witness did a pratfall, courtesy of Brevetti's extensive questioning. No, he had never read a manual or received training in how physical evidence should be collected. She pointed out the FBI recommends glass shards be wrapped in cotton and placed in a box, and a chart made of where the samples were found. No precautions had been taken to keep the chips from bumping together and becoming even smaller chips, perhaps erasing important patterns in the process. Chany had just put them loose into a paper sack.

As with fingerprint expert Peters and forensic lab chemist Eustace, Chany was unable to provide anything of value. None of them laid a finger on Olivia Riner.

On Friday, June 19, a day after his three expert witnesses seemed to blow up in his face, George Bolen decided the real problem was with the press. Before the jury filed in, Bolen said he had a matter of utmost importance to discuss, then launched into a complex tirade of how a police videotape had fallen into the hands of the media. He pointed back to January 14 and the "Now It Can Be Told" show hosted by Geraldo (Bolen drawled out the word to mimic an Hispanic accent) Rivera, and charged portions of the broadcast tape were doctored to present something that was "clearly a lie." Stripped of the histrionics, Bolen was trying to say the tape's alleged laughter and voices attributed to Gallagher and Leah actually had taken place some three minutes before they appeared on the screen.

His voice grew sharp as he paraded before the press rows and charged the same falsehoods were now being broadcast again and the print media were picking up the erroneous information. "The two voices in question are absolutely not John Gallagher and not"—he slapped the podium with his hand—"Leah Fischer!" He said such claims were "terribly prejudicial to the People's case." He told the court it was his personal practice not to comment to the press about a case before, during, or after a trial.

He wanted the jury to be polled again to see if they had been tainted by the false reporting. The judge reluctantly agreed.

Brevetti denied her staff had released the tapes. Anyway, she wanted to know, if the voices were not those of John and Leah, whose were they? Bolen refused to divulge names.

The attack came in the week that was the twentieth anniversary of the Watergate scandal, which drove a lying President from office. The reporters were at first astonished, then amused, by Bolen's charges. Since he offered no proof of what he said, the press viewed the gambit as a desperate try by the lawyer to have the jury proclaimed tainted so his case, growing weaker by the day, could be thrown out in a mistrial.

The media issue was not over for the day. The CBS station, Channel 2, had aired an interview with former police chief Oliva the previous night, and on camera Oliva said, "I think we did a thorough investigation . . . We had a lot of suspects and a lot of conjecture, and the calculations of the investigator reduced it to Olivia Riner."

The statement, made on June 19 as the trial was in its third week, was the first time someone in authority had mentioned there were other suspects in the case. Brevetti wanted to know who those others were, for she had been told repeatedly since December that her client was the only person suspected. The issue was left open.

Silverman, who noted with a grumble that Bolen had six months to raise his objections to the press about the Geraldo show instead of waiting until the middle of the trial, dutifully polled the jurors about the questionable videotape. None had seen it. The trial would continue.

Chapter Thirty-One

LEAH

THREE TEENAGE GIRLS MANAGED TO GET SEATS IN THE standing-room-only court and, before the trial, began to chat among themselves.

Girl One: "How could somebody kill a baby?"

Girl Two: "But she didn't do it."

Girl Three: "A person is innocent until proven guilty. I got that from television."

At 10:58 A.M. on the final day of the third week of trial, a tall young woman, conservatively dressed, took the witness stand. Her long brown hair, with sunny highlights, was curled, swept back and held in place by a white bow. She wore a dark blue suit and a white blouse, tiny earrings and a gold chain necklace. With her father, boyfriend, and a small cheering section of friends in the back row, Leah Fischer, half sister of the slain child, put her hand on the Bible and became witness number nineteen in the case against Olivia Riner.

George Bolen lost no time in disposing of the matter that Leah and John Gallagher had hatched a plan to insure his pickup truck despite his driving record. She said that in the "last few weeks" John had finally been listed as an operator of the vehicle, which was still registered in her name, thus admitting they had previously misled the firm.

Running through her background, Leah said she had decided to stay at 5 West Lake Drive following the divorce of her parents because "I lived there all my life. I didn't want to change." She had known and "seriously" dated John for five years.

Bolen had her describe her back bedroom on West Lake Drive—a dresser and desk along the right wall, a wicker shelf on the left, the platform bed beneath the window, and a walk-in closet at the far end. For the winter, an air conditioner had been taken out of the window, which she testified was covered with blinds that were closed and "always kept locked." The comment validated the fortress theory.

To further buttress that claim, she further testified that a leftover Thanksgiving decoration of dried corn husks was affixed to the front door and made a swishing noise when the door was opened. This would provide still another signal if an intruder entered through that portal.

Bolen had Leah describe her relationship with Denise. Leah said she had thrown a surprise shower for her pregnant stepmother in August, and that she and John had visited Denise at the White Plains Hospital the day Kristie was born the following month. To welcome the baby, she gave Kristie one of her own favorite stuffed animals, a white bear, which was thereafter kept in the nursery. Bolen asked if she had ever taken life insurance out on her baby half sister, and Leah, appearing shocked, said she had not.

The prosecutor reached beneath his table and produced a new, gray car seat that instantly became a magnet for jurors' eyes. Leah testified that the gray Evenflo carrier with silver straps and white plastic buckles looked exactly like the one that had been burned, and Bolen entered it as People's Exhibit Number 2.

Turning to her personal life, Leah testified that she and John did break up and reconcile, and said "Sure" when Bolen asked if since then they had the occasional fight or argument. Later, in cross-examination, Leah would reply,

"I don't know what you're talking about," when Brevetti asked about the August fight that both her father and boyfriend had confirmed.

Her relationship with Olivia was described as good, and she said they would spend time talking and watching television together. The family's cats seldom made any noise, she said, contradicting Olivia's statement to police. Leah would feed them in the laundry room prior to going to work.

She confirmed that on the morning of December 2, she and John returned to the Fischer house, and she got ready and left for work, arriving there at 8:30 A.M. Bolen asked how she left the door in her room upon exiting. "I kept it open" when not at home, Leah said. "If my cats were inside, I didn't want them to be trapped."

It was another significant point. If she had left the door open to her room and authorities found it closed, then there was a question of who had shut it, with the logical answer being Olivia. Bolen pursued this and asked how she left the door if she knew the cats were not in her room. "I usually left it open," she said.

She arrived back at the house that afternoon around 5:30 P.M. to find the tragedy unfolding and her father standing with Olivia. "My father asked her what happened. She said she was feeding the cats and closed the door to the baby's room because the baby was on the floor."

Satisfied with the strands of circumstantial evidence Leah had provided—the open door to her bedroom, the window to her bedroom always locked, that it was impossible for anyone to sneak in the front door, the clearing up of the truck insurance bobble, the allegation that Olivia said she had closed the baby's door— Bolen rested his questioning at two minutes before noon.

Two minutes after noon, Laura Brevetti moved to the podium to start her cross-examination. After what Brevetti had done to Gallagher and almost every other witness,

Leah Fischer gave her only curt answers. That cold attitude suited Brevetti just fine.

The lawyer went quickly to the personal side of things, comfortable in a woman-to-woman exchange that might have made a male lawyer balk. Leah said she had at least a fair relationship with Denise.

Into the year 1991, her boyfriend, John Gallagher, had been allowed to sleep over at 5 West Lake Drive "maybe" five times a week. "In the fall of 1991, that routine changed, correct?" asked Brevetti. Leah confirmed that it had and that she had begun to stay at John's house from three to five nights per week.

"Isn't it true that John Gallagher was no longer allowed to stay overnight during the weekdays?"

"Yes." To clarify, Leah added that John was now allowed to stay overnight only with advance permission from both Bill and Denise Fischer, whereas before, he could stay anytime he wanted. But she said that neither she nor John were resentful that the overnight visits were curtailed after the arrival of the baby and the nanny. In his testimony, Gallagher had waffled on the issue, saying he could still sleep over anytime he wanted.

Leah denied arguing with Denise about the new rules and denied that Gallagher wanted Leah to live with him at his home in Mahopac. As questioning continued, Leah said that John, even before the new house rules were instituted, had throughout their relationship sat in his truck in the driveway, awaiting her arrival, even if someone was already home at 5 West Lake Drive. She emphasized that Gallagher always slept on the couch, but she also said "Yes" when Brevetti inquired if they had been "intimate" during the many years they had spent nights together.

Brevetti backtracked to the Sunday the day before the fire, and Leah said John had come over about three P.M. and that she had a specific recollection that they went to an inn for lunch. Gallagher had testified he arrived at two P.M., stayed two hours, did not have lunch and went straight to his house.

Brevetti asked about Monday morning, and Leah stated she arrived between 7:00 and 7:15 A.M., saw the doors to both the nursery and Olivia's room closed, and got ready for work. She did not remember if John came inside. Brevetti read back some of Leah's grand jury testimony that indicated the possibility she did not see anyone, including John, inside the house. "He must not have been there," she now testified. Gallagher had testified both ways, eventually settling that he had probably gone inside.

Now the defense lawyer asked about the bedroom door that Leah had emphatically said she always left open. Brevetti attacked. "You kept your door closed most of the time to hide the mess," she said. The jurors were again handed a different version of an event. Was the door open to protect the cats or left closed to shut off the mess within?

Brevetti queried about the window that Leah said was always kept locked. That morning, she had not checked to be sure the lock was closed, and it could not be seen behind the closed blinds.

Now it was the defense team's turn to examine that pesky truck insurance issue, a point that raised a few eyebrows among jurors asked to believe the credibility of the two witnesses involved. Leah was clearly on the defensive, saying they had put the truck in her name only as a move to save money, denying Brevetti's assertion that Gallagher could not get insurance and had turned in his license because it was suspended. Brevetti produced a photostat of Leah's signed insurance application, upon which a negative response was marked as to whether anyone would use the pickup truck who had serious traffic violations or license suspensions during the past five years. Leah said she did not recall signing such a statement, but that since it was there before her, "I must have."

Brevetti turned the dagger, asking if the reason Gallagher's insurance premiums would have been so high was because of traffic violations. "You knew you had to check 'No,' " the lawyer charged. Leah confirmed this. Brevetti then used naughty words such as "lied to" and "defraud" in referring to the insurance incident and then ended her cross-examination.

With Leah still on the stand, Bolen rose to address a matter that had been "floating around" during the lunch hour and various breaks. Trial watchers indeed had been puzzled. The prosecution had asked Leah everything but, "Did you do it?" Bolen patched that hole.

"Did you murder your half sister?"

"No. I did not," Leah Fischer shouted.

"Did you set a fire in your own house?"

"No. I did not."

Brevetti, too, had a final question, and asked Leah if she had received immunity from prosecution in exchange for her grand jury testimony. Bolen leapt to his feet to object, and Silverman flashed obvious anger, striking down the question and ordering the jury to ignore it. Then he had the jury removed from the room so he could scold Brevetti.

"You should ask my permission to ask that question, and you did not do it," Silverman barked at Brevetti, clearly irate. A repetition of such a breach could result in the judge declaring the defense lawyer in contempt of court.

Silverman said it was an unfair question because it suggested something that was not true. In New York, every witness appearing before a grand jury, unless that person is a target of the investigation, is automatically granted immunity from prosecution. In this case, that included both Leah Fischer and John Gallagher.

Bolen, angry and frustrated, said everyone testifying in the Riner case had been given immunity. He sizzlingly claimed that, despite the judge's instructions, there was no way that the minds of the jury could be wiped clean now of the possibility "that this young lady was a target [of investigation] when she was not."

Silverman, frustrated at the breach, abruptly declared he had heard quite enough on the issue, and adjourned court for the week.

Chapter Thirty-Two

SURPRISE, SURPRISE

FOR LAURA BREVETTI AND HER DEFENSE TEAM, EXHAUSTION was setting in, their routine of twenty-hour days taking a toll. She felt as if she were in the center of a hurricane of swirling information, and worried she might lose her perspective. Bolen's meandering questions, in which he sometimes told a witness to "fast forward" to some entirely different place, kept Brevetti and Chris Rush on their toes. What worried them most was Bolen's reputation for carefully drawing a web of evidence, and then producing a surprise witness to demolish the defense. In the Riner case, the life of each prosecution witness was chronicled in the war room at the La Reserve, and Rush would spend each morning up in Mount Pleasant, passing out subpoenas and gathering scraps of information. Everything known about the witnesses was catalogued. It was the unknown that worried them.

Sure enough, there was a surprise witness. When court began on Tuesday, June 23, a slight, balding man carrying a briefcase came through the doors at 10:02 A.M. John F. Marble looked like what he was, a businessman. He had flown in, at taxpayer's expense, the night before from his job as operations manager for the Concord Beverage Company in Concordville, Pennsylvania.

Marble testified his company produced the Vintage brand of sodas and tonic water that came in clear plastic bottles with light blue bottoms. He described the molding process and the date code stamped into each bottle, which could identify it down to the very shift on which it was produced. Bolen gave him the warped bottle found in the nursery, and Marble read off the code number—MAR2692CB1—and confirmed it was produced by his company.

Brevetti, not having a clue why this man was a witness, hoped to find the answer through a detailed quiz on how the bottles were made and distributed. Mystified, she gave up.

Silverman tried. He asked Marble if, at any given time, thousands of such bottles could be found in the New York metropolitan area. That was incorrect, said Marble, a better range would be in the hundreds of thousands.

The surprise witness then left the courtroom, having proven the State of New York had discovered where the burned bottle was made. Where it was purchased, when, by whom and for what purpose was never determined. Neither was the purpose of Mr. Marble's testimony.

Civilian police dispatcher Marie Solimando followed the mystery witness to the stand. Testifying in her first trial, Solimando said that at one point she noticed Olivia's "eyelashes had some singe on them." Solimando described Olivia changing clothes in the detectives' office, and said she folded the removed articles and put them in a brown paper bag.

Brevetti asked the nervous policewoman, whose eyes were flitting around the court, if Olivia was given a cloth with which to wash her face. Solimando said no. Staying with the questions about Olivia's long eyelashes and hair, Brevetti asked if Solimando noticed whether the defendant had hair below her shoulders. Solimando said when Olivia changed clothes, she noticed the young woman had underarm hair. Silverman smiled but did not laugh, although others did.

She described how Olivia was placed in the cell and

slept about four hours on the wooden bench without pillow or mattress, and how she had gone to sleep, weeping.

Before the assistant medical examiner, Kunjlata Ashar, came to testify, Bolen asked the judge to allow the jury to visit 5 West Lake Drive. It was the only way, he said, for them to get "a true overall picture" of how small the house actually was and the exact distances between rooms.

Brevetti, in opposition, argued the house was undergoing extensive remodeling and even the basic floor plan had been changed. Silverman agreed. The house had been altered so much that a jury visit would be useless, he said. "That scene [of December 2] really no longer exists," Silverman ruled, dealing Bolen another setback.

Ashar, a University of Bombay graduate who had been with the Westchester County medical examiner's office for nine years, described the extensive autopsy performed on Kristie Fischer. She said the child was burned over 85 percent of her body, but that no signs of disease, broken bones, bruises, and/or hemorrhage were discovered. Ashar was unable to pinpoint the time of death, other than saying it happened after the deadly blaze started. She had discovered the baby was breathing at the time of the fire. Moving again to keep emotions out of the trial, Silverman told the jury that the testimony "doesn't necessarily mean that the baby had to be conscious" during the fire.

The physician said the cause of death could have been asphyxiation or the severe burns on the body or both.

Brevetti had the medical examiner's assistant confirm she "did not find any evidence of injury" prior to the fire. She further could not verify or rule out whether the baby might have been smothered, although the contents of the lungs proved the baby had inhaled during the fire.

* * *

The day's minor trial elements were overshadowed by the *Reporter-Dispatch* newspaper's lead editorial that morning. Saying the performance of the Mount Pleasant police in the Riner case "in many aspects lacked professionalism," the newspaper pointed out that the crime scene was not preserved, dusting for fingerprints was late, no photographs were taken until after the scene had been disturbed, and that Joe Butler did not take notes.

The editorial said many small police departments do not have the resources to do the technical tasks needed in modern criminology. The county, it said, already had a bomb squad, forensic team, and undercover narcotics squad to help local departments, so what was needed was a task force of experienced detectives that could be attached to an assistant district attorney specializing in major crimes.

Chapter Thirty-Three

ARSON

THICK RAIN SQUALLS MARCHED INTO WESTCHESTER OVER THE weekend, and the gray, leaking sky added to the dreariness inside the courtroom as Silverman launched the fourth week of trial. In a seating change, Chris Rush moved to the defense table to temporarily replace Elan Gerstmann, for the defense was about to go on the offense. This would be the day Brevetti linked the Riner case to a string of arsons and burglaries that plagued the Thornwood area.

Silverman had signed the requested subpoenas, but it was far from certain whether he would allow such an explosive issue into the proceedings. If the jury learned of other arsons, their conclusions would be affected. Therefore, the arguments were made with the jury out of the courtroom.

The defense theory was that the Fischer house was burned by an intruder who had knowledge of it and access to it and was working with one or more people acting as lookout. Brevetti also wanted to pull John Gallagher's name into her scheme and castigate the police for not conducting a thorough investigation.

There had been indications from the start that Brevetti would try to get other arsons into evidence, and Rush had spent hours investigating them. It was time to put the results on the table.

Brevetti claimed that there were characteristics of burglary and arson involved in the West Lake Drive fire similar to patterns that had surfaced in other area fires. She added that on December 5, the *New York Times* quoted Police Chief Oliva as saying police were looking for a possible connection between all of the fires. After that, only denials of linkage were issued by police because, she said, they chose to arrest Olivia rather than conduct a thorough investigation.

Brevetti said the rash of fires were linked by the common use of flammable liquids as accelerants and the methods employed in setting them. The police, she claimed, had suspects who were part of a burglary ring that targeted automobile parts stores and gasoline stations, people who were also involved in the area's stock-car racing circles.

She cited memos from Mount Pleasant police officials for cops to watch for two individuals in regard to the fires—memos written months *after* Olivia was arrested and charged.

Brevetti argued that twenty suspicious fires were set in the area during the eleven months spanning March 1991 to February 1992, a time frame that covered the deadly December blaze at the Fischer house. The defense attorney drew striking similarities between those fires and the one in which Kristie Fischer had died—flammable liquids were used to start thirteen of them, and many happened at night.

Silverman was not impressed. The judge reminded Brevetti that to get any of this material into the trial, she would have to "establish a reason to believe" the same person who set those other fires also set this one.

Brevetti brought up the arson at the Valhalla Volunteer Ambulance Corps headquarters on March 11, 1991. The similarities were impressive. It happened during darkness; three fires were set, two on beds and one on a chair; the fires were in a bedroom area; the possible ignition source was wooden matches, and flammable liquids were found.

Police said it was an inside job, done by someone with access to the building.

She did not mention the police reaction that night, when surrounding roads were sealed off, hundreds of passing motorists were questioned, and a door-to-door search conducted for a culprit. None of those were done with the fire on West Lake Drive.

Then Brevetti ran down a laundry list of other suspicious burns, including the April 1991 fire where a window was broken in a professional building and flammable liquid poured through. In February 1992 two fires occurred in the Eastview Court area, close to Nanny Hagen Road, and police found a plastic soda bottle near the scene. Lab specialist Chris Chany said it contained paint thinner.

As early as June 1991 Detective Bruce Johnson wrote police agencies to watch clinics and hospitals for victims of flammable burns. "They were aware they had a problem with highly flammable liquids being used to start fires in the area," Brevetti said.

Silverman interrupted again to ask whether anyone was home in the buildings or if there were any personal injuries when the suspicious fires began. She said there were not. He said there was an important difference between a fire being set and an arson with the intent to harm someone.

Brevetti then accused Eric Trimpe, who lived at 356 Nanny Hagen Road, only a quarter mile from the Fischer residence, of starting several fires, describing the twenty-nine-year-old man as a "pathological fire setter." She said he was the one who torched 5 West Lake Drive. And she claimed he was assisted by a lookout, none other than John Gallagher.

Brevetti said Trimpe had been arrested a half-dozen times over the past ten years, carried several felony convictions on his record, and had even fought his way out of the police station. She also ran through the records of a couple of his pals who had been involved with him in some arson-burglary cases.

Six weeks after the fire at the Fischer house, police got a search warrant to search the Trimpe residence. In a confrontation, Trimpe's dog bit one of the investigating officers. Trimpe was not arrested for arson, but was charged with harassment. He was also never charged with the fires at Eastview Court, although police questioned him about them. Trimpe also was questioned in connection with a suspicious fire at 400 Nanny Hagen Road. It had snowed, and police followed footprints from the scene to the doorstep of Trimpe's house. He was not arrested.

Chris Rush turned up a police memo instructing officers to check the homes of Trimpe, his friends, and the burned-out Fischer house every hour. He drew a chart of targets that had been burglarized to show there was a common thread of auto-related businesses. Although unspoken, it was not lost on listeners that Bill Fischer owned an automobile repair shop.

In her effort to link Gallagher and Trimpe, Brevetti cited two sources, one of them an anonymous former Mount Pleasant cop who, she said, had seen the two men "in each other's company" and also at the police station. The second source was a television interview in which Trimpe said he knew Gallagher from high school, was also involved in automobile racing, and had seen the fire engines arrive at the burning Fischer residence on December 2.

Rush would recall later an encounter when he knocked on Trimpe's door as part of the defense investigation. "Trimpe started to come at me. I told him that if he came through that door, he wouldn't be going back." Trimpe apparently saw reason in the warning from the big ex-cop and remained inside.

After her lengthy analysis, Brevetti said that in contrast to her client, John Gallagher was the one who had motives for what happened at 5 West Lake Drive. She listed them as the change in normal patterns: he was not permitted to sleep there, the birth of Kristie, arrival of the nanny, and he was no longer permitted to enter the house if his girlfriend was not there.

As she wrapped up her argument, George Bolen paced the room. But he really did not have to say a word. Silverman made it clear he was not buying the Brevetti scenario.

"That is the spin you tried to put on it," the judge said. "I've got to tell you it is a lot of nonsense," and he added that none of her ideas contained motive enough to kill an infant. "You're conjuring up a fantastic story that has a lot of interesting elements, but what proof is there that anything you have just said has any credence?"

"This is a theory based on a hunch that may or may not be correct. The evidence in question must raise more than a suspicion that a third party may have been involved in a crime."

Bolen was allowed to rebut the defense arguments. "What we have here is a further direct attempt to besmirch the character of John Gallagher . . . who had nothing to do with the setting of this fire." Anyway, the suspicious fires had been misrepresented; most were only minor nuisance burnings of such things as piles of wood, garbage cans, and the exteriors of houses, the prosecutor said.

He read Trimpe's rap sheet, and while admitting he was a "troubled man," emphasized that Trimpe had never been arrested for arson. If Brevetti's yarn was placed in proper context, Bolen said, it would show that proof is "just not there."

Silverman ruled immediately against Brevetti. The narrow window provided by the law demanded a direct link be established to involve a third party and the crime in question, almost an impossibility. In order to accomplish that leap, the defense would not only have to demonstrate that Olivia was innocent, but would have actually had to solve the crime!

The judge said that there was "at most a suspicion that Trimpe may have been involved." A suspicion is not evidence, and he would not allow what he considered "wild speculation" to go before the jury.

The judge had ruled. The jury would never hear a word about any of the suspicious fires that had occurred in the Thornwood–Mount Pleasant area. As far as the Olivia Riner case went, it was as if those arsons and burglaries, many of which happened before she even arrived in the United States, had never happened.

Chapter Thirty-Four

THE WINDOW

IT WAS TIME FOR BRUCE JOHNSON TO TAKE THE STAND AGAIN. George Bolen's office sent a fax to Laura Brevetti to alert her defense witnesses that their time to appear was approaching. He did not say Johnson would be the final prosecution witness. There were a number of persons whom Bolen had not called to the stand, and the betting in the hallway was he would play another emotion card by putting Denise Fischer on the stand. Then he could rest his case after the jury heard from the grieving mother.

Meanwhile, the courtroom doors opened and Detective Johnson, the strongest witness Bolen had, moved forward to begin his testimony. He smiled easily at the jurors as he settled in for a long stay to recount in detail his story of the arrest of Olivia Riner.

Bolen asked about Johnson's movements on December 2. The detective confirmed he saw the window in Kristie's nursery was locked, although broken, and that in Leah's room the dual frames met in the middle, with the thumb lock pushed into the "up" and locked position. Bolen wanted this on the table early to shore up his fortress idea. The window in Olivia's room was unlocked and the pane moved to the left.

Johnson testified that on December 5 he had picked up the remains of the burned car seat, and that on the morning of December 11 he had been at the house to comply with the court order that allowed the defense team to look inside the house. Before court adjourned for the day, Bolen asked about the pictures Johnson snapped of Olivia at the station to prove her eyebrows were singed. The photos, replied the detective, were too dark, and the eyelashes did not photograph well.

On Wednesday, June 25, the jurors found the padded headsets waiting on their chairs as they entered the court at 9:52 A.M. Johnson resumed on the stand and carefully went through his story. He described his first talks with Olivia, how she said she had been in the living room and also in the laundry room when the first fire was discovered. Silverman interjected, as if drawing a line to something he did not want the jury to overlook. "She told you two different things, it is your testimony?" asked the judge. The detective said that was so.

Bolen was thorough and cautious, although his questioning was all over the map, making it hard to follow his thinking. Johnson answered questions in long narrative form, which, combined with Bolen's questions, gave a detailed overall description of that evening. They covered all major facets, from his ability to understand the Swiss girl to the fact that the police department on that night only had four evidence cans in stock and Johnson ordered more from Berger Hardware the next day. Johnson took the jury from the front lawn of 5 West Lake Drive to the police station, throwing in some information from later investigations, such as Olivia was unable to turn on the light in her room because the bulb had blown.

Olivia, wearing a white outfit, was almost animated as she sat at the defense table watching Johnson, listening to Maya, and making a few notes. Bill Fischer and his daughter Leah sat in the third row, both of them staring straight ahead without emotion when Johnson said Olivia told him "she loved the baby very much."

As the trial moved into the afternoon, Silverman explained the workings of the headsets to the jurors and said they were about to hear the tape recording of Johnson's interview of Olivia. Although garbled at times, they would be able to follow along on the transcript that opposing counsel had reluctantly agreed upon, and "about ninety-nine percent of the words you will understand."

They put on the headphones, and after five minutes of blundering with the machinery, only a loud hiss was heard. Bolen went to fetch a technician. Finally the tape rolled, pouring Olivia's words directly into the jurors' ears. The words were also faintly broadcast from the tape deck for the audience. In the jury box, the press rows, and the hands of Bill Fischer, transcript pages were turned. It was the first time Fischer had heard the familiar Swiss voice since December 2, and Olivia was talking about the major event of his life. He followed her taped voice, word by word, on the written page. And it was the first time the jurors heard her voice, giving them a chance to match it with their visual impressions gathered over the past weeks.

When the hour-long tape was done, Bolen resumed questioning Johnson until 4:26 P.M. and adjournment of the trial's fourth week.

Week Five started right where Week Four left off, with Johnson back on the stand. The temperature outside was scorching and the courtroom air conditioner groaned to cool the proceedings, which got under way at 10 A.M. Silverman announced that he expected testimony to conclude this week, but he would not give the case to the jury on a Friday.

Bolen decided enough was enough and questioned Johnson for only eleven minutes before turning the witness over to Brevetti. The detective and the defense lawyer greeted each other like old acquaintances, all smiles and politeness.

The first thing Brevetti wanted to discuss was who was actually in charge of the scene on December 2. The answer was vague. Johnson said he was "somewhat" in overall charge, while Lieutenant Alagno was the senior officer on the scene, directing all actions. Her questions for the next few hours were not pointed, not even very interesting. She picked at some of the strange elements Bolen had entered into his arguments. She asked Johnson if some of Bolen's comments, which involved such things as tree houses, skunks, raccoons, the existence of a Beer Garden restaurant, the location of a shopping center and the like, had anything at all to do with his investigation. The detective said no, they did not. Brevetti took him through the story and questioned parts of it, but the jury was puzzled. Bolen was puzzled, too, feeling in his lawyer bones that something was afoot here, and so nervous that he shifted his chair six times in one thirty-second period.

Clearly, the defense attorney, who looked rested, even eager, was stalling. Silverman called a lunch break, and the uniformed court officers shooed everyone not directly involved in the case off the fourteenth floor. There was secret stuff to be done, and when it was completed, the defense team sat around a gray metal desk in a court hallway, sharing box lunches that had been ferried up. They were laughing and in a good mood. They knew what was coming.

When the doors to the court opened at two P.M., it was as if a stage set had changed. Four huge 27-inch Toshiba Black Stripe television sets were on stands, two facing the jury and two facing the audience. A smaller one with a JVC videocassette player attached was on the defense table. From the start of the trial, one defense plan was to contrast the allegedly sloppy work of the police and prosecution with their own crisp, technologically adept, efficient style. Where Bolen had used only a single dusty television set mounted on a rickety metal stand for his videos, Brevetti had erected a small film-screening studio. It looked nice, but what was the purpose? Investigator Chris Rush, an electronics expert, sat back in his seat, confident and relaxed. He was ready for the big show.

Brevetti resumed questioning, covering Johnson's taking notes at the Fries home, the actions of the nervous cats, Olivia telling him the door to the nursery was never locked but was when she tried to open it. A dozen other questions flashed by, and the detective answered with a staccato of yesses and nos. He had not looked for footprints on the frozen December ground and did not request a medical report on Olivia's condition at the fire scene. She established again Olivia's statement that she was alone in the house, that no one else could have been inside without her knowledge. Brevetti seemed impatient, and everyone knew it had something to do with the black television sets that loomed like big eyes over the court.

Eventually she went to Johnson, stood beside the witness box, and had him describe precisely the window in Leah's bedroom. She held up a single finger as Johnson confirmed the panes were together so the middle bars appeared as one, not two separate frames. The hasp to secure it was in the up, or locked, position, the detective confirmed once again.

Brevetti picked up a remote control, as if it were a conductor's baton, and the blue screens of the television sets flickered to life with the familiar tape made by Henry Flavin. Everyone could see the confusion, the smoke, the flames. From the audience rows Bill Fischer watched his house burning.

Brevetti hit the stop button on her remote and the film halted with the tape counter reading 0:05:37. For months, the film had been in the hands of the prosecutor and the police, who had viewed it time and again. However, they apparently only saw what they wanted to see—a fire devouring the rear bedroom. But Brevetti, Rush and the defense team were looking for something different when they examined the same pictures. And they found it! For six months, the critical piece of evidence on the film had lain hidden from the prosecution—hidden in plain view. When displayed and explained in court, it would mortally wound the case against Olivia Riner.

It was a picture of the window in Leah's room, several straight lines dark and parallel before a cloud of gray smoke. Brevetti asked Johnson if he could describe the relationship of the straight lines, which were the frames of the sliding glass window. Together or apart? The detective said he did not know. Silverman interrupted to say, "For the record, there appears to be space" between the two frames. But it was at an angle, and although light showed between the window frames, it was not conclusive.

Brevetti toyed with the remote and the film rewound slowly, inch by inch, putting the fire in reverse, until she stopped it at 0:04:57. Here was a square of angry orange-gold flames in the bedroom providing an exact and bright background for the window.

There were two bars, with plenty of space between them, in the middle. The window was open.

The judge commented that the detective had testified that he personally examined the window and found it was both closed and locked.

"Who closed the window, Detective Johnson?" Brevetti barked.

"I don't know," replied a bewildered Johnson.

"You see now on the tape that it appears to be open, don't you?"

"Yes," he said, looking like a boxer who had just taken a heavy blow. His voice was low, strangled when answering.

"Who was opening and closing those window frames?"

"I don't know. The heat—"

"You have no idea what the status of that window was, whether it was open or closed before or during the fire," Brevetti hammered, her voice rising. "As far as you know the window could have been open before the fire."

"I don't know."

"You testified Friday that it was closed and locked before the fire—"

Bolen jumped up to object and was sustained by Silverman. Brevetti had made her point and he wanted her to quiet down.

It really didn't matter, for Laura Brevetti had lied to the jury.

She had promised them before the trial started that she was not a Sherlock Holmes or a Perry Mason, and just now she had solved the Riddle of the Locked House, something straight out of a mystery thriller. And they had seen it all! Jury duty was better than a ticket to the circus!

As Brevetti quietly resumed her questioning of a shocked Detective Johnson, at her feet lay the debris of George Bolen's carefully constructed theory that 5 West Lake Drive had been impregnable on the night of December 2. His entire case had been pegged to the fact that the house was secure, Olivia was the only one in it, and therefore she had to be the one who committed the crime. Now, thanks to the miracle of modern technology and long hours of sweat by the defense team, that theory was in ruins.

The jury already knew the front door was unlocked, because Bill Fischer had entered without Olivia's knowledge. They knew the window in Olivia's room was open and the window in the baby's room had a huge hole in it. Now with this explosive television demonstration, the window of Leah's room had been shown, without a doubt, to have been wide open, not closed and locked as they had been told repeatedly by the State of New York throughout five weeks of tedious trial.

Although Brevetti's questions returned to more mundane matters, the spellbound jury never took their eyes from her again all day, fearing she might pull another trick.

She had one more major point, and had Johnson confirm that, although the majority of his nine hours of questioning had been done overnight on December 2, he did not sit down to re-create the conversations from his notes and recollections until the following Sunday, six days later.

He confirmed that on the transcript of the tape, Olivia was documented as saying in broken English, "I no light no fire." But that in his official reports he quoted her as precisely saying, "If anyone was in the house I would either hear them or see them from anyplace I had been downstairs." Important stuff, questioning his memory the same way she had questioned the recall ability of Joe Butler, but pale in comparison to the open window.

Olivia got a surprise gift on the way home that day when two women from White Plains gave her a small bouquet of pink carnations. The flowers could have been for them all. "The sleepless nights paid off," said a jubilant Rush. His investigation of the arson-burglary ring had failed to get into court, but his slow, careful scan of every frame of the Flavin videotape had paid off handsomely.

Brevetti had been given a copy of the Flavin videotape, and the defense found the damning section that showed the open window even before the trial began. It had been paramount that it be kept secret, and throughout the trial Brevetti had dropped little testing questions to see if the prosecution had discovered the vital pictures hidden in the Flavin tape. Rush, in a visit to the district attorney's complex of offices, had glanced at the electronic gear to see if it had been used, and was happy to discover it was covered with a layer of dust.

The secret held.

Brevetti recalled her own excitement when she saw the details of the window so clearly outlined against the backdrop of angry fire. She reached out her hand and slowly curled her manicured crimson fingernails into a fist of sharp talons. "I saw that frame and realized, 'I've got you by the balls, Detective Johnson.'"

Chapter Thirty-Five

END GAME

EVENTS MOVED SWIFTLY NOW. THE TRIAL HAD TAKEN A BI-
zarre new turn with the crushing evidence on the videotape and, perhaps for the first time, the shift in public
opinion reflected in the jury box. The adage that someone
is innocent until proven guilty became tangible and real.
The prosecution had built a flimsy case on weak circumstantial evidence and had not come close to proving beyond a reasonable doubt that Olivia had burned the
house and killed Kristie Fischer.

There were a few more bomblets yet to drop as the calendar changed from June to July. The jurors were becoming very unsympathetic to Johnson, particularly after he
hedged when Brevetti asked whether the emotional telephone call between Olivia and her father in Switzerland
had been conducted in private.

"Did I tape-record it?" Johnson asked.

"Did anyone? " Brevetti shot back.

"No, not to my knowledge," he said.

Brevetti then had him confirm that every word coming
into the Mount Pleasant Police Department over telephones is taped automatically, including that transatlantic
one exchanged between Olivia and Kurt Riner.

And what about the burned baby seat that had eventually risen to such importance that it was the very first
piece of major evidence presented by the prosecution?

Johnson said he picked it up at the wrecked house three days after the fire and put it into a garbage bag. It was taken back to his office and leaned against a wall in the hallway, then moved into the detectives' office to lean against a wall there. It finally was taken to the crime laboratory on January 22—fifty-one days after the fire. After spending so long in unprotected areas frequented by other people, apparently there was no need to test it for anything.

Bolen had a final chance to question Johnson, and brought his usual skeletal television stand and set into court. It appeared somewhat ridiculous in comparison to the extensive setup Brevetti had used. His question proved nothing. When he showed the Flavin videotape to counter Brevetti's show-and-tell episode, he turned the single screen so that no one in the audience could see it. It didn't matter, because when he managed to stop the tape at an important part, Judge Silverman came over and placed a finger on the screen. "What's this here?" asked the judge. Silverman saw two shadows of window frames, not one, coming down in separate lines, not overlapping. In other words, Bolen's presentation also demonstrated that the window in Leah's room, the window that he had thought he'd proven to be locked, actually was wide open.

Detective Johnson left the witness stand for the last time, and soon afterward, at four minutes after noon on Wednesday, July 1, the sixteenth day of the trial, Bolen announced that the prosecution rested its case. There was a stirring in the courtroom. He had chosen not to call Denise Fischer after all. She sat in the courtroom audience beside her husband.

Laura Brevetti barely rose from her chair. She held out a single sheet of paper that was the report from medics who attended Olivia at the fire scene. The report described her as being "hysterical." With that in evidence, at 12:14 P.M., Laura Brevetti stunned the court. "The defense rests," she said.

The decision not to call a single witness sent a loud message to the jury. Brevetti, who performed magic for them yesterday, was saying the prosecution had failed so badly that she didn't need to fight back. She later explained that "every prosecution witness had turned into a defense witness."

Silverman tended to agree, telling reporters he had a "strong opinion" about what the verdict should be. Speculation was rife that if the jury came in with a vote to convict Olivia, he would overturn it. Silverman told the jury their work was done for the week, to take a long Independence Day holiday weekend and come back next week to begin deliberations.

The following day, Silverman and the two lawyers worked out the wording for the charge he would give to the jury.

Bolen came up with a surprise, asking the court to drop the second count of the indictment against Olivia. Even he did not believe he had proven that she exhibited the "depraved indifference to human life" with which she had been charged.

The remaining three murder counts and the arson count would go to the jury.

Before leaving the courthouse, Olivia was given a huge floral display with burgundy orchids by a family that had been following the trial. "A three-month-old baby died and someone out there killed her. It looks like the police department made a mistake," said one of the donors.

The closing arguments, heard on Monday, July 6, were anticlimactic, although Brevetti and Bolen had spent the holiday weekend preparing for their two and one-half hour summations. There was nothing new.

Brevetti went first, and after calling the prosecution's case "pitiful" and loaded with "irrelevant" facts, said "gaps as large as the Grand Canyon" existed in the investigation and charged the jurors to challenge the purported alibi of John Gallagher. "He is a walking reasonable doubt," she said. Further, she took a swipe at the hurry-up investigation done by the Mount Pleasant police. "There's something rotten when the police don't look farther than what's at their feet, and base their actions on what proves to be wild speculation," she said.

Bolen, who had to breathe new life into a case that had suffered repeated damaging blows, told the jurors that the facts were circumstantial, but solid. Olivia's eyebrows were singed, she pronounced her name two different ways when she telephoned for help, and she had been "scrounging for accelerants" on December 2. No evidence had been presented to support that final statement.

"No one secretly entered the house by sneaking through any windows, nor did anyone enter by picking locks," Bolen said. "The finger of guilt points unerringly at her." Putting a peculiar ending to his case, the assistant district attorney mentioned again that the four cats were involved and that Riner told Bill Fischer, "I went to feed the cats, and I closed the baby's door."

"One thing we know is that the cats didn't do it. But they saw who did it," he proclaimed.

The judge turned the case over to the jury after giving them a lengthy charge on precise points of law that should be considered. Once outside the court, Olivia, flanked by her parents, broke her long silence, telling reporters through an interpreter that "I have a basic faith in the system. I am hopeful that the outcome will be fair."

Likewise, the Fischers also opened up to reporters after the jury was sequestered. They had sat silently while the defense punched holes in the prosecution case, but had not changed their own minds about what happened to their baby daughter. "I know she started it," Bill Fischer said. "No one else could have gotten into that house. She never tried to get the baby out. Never tried."

John Gallagher was more vehement. He said he felt like going up and punching Laura Brevetti right in the nose. When Brevetti heard that, she almost laughed aloud, as did Chris Rush, who had moved near her shoulder just in case something might flare up. "Let him try," mocked Brevetti. "I've been threatened by better crooks than John Gallagher."

The jury deliberated for a little more than twelve hours, from lunchtime to almost midnight, before reaching their verdict. Forewoman Shanet Yancy read it aloud. There were four counts to be decided, and to each, Yancy said, the decision was a unanimous "not guilty."

Olivia Riner broke into a smile and hugged Laura Brevetti as the courtroom crowd erupted in a standing ovation. Remaining seated were the Fischers, who had felt hammer blows with each innocent verdict that was announced, then felt bewildered and angry at the wave of applause. The family felt the crowd had forgotten that their three-month-old Kristie had died, and were unable to see past their hurt to the point that, perhaps, their nanny might not have been responsible.

From his bench Silverman confirmed the verdicts were true and correct, then told Olivia she was free, could remove the electronic anklet she had worn for six months and could return to Switzerland whenever she wished.

Members of the jury told reporters that while a couple of men had initially wanted to pass at least one guilty verdict, the outcome actually had been inevitable. "The prosecutor had certain little things to prove his case . . . and they fell apart," said forewoman Yancy. "The facts basically were not there," added Irwin Wilmot of Rye. Annette Feigin of Scarsdale added the clincher was the videotape showing the open window.

Bolen, appearing at a news conference, said he accepted "total and complete responsibility" for the outcome of the trial. But he pointed out there was a difference between verdicts of not guilty and actual innocence. "In my opinion, yes, Olivia Riner did this particular crime."

It no longer mattered that Bolen remained convinced of her guilt. He had his chance and had lost.

The nanny murder case was over.

Chapter Thirty-Six

GOING HOME

As Olivia Riner was set free and prepared to return to Switzerland, the finger-pointing began around Mount Pleasant and White Plains, and there was enough blame to go around.

The *Reporter-Dispatch*, in a lead editorial, declared the jury acted in the only way possible. "There was little evidence to support police accusations. The investigation was narrow and unprofessional, and the testimony of police at the trial was filled with holes and contradictions." The newspaper stated that what was needed to prevent a repeat of "this travesty of justice" was a full-time major crime-scene unit in the county to be at the disposal of police departments. It also said the Town of Mount Pleasant needed to revamp its entire police organization.

The county Board of Legislators began looking into the possibility of establishing a major crime investigation unit, as political figures of all stripes rushed to be on the side of the angels in this disturbing case. Police chiefs of several towns agreed that a specially trained unit should be formed.

District Attorney Carl Vergari said the police did a thorough and competent job. He added that the case was done, finished, and would not be reopened. In that, he was quickly proven wrong.

The Mount Pleasant Town Board, trapped in a political

web of its own, did not need a lot of questioning from the citizenry. If Olivia was innocent, then the crime was unsolved, and that wasn't good enough. The board voted to spend $50,000 to hire an independent consulting firm to investigate police actions in the death of Kristie Fischer. But the company they hired did not have subpoena powers nor permission from the court to examine all of the records.

A few weeks later a state investigative body was also set up, but was given the needed authority to crack open the closed books and examine the details. In both situations, charges that they were politically motivated bloomed.

In retaliation for the apparent slight, the Mount Pleasant police charged that the town board was abandoning them and merely looking for a scapegoat.

Further community unrest surfaced when Mount Pleasant supervisor Robert Meehan said he thought the sudden retirement of Police Chief Oliva "was related to the case." Oliva, with a political base of his own, immediately denied the inference and said he was proud of the way his former troops had handled the Riner episode.

District Attorney Vergari also charged that Swiss law enforcement officials refused to cooperate with Mount Pleasant police and would not provide background information that would have helped develop a motive. Eric Dardenne, the Swiss deputy consul in New York, said the statement was "groundless" and that all requested information had been supplied. "Probably the information we gave didn't please Mr. Vergari . . . [Riner] has a good reputation," said Dardenne.

Despite their protests that everything had been done correctly with the Riner investigation, the Mount Pleasant police changed their operations. On Thursday, July 16, Miguel Florentino of Manhattan was shot to death on Clove Brook Road in Valhalla. In stark contrast to the lazy, uncontrolled approach used in the nanny case, the police established a crime scene, saturated the area with forensic specialists, and called for expert help in the investigation. A suspect was arrested three days later.

For the individuals most involved in the Riner case, life went on, although all had been indelibly stamped by their experiences.

Laura Brevetti resumed her high-profile career in Manhattan, with television people planning a movie about her. George Bolen was soon back at work as an assistant district attorney. Lawyers may clash in the courtroom, but in the end it's just a job and tomorrow is another day.

The Fischers stuck with their conviction that Olivia Riner had killed their daughter Kristie, and accused the media of tilted coverage. They never wavered in their support for John Gallagher, and in news interviews, Bill repeatedly said he loved John "like a son." There were plans for the four of them to move into a new two-story house— Bill and Denise living upstairs, and Leah and John downstairs.

Judge Silverman sharply criticized how the case had been built, citing such things as arson investigator Joe Butler's lack of notes and the failure of investigators to thoroughly look into Gallagher's story before clearing him. The judge said he thought Gallagher had nothing to do with the murder and had been slammed unnecessarily by the media.

In November, Silverman was elected to a 14-year term on the Supreme Court, after once again having to wait for the late paper ballots to be counted before he was declared the victor.

The Swiss consul general gave a reception at his Park Avenue offices in New York for Olivia, her family, the people from the defense team, and several special guests on July 10. Three days later, on Tuesday, July 13, she was back at

John F. Kennedy International Airport, being escorted for a final time by her friendly guardian, Chris Rush.

They had grown close during the long trial, as the tough former cop grew to admire the inner steel of the Swiss nanny. Olivia looked upon him as a special uncle into whom she could always stuff one more rich Swiss chocolate. Alone for a final moment at the airport, she gave him a Swiss Army knife. Rush took off his trademark Blueblocker sunglasses and gave them to the girl he had watched over like a child of his own. With tears in her blue eyes, she put them on. They were too large, and tilted to one side, but she wore them anyway. As she left, Olivia whispered that she was a little afraid of going home.

Brevetti, who said the flight home would mark the end of "eight months of pure torture" for her client, joined Olivia aboard Swissair flight 101 from New York to Zurich. The lawyer spent only a day there, then flew back to New York. The cost of the expert defense was estimated at about a half-million dollars. Kurt and Marlies Riner were $75,000 in debt, due to living and travel expenses.

Once back in Switzerland, Olivia was feted like a Homecoming Queen. Her arrest and trial had blazed across the headlines throughout the country, and a crowd of friends and well-wishers was on hand to greet her. "I am starting a new life," she told the gathered media. "My American nightmare is over."

Since her father was a member of the town's volunteer fire department, Olivia and her family were driven home in a boxy red fire truck from Wettingen. With blue lights flashing and the odd European-style siren giving its distinctive boop-beep-boop-beep whoop, the truck disappeared into the ancient streets of northern Switzerland.

The crew of Swissair 101 breathed a sigh of relief. They had dodged a major faux-pas. Before they knew Olivia would be on their passenger list, they had chosen a film for the long transatlantic flight. There were a pair of movies available, and without much thought, they picked a French drama with English subtitles.

Left behind in New York was the recent Hollywood box-office smash hit, *The Hand That Rocks the Cradle*.

Detective Bruce Johnson, still maintaining a good humor, often sorts some of the papers in a special brown accordion file in his office. In there is his least favorite book in the entire world.

When he first read it, as the result of an anonymous tip, he started the investigative wheels rolling between Mount Pleasant and Switzerland. A kiosk at the train station in Baden, across the river from Wettingen, had two copies in stock and sold one in October 1991. Swiss police at first assisted in tracking down the kiosk owner to try to determine who may have purchased the book of four short stories printed in both French and English. Then, inexplicably, the Swiss stopped cooperating. Even a plea to the FBI resident station in Switzerland could not get the Swiss police to come through with any information on who bought the book.

One of the stories, written by author Patricia Highsmith, told of a troubled young girl who arrived one day to fill a child care job with a family in Westchester County, New York. She became so happy with her new position and with the children in her care that she dreamed of doing something truly noble, something that would win her the everlasting love and respect of the family, who would then want to keep her with them forever.

One evening the governess set a series of fires in the home where she was employed. As flames climbed the walls, she dramatically rushed forward to rescue the children.

The story is entitled "The Heroine."